Native Authenticity

Native Traces

Gerald Vizenor and Deborah L. Madsen, series editors

Native Authenticity

Transnational Perspectives on Native American Literary Studies

Edited by

Deborah L. Madsen

Cover, *San Geronimo Feast in Taos*, painting by Pierre Cayol.

Published by State University of New York Press, Albany

For information, contact State University of New York Press, Albany, NY
www.sunypress.edu

Production by Kelli W. LeRoux
Marketing by Anne M. Valentine

Library of Congress Cataloging-in-Publication Data

Native authenticity : transnational perspectives on Native American literary studies /
   [edited by] Deborah L. Madsen.
      p. cm.
   Includes bibliographical references and index.
   ISBN 978-1-4384-3167-3 (hardcover : alk. paper)
   ISBN 978-1-4384-3168-0 (pbk. : alk. paper)
   1. American literature—Indian authors—History and criticism   2. Indians in
literature.   3. Indians of North America—Ethnic identity.   4. Authenticity
(Philosophy) in literature.   I. Madsen, Deborah L.

   PS153.I52N35 2010
   810.9'897—dc22   2009034852

10 9 8 7 6 5 4 3 2 1

Contents

Preface

This book brings together original work by some of the foremost scholars of Native American studies in North America and Europe in order to map one specific and highly charged aspect of the contemporary theoretical field of Native American Indian studies. The issue of "authenticity" or "Indianness" generates a controversial debate in studies of indigenous American literatures. The articulation of Native American Indian identity through the prism of Euro-American attempts to confine "Indian" groups to essentialized spaces is resisted by some Native American writers, while others recognize a need for essentialist categories as a key strategy in the struggle for social justice and a perpetually renewed sense of Native sovereignty. This volume addresses the complexities of the efforts, both literary and scholarly, to negotiate the discursive space opened by the diverse reimaginings of indigenous identities. Pressure from neocolonial essentializing practices are in conflict with a politics of cultural sovereignty that demands a notion of "Indian" essence or "authenticity" as a foundation for community values, heritage, and social justice.

Contributors to this volume participate in the scholarly and pedagogical search for an intellectual paradigm for Native American literary studies that is apart from, yet cognizant of, powerful colonial legacies. Essays in this volume are focused upon the diverse and sophisticated responses of Native American Indian writers and scholars, while offering comparative perspectives upon Native Hawaiian, Chicano, and Canadian First Nations literatures. The complex politics of Polynesian authenticity versus Native American indigeneity is engaged by Native Hawaiian writers as they negotiate conflicting demands upon personal and tribal identities. Related to this questioning is the authenticity debate in Canadian First Nations writing, where the claim to authenticity rests upon a claim to historical precedence; also related is the highly contentious

claim by some Chicano/a writers to an indigenous heritage as a claim
to authority and "American" authenticity.

The primary issues explored in this collection could be summarized
as colonialism and the possibilities for Native heritage in the present
moment; the ongoing influence of Euro-American imperialism upon
Native land rights and land title; the hermeneutic basis for articulating
Native tribal sovereignty; and methodological issues for scholars (Native
and non-Native) who want to resist the dangers of recapitulating in
their own work the domination and destruction wrought historically
in Native American Indian communities and upon the individuals of
those communities. The introduction presents an overview of theoretical
perspectives on these issues by tracing a range of definitions of what it
means to be Indian.

In the first of the chapters presented here, Paul Lyons addresses
the colonized condition of the indigenous peoples of the Pacific and
especially Hawai'i. The political contexts of contemporary debates over
indigeneity and "Indianness" emerge clearly from this essay. Lyons engages first the difficult ethical issue of how a non-Native critic can pose
the question of Native authenticity. He goes on to discuss the dynamic
nature of indigenous Pacific writing that at once resists confinement to
the past while exploring specifically Pacific forms of storytelling, perception, and knowing.

David Moore, in the next essay, discusses relations between
authenticity, individual and community identity formation, and tribal
sovereignty. Moore's understanding of the permeability of communal
boundaries (of both the U.S. and the tribes) offers a framework within
which he traces the dynamic relationship between what he calls cycles
of selfhood and cycles of nationhood in Native American writings from
the period of the early Republic to the present. Moore's emphasis upon
the foundational role of tribal sovereignty in the politics and culture of
authentic "Indianness" is then taken up in Lee Schweninger's " 'Back
when I used to be Indian': Native American Authenticity and Postcolonial Discourse," which addresses directly the context of colonization and
U.S. imperialism raised by Moore. In this chapter, Schweninger argues
that borrowing from postcolonial studies in order to theorize issues of
authenticity can help readers of Native American literature to understand and address the postcoloniality of the United States. Like Lyons,
he explores what it means for a non-Native scholar to engage the issue
of Native authenticity. He works through the writings of such Native

American authors as Louis Owens, Mark Turcotte, and Gerald Vizenor to identify the literary strategies by which authenticity can be resisted without reinstating it through essentialization. Within the context of U.S. influence over Native American cultural production, highlighted by Lee Schweninger, how is it possible to read the rhetoric of "Indianness"? In her essay, "The X-Blood Files: Whose Story, Whose Indian?" Malea Powell offers a mixed-blood view of recent developments within the field of Native American studies, with an emphasis upon indigenous responses to imposed colonial measures of authenticity such as blood quantum and federal recognition. Hers is a carefully nuanced interpretation of the ways in which "real" versus "fake" Indians have been defined, in order to distinguish modes of being, writing, and living "like" an Indian, in the works of prominent Native American theorists and writers.

Having introduced the issue of how to read the rhetoric of "Indianness," the focus turns to the question, how is "Indianness" lived and written? Joy Porter's essay, "Modernism, Authenticity, and Indian Identity: Frank 'Toronto' Prewett (1893–1962)," explores one complex example of living "Indianness" in the early twentieth century. The nickname "Toronto" derives from the Indian ancestry claimed by, and for, this Canadian poet as he moved in the influential literary circles of post–World War I England. Prominent members of the Bloomsbury set such as Siegfried Sassoon, Robert Graves, Virginia Woolf, and Lady Ottoline Morrell were counted among the admirers of his poetry and, importantly, his "Indianness." Porter argues that, despite the veracity (or otherwise) of Prewett's indigeneity, his significance lies in the correspondence between the poetry he wrote and the desire of modernist sensibilities to encounter living embodiments of "Indian" stereotypes. The philosophical and hermeneutic bases upon which determinations of "Indian" versus "non-Indian" identity are made provide the focus of Helmbrecht Breinig's essay, "Transdifference in the Work of Gerald Vizenor." His wide-ranging discussion of Vizenor's poetry and fiction addresses the tension or rhetorical indecidability between difference and binary differentiation that allows us to live with uncertainty but that Vizenor's work refuses to resolve. Distinguishing his concept of "transdifference" from Homi Bhabha's "hybridity" and Jacques Derrida's "différance," Breinig argues that the simultaneous confrontation with contradictory and irresolvable elements of experience is more akin to John Keats's understanding of "negative capability," and it is this rhetorical achievement that characterizes Gerald Vizenor's writing.

The next two chapters address the difficulties and complexities of authentic "Indianness," or the formulation of indigenous identities, in "border" communities that offer productive comparisons with Native American Indian experience: indigenous Mexicans and Canadian First Nations peoples. In "Traces of Others in Our Own Other: Monocultural Ideals, Multicultural Resistance," Juan Bruce-Novoa explores the often fraught relationship between indigenous communities and identities on each side of the U.S.-Mexican border, through understandings of indigenism and "Chicanismo." While the former offered a strategy by which the biological claim to indigeneity could validate political claims to land and "roots," the latter, "Chicanismo," used strategic distinctions between Mexican and Native peoples in order to affirm Chicano identity, despite the traces of European cultural influence in even such early writers as Cabeza de Vaca and Villegra. Where Juan Bruce-Novoa attends to the complex discourses of indigeneity south of the U.S. border, the penultimate chapter of the collection takes us to the northern border between the U.S. and Canada. Richard J. Lane, in "Sacred Community, Sacred Culture: Authenticity and Modernity in Contemporary Canadian Native Writings," attends to the changing practices of the Native potlatch concept, a concept rendered paradoxical in European epistemologies that cannot account for the giving of a gift in which ownership is maintained. Lane takes as his starting point the immensely important foundational claim that Canada's First Nations have existed in the land since "time immemorial" and, through the interrelated contexts of land title, self-governance, and Native metaphysics, he argues against the notion of Native authenticity as located in a past moment. Rather, he uses Walter Benjamin's term "now time" to argue that Native authenticity is not "eccentric"—neither too late (for being located in a lost mythic past) nor too early (for arising after colonialism)—but is located temporally and spatially here and now. His discussion of Linda Griffiths' and Maria Campbell's *The Book of Jessica: A Theatrical Transformation* and Joseph Dandurand's *Looking into the Eyes of My Forgotten Dreams* and *Please Do Not Touch the Indians* explores the rhetorical interplay of the Native claim to presence as a claim both to mythic identity and history, and also as an assertion of modernity.

The book concludes with a conversation between the acclaimed Anishinaabe writer, theorist, and scholar Gerald Vizenor and his long-term collaborator, A. Robert Lee. This interview, "Postindian Reflections: Chickens and Piranha, Casinos, and Sovereignty," offers an update of some of the issues related to Native authenticity that Vizenor and Lee raised in their collection of interviews, *Postindian Conversations* (1999). The emphasis here is placed upon the issues of relevance to this volume: sovereignty, the challenge to sovereignty posed by developments such as tribal Indian casinos, the "authenticity" issue, and the strategies by which the notion of an "authentic Indianness" has been exploited by the American Indian Movement (AIM) and by a whole tradition of creative writers.

None of the essays presented here intends to have the final word on approaches to Native American "Indianness." What the volume does intend to map out is the range of methodological positions that characterize the contemporary field of Native North American Indian literatures. This book is an attempt to provide a clear yet comprehensive guide to this politically and culturally sensitive debate, which exercises a profound influence over Native American Literary scholarship. Some of the essays (Bruce-Novoa, Schweninger) originate in the 2003 MLA panel that I organized, "Authenticity and Identity in American Ethnic Literatures"; others (Breinig, Lee and Vizenor) were originally presented at the conference on Native American Literature that I hosted at the University of Geneva in 2004. The remaining essays were commissioned for this collection in order to fill out and to complete the survey of approaches that we have sought to present. What the essays collected here attempt to do, by engaging diverse aspects of the problematics of Native authenticity, is to contribute to the ongoing contemporary conversation that tries to formulate clearer and more effective ways to pursue social justice through the creative and scholarly activities of reading and writing.

I am grateful to my graduate assistant, Erika Scheidegger, for preparing the initial transcript of the Vizenor-Lee interview and for proofreading the typescript of this volume. The support of the Swiss National Science Foundation, the Department of English at the University of Geneva, and the Embassy of the United States of America in Bern has made this project possible from the early stages. I thank all the contributors for their patience and unstinting effort to bring this book into being. Finally, I owe a particular debt of gratitude to Alfred Hornung for his sustained support and friendship over the course of many years.

INTRODUCTION

Contemporary Discourses on "Indianness"

Deborah L. Madsen

Mixed bloods are neither here nor there, not like real bloods.

—Gerald Vizenor, *Griever: An American Monkey King in China*

In this introduction, I want to offer a survey of the diversity of understandings of "Indianness" that characterize contemporary Native American literature. Native American Indian literary study is based on the assumption that such a thing as "Native Americanness" or "Indianness" exists to define the category of literary expression that is the object of study. In this respect, all Native American Indian literary study rightly supports and is consonant with Native claims to sovereignty, self-determination, and self-identity. However, the claim to self-identity, to "Indianness," is complicated by the long history of colonial relations that characterizes the contemporary United States. The right to define "Indianness," to determine who can speak as a Native American Indian, is a matter of very considerable complexity as a result of centuries of federal U.S. intervention that compromise tribal self-government and the sovereignty of tribal nationhood. How the sovereign claim to determine tribal membership, by defining "Indianness," affects the practice of literary scholarship and teaching is my subject here.

1

It may seem self-evident that Native American literature is that which is written by Native American authors. However, broad ethnic categories are problematic, and not only in a Native context. Issues of history, the political construction of the category, language, and questions of cultural specificity all come together to make ambiguous the answer to the question of whose work qualifies to be read under particular ethnic tags or banners. As with the category of Asian American writers, the issue of what is being hyphenated with America (and how) is an urgent question for students, scholars, and writers of Native American literature. The seemingly simple assumption that a Native American writer is someone legally defined as a Native American Indian is complicated by the many and highly politicized mechanisms by which that legal definition has been formulated and is applied. A blood quantum of a specified percentage of Native American Indian descent is the criterion most frequently invoked but this is a form of identification formulated and imposed by the U.S. federal government, not a form of self-identification arising out of Native lifeways. Alternative, culturally based forms of tribal identification based on the practicing of traditional lifeways and active engagement in tribal affairs have been adopted by some tribes in place of blood quantum; however, by divorcing tribal identity from issues of tribal blood and genetic inheritance this strategy opens the possibility that an individual who possesses no tribal blood can "become" a Native American Indian. As I will explore in more detail here, Wendy Rose's critique of "whiteshamanism," the form of cultural imperialism that appropriates control of Native cultures through the exercise of knowledge as power, brings this problem into sharp relief. We might also think here of the recent controversy concerning the authenticity of Ward Churchill's "Indianness." And a useful historical case study of the consequences of divorcing "Indianness" from tribal blood is provided by the experience of the Pueblo people who, as Jana Sequoya-Magdaleno describes, were declared non-Indians by the Supreme Court of New Mexico in 1869 and by the U.S. Supreme Court in 1877 on the grounds that they were:

> "a peaceable, industrious, intelligent, and honest and virtuous people . . . , Indians only in feature, complexion, and a few of their habits." However, this legal determination was less in recognition of common humanity than of federal and state economic interests in opening the land to settlement and development under the Homestead Act; for if the Pueblo

were not Indians, then they were not protected by rights of dependency established by John Marshall's Supreme Court decision (*Cherokee Nation v. Georgia*, 1831). (90)

As this example highlights, the ways in which "Indianness," as tribal affiliation and traditional cultural practices, can be enacted are subject to interventions by the dominant colonizing influence of Euro-America and are historically contingent. Consequently, how "Indianness" is possible changes and is specific to places and moments in the ongoing colonial history of Native North America.

One way to avoid the pitfalls of any focus on "Indianness" as a tribal identity has been to refocus on the hyphenated status of Native American Indian writers in the colonized position in which they are placed in the contemporary United States. The focus of attention then moves away from issues of traditional, tribal cultural practices and life-ways toward the relationship between Native and migrant American identities and the complexities arising from that hybrid condition. Favored writers within this kind of scholarly framework tend to be urban rather than reservation-based writers, who explicitly claim a mixed-blood status and a heritage constituted by the complex history of Native American colonization and conquest. A significant difference between a mixed-blood writer and a writer of single tribal heritage is that the former is more likely to invoke a pan-Indian definition of Native American identity. In other words, the writer who sees him- or herself in terms of only one tribal heritage is less likely to address the diversity of Native American tribes. Geographical, linguistic, cultural, historical differences among the more than five hundred recognized Native nations of North America alone are effaced by the pan-Indian perspective in favor of a sense of "Indianness" that transcends the specificity of each individual tribe. "Indianness" becomes even more complicated when considered in this context of tribal diversity, for example, when we ask the question, Can the Native peoples of Alaska be seen as somehow the same as tribal nations in Florida, in the Pacific Northwest, in the Northeast, or in the woodland regions of the Great Lakes?

In what follows, I want to offer a (necessarily selective) survey of the very rich field of approaches to the concept of "Indianness" in contemporary scholarly writings about American Native peoples. A history of colonial and neocolonial interventions on the part of governments, schools, churches, and missions has produced a complex array of definitions of what it means to be Indian. As noted previously, the definition of tribal identity and tribal membership can be measured by blood quantum, by place of residence (reservation or off reservation), or by cultural identification—by descent or consent—with highly charged debates raging over the methods by which tribes are formed and known, and the place of mixed-blood people within this range of identity formations. In the case of indigenous communities that are not encompassed by definitions of U.S.-based Native American Indians, such as Canadian First Nations peoples, indigenous Mexican, and Native Hawaiian peoples, these questions of identity and identification become even more problematic. This introductory chapter, like those that follow, offers a wide-ranging account of the various theoretical positions that characterize the field of Native American literary studies: from tribal-centered to poststructuralist inspired positions.

Appropriating "Indianness"

In a manner that crystallizes the ironies, complexities, and politics of Native or indigenous self-naming, M. Annette Jaimes opens her essay "Federal Indian Identification Policy: A Usurpation of Indigenous Sovereignty in North America" with the following epigraph from the Native scholar and activist Ward Churchill:

> I'm forever being asked not only my "tribe," but my "percentage of Indian blood." I've given the matter a lot of thought, and find I prefer to make the computation based on all of me rather than just the fluid coursing through my veins. Calculated this way, I can report that I am precisely 52.2 pounds Indian—about 35 pounds Creek and the remainder Cherokee—88 pounds Teutonic, 43.5 pounds some sort of English, and the rest "undetermined." Maybe the last part should just be described as "human." It all seems rather silly as a means of assessing who I am, don't you think? (123)

As Jaimes goes on to point out, the appropriation of the right to determine membership of sovereign Native nations is a typically colonizing move: a move reminiscent of the Nazi quantification of "Jewishness" and of South African efforts to distinguish by blood "blacks" from "coloreds" under apartheid. The effect of such imposed restrictions on membership of a cultural community is felt not only by the group itself, which finds itself truly powerless in such a fundamental matter as self-determination, but also by individuals who are seeking to define for themselves a sense of personal and cultural identity. The blood quantum standard for Native tribal membership was introduced as part of the 1887 General Allotment Act, which identified those Native people (of one-half or more Indian blood) who were eligible to receive a federal land grant. Those who did not meet the requirement were disenfranchised or dispossessed of their previous treaty entitlements to land, and other federal payments and benefits (Jaimes 126). The longer term consequences of this colonialist strategy include what Jaimes describes as a situation where "the limitation of federal resources allocated to meeting U.S. obligations to American Indians has become so severe that Indians themselves have increasingly begun to enforce the race codes excluding the genetically marginalized from both identification as Indian citizens and consequent entitlements" (129). The abolition of blood quantum identification in favor of self-identification, as part of the 1972 Indian Education Act, was seen by many Native people as "the federal attempt to convert us from being the citizens of our own sovereign nations into benign members of some sort of all-purpose U.S. 'minority group,' without sovereign rights" (Ted Means, statement to the South Dakota Indian Education Association, Pierre, SD, 16 November 1975; quoted in Jaimes 131).

Tribes such as the White Earth Anishinaabeg, the Haida of Alaska, and Oglala Lakota on the Pine Ridge Reservation in South Dakota have begun instituting their own processes for determining membership of the nation: by criteria such as residency, familiarity with tribal cultural practices, service to the tribe, by marriage to a tribal member, adoption into the tribal nation, and birth (Jaimes 134–35). One consequence of self-identification, however, is conflict with the federal and state authorities who refuse to accept any form of Native tribal membership except that validated by federal means, such as blood quantum. To confuse the situation even further, distinct federal and state agencies define "Indianness" quite differently: at one extreme the federal Census Bureau accepts self-identification, other agencies accept only residence on a federally recognized reservation, still others demand a minimum blood quantum that also varies: "one-half blood was the standard utilized in the case of the Mississippi Choctaws and adopted in the Wheeler-Howard Act;

one sixty-fourth was utilized in establishing the Santee rolls in Nebraska" (Jaimes 136).

Complementing analyses such as Jaimes's of the legal disempowerment of Native people, in matters of defining tribal membership and "Indianness," are studies of what Wendy Rose (1992), following Geary Hobson, calls "whiteshamanism." The term refers to non-Native producers of cultural knowledge who claim a superior insight into Native customs and spirituality. Hobson names white American poets such as Louis Simpson, Charles Olsen, Jim Cody, John Brandi, Gene Fowler, Norman Moser, Michael McClure, Barry Gifford, Paul Steinmetz, David Cloutier and, above all, Jerome Rothenberg, who see themselves as poet-shamans (Rose 403). Wendy Rose extends the remit of whiteshamans to include anyone (not necessarily poets, not necessarily whites) with pretensions to the status of an expert on Native cultures despite a patent lack of knowledge of Native lifeways. She cites Carlos Castaneda and Ruth Beebe Hill as models of this kind of whiteshamanism, along with " 'Blackfoot/Cherokee' author Jamake Highwater's (aka: Jay Marks, a non-Indian) extended repackaging of Greek mythology and pop psychology in the garb of supposed 'primal Native American legends' " (403). Ward Churchill, in a 1988 essay, relates this same phenomenon to what he calls "New Age Hucksterism." The effect of this whiteshaman movement is seen by Rose, and others, as "part of a process of 'cultural imperialism' directly related to other claims on Native American land and lives. By appropriating indigenous cultures and distorting them for its own purposes . . . the dominant society can neatly eclipse every aspect of contemporary native reality, from land rights to issues of religious freedom" (404). These "wannabe" Indians are obviously playing at being Indian by impersonating stereotypical images and iconography of "Indianness," or "the Indian," and if the impersonation is sufficiently powerful as a way of embodying and animating those stereotypes then the whiteshamans may "become" "real" Indians, as Rose wryly comments, "even when actual native people are present. Native reality is thereby subsumed and negated by imposition of a 'greater' or 'more universal' contrivance" (405).

Against this extensive critique of the cultural imperialism of whiteshamanism, Rose provides a corrective that articulates many of the fears of non-Indian scholars of Native American literature and culture:

> The fear exists among non-native writers that we are somehow trying to bar them from writing about Indians at all, that Indian people might be "staking a claim" as the sole interpret-

ers of Indian cultures, most especially of that which is sacred, and asserting that only Indians can make valid observations on themselves. Such fears are not based in fact; I know of no Indian who has ever said this. Nor do I know of any who secretly think it. We accept as given that whites have as much prerogative to write and speak about us and ours as we have to write and speak about them and theirs. The question is how this is done and, to some extent, why it is done. (415–16)

The emergence of critical emphases upon "tribally centered" literary critical praxis and methodologies of reading have exacerbated such fears as Rose describes, especially among non-Native scholars of Native American Indian literatures. What this might mean, in critical practice, is described by Kimberly Roppolo as a strategy for reading from the perspective of Native American cultural perceptions and understandings rather than working against Western cultural assumptions. Roppolo (2001) clarifies this proposition by quoting Kimberly Blaeser's call for

> a critical voice which moves from the culturally centered text outward toward the frontier of "border" studies, rather than an external critical voice which seeks to penetrate, appropriate, colonize, or conquer the cultural center, and thereby, change the stories or remake the literary meaning. (Blaeser quoted in Roppolo 263)

As Roppolo observes, this call brings into focus the relationship between individual tribal cultures and an intertribal culture that would provide the basis for this generalized tribal-centered approach to literary texts. Such intertribalism exists in movements like AIM (the American Indian Movement), the legacy of Native residential schools, the Native American Church, and educational Native American studies programs. What this intertribal critical method needs to oppose is the "anthropologism" of Western or non-Native approaches to Native American literature, the placing of the Native, and Native cultural artifacts, as the object of analysis rather than as a subject involved in the activity of analysis and meaning-making. This anthropologism should be seen as analogous to the whiteshamanism denounced by Wendy Rose.

Just as this whiteshamanism or anthropologism assumes and draws upon a generalized perception of Native American Indians, so too does the concept of "pan-Indianism" or intertribalism. Kathryn Winona

Shanley describes how "[p]aradoxically, pan-Indian movements preserve the sovereignties that keep the peoples distinct from one another. In other words, threats to cultural distinction and to self-determination drive pan-Indian movements and alliances that, in turn, tend to generalize identities and issues" (4). However, the late-twentieth-century wave of Native American writers, such as N. Scott Momaday, Gerald Vizenor, Leslie Marmon Silko, and Louise Erdrich, even when of mixed heritage, do write from a tribally specific setting and context. This suggests the need for scholarly negotiation between pan-Indian and tribally specific critical and cultural contexts.

Perhaps the Native American Indian scholar and critic who best exemplifies this move away from European critical paradigms of literary analysis toward Native inspired models is Elizabeth Cook-Lynn (Crow Creek Sioux). In her book, *Why I Can't Read Wallace Stegner and Other Essays: A Tribal Voice* (1996), she attributes the shape of her own academic career, as a tribally identified person working as a teacher and intellectual within the framework of the U.S. colonialist educational system, to the rise and fall of affirmative action. Cook-Lynn describes her career as a process of discovering the extent to which education operates in the United States as a form of imperialist socialization, educating Native children to a life of marginalization and subservience:

> My work has turned out to be unabashedly based on the idea that there is probably nothing unhealthy in Indians dropping out of racist and damaging school systems to which they are routinely subjected. It appears instead that there is something systematically unhealthy in the schools, themselves, in their false history based on the assumptions of a European body of thought which suggests that the American Indian experience is somehow a lesser one. (x)

In a later essay she locates her experience in relation to the field of Native or Indian studies: "Indian Studies scholars who have been studying Indian histories and lifeways in the past two or three decades have been doing so for the purpose of petitioning for redresses of grievances in this democracy. In the process of that engagement they have helped everyone to understand that the need for transformation is urgent and compelling" (1996, 39–40). It is in this broader context of activism and social justice that Cook-Lynn argues that only tribal models of literary criticism can act as vehicles of tribal intellectual empowerment (1996, xiv), not so much counteracting as providing an alternative intellectual methodology and environment for Native American Indian writers and critics. Working in a similar vein is Craig Womack, who addresses his book *Red on Red: Native American Literary Separatism* (1999) to "Creek people, specifically, and Native People, more generally" (1). This address supports what he calls "[m]y greatest wish . . . that tribes, and tribal members, will have an increasingly important role in evaluating tribal literatures" (1). Going further than this, though, Elizabeth Cook-Lynn claims that methodologies that do not arise out of this tribally specific context are necessarily inferior: "I maintain that when the ethical relationship between tribal nationhood and the imagination is ignored or falsified, flawed scholarship is the result" (1996, xiii). It is this kind of claim that non-tribal, and particularly Euro-American, scholars and critics find threatening.

The field of Native American literature is enriched by the increasing diversity of approaches. Few scholars would dispute this. However, the claim that non-tribal approaches must produce "flawed scholarship" can be alienating and threatening. In her introduction to *Why I Can't Read Wallace Stegner and Other Essays*, Cook-Lynn also offers a more modulated vision of the scholarly terrain of Native American literary studies, when she writes:

> Now that this [Native American Indian] culture is being examined and criticized by those persons whose intellectual backgrounds are deeply embedded in the oral traditions of the native tribes of America, new visions are in the offing, mistaken ideas about the native past can be reexamined, and concerns that have not been part of the broad public dialogue can now be addressed. (xiii)

But this is not what Elizabeth Cook-Lynn does in the essays that follow her introduction; in these essays she is concerned to expose the consequences of colonialism for Native American literature and culture, rather than provide a proactive tribal-centered approach to literary texts. In her chapter entitled "The American Indian Fiction Writer," for example, she offers a clear condemnation of contemporary Native American Indian "canonical" writers as collaborators with white American colonialist values. In an article entitled "Cosmopolitanism, Nationalism, the Third World, and First Nation Sovereignty" (1993), she contends that

> The American Indian writers who have achieved successful readership in mainstream America seem to avoid that struggle [between tribal nation status and enforced denationalization] in their work and move into thinking about Indian populations as simply gatherings of exiles and émigrés and refugees, strangers to themselves and their lands, pawns in the control of white manipulators, mixed-bloods searching for identity. . . . (86)

Echoing the vocabulary of Wendy Rose's whiteshamanism and Kimberly Roppolo's anthropologism, Cook-Lynn argues in the chapter entitled "End of the Failed Metaphor" that "Indigenous people are no longer in charge of what is imagined about them, and this means that they can no longer freely imagine themselves as they once were and as they might become. Perhaps a separation of culture and place and voice has never been more contextualized in modernity than it is for Indians today" (1996, 143). The specific "failed" metaphors that Cook-Lynn discusses are the tropes of Mother Earth and the Trickster. Of all contemporary writers, it is Rudolfo Anaya, "The New World Man," who is condemned as a "collaborator" with European colonialists for celebrating the figure of the Native woman Malinche:

> To accept the indigenous woman's role as the willing and cooperating recipient of the colonist's seed and as the lone repository of culture is to legitimize the destruction of ancient religions, the murder of entire peoples, the rape of the land, not to mention the out-and-out theft of vast native homelands. To do so dismisses the centuries of our modern American Indian histories when our fathers fought and died and made treaties in order to save us from total annihilation. (147)

Against images of the critic as "collaborator" with the colonizing "enemy," Native scholars like Greg Sarris propose understandings based on dialogue, with the critic attempting not to "possess" or "master" Native literary texts, but instead attempting to move toward the writer in a common goal of intercultural communication. In *Keeping Slug Woman Alive* (1993), he opposes critical paradigms that seek explanatory meta-discourses, which distance the scholar from the subject or text under study. Using a performative as well as expository method, his essays, as he describes, "collapse the dichotomy between personal narrative and scholarly argument . . . to create a document representing exchanges that open the world people share with each other" (6). It is this opening of dialogues that Sarris stresses; he recognizes that storytelling, including the creation of critical narratives, is a complex process that can be variously oppressive or liberating. What Sarris seeks is a dialogical or conversational strategy that will open up possibilities: "that can open the intermingling of the multiple voices within and between people and the texts they encounter, enabling people to see and hear the ways various voices intersect and overlap, the ways they have been repressed or held down because of certain social and political circumstances, and the ways they can be talked about and explored" (5).

From "Indianness" to "Postindianness"

The power of stories shapes the work of critics like Jana Sequoya who, in her 1993 essay "How(!) Is an Indian? A Contest of Stories," locates the debate over "Indianness" explicitly in the context of the politicizing and prescriptive power of competing cultural discourses that impact upon the material conditions in which Native American Indian people must formulate identities:

> The question of who and how is an Indian is an ongoing context of stories in North America, a contest in many ways emblematic of global struggles to contain and control difference in modern societies. At stake are the social, political, and economic conditions of possibility for Indian identity within the encompassing national context. Who, what, where, and when can that Indian be, which the founding narratives of the North American nation construed as either absent—the empty land scenario—or inauthentic. Inauthentic, that is, by comparison with the imagined "Original" Indian, whether of the Golden Age or demonic variety; inauthentic because rather than vanishing, American Indians in all our diversity are still here, alive and kicking against the odds. (453)

She goes on to argue that what is at stake as Native communities and individuals struggle with imposed stereotypes is "the replacement of traditional Native American structures of identity with those of Euro-America" (455). In a later essay, "Telling the *différance*: Representations of Identity in the Discourse of Indianness" (1995), she makes the telling point that in fact the entire debate concerning "Indianness" is an artifact of the colonization of Native people and the subsequent "Othering" process of discursive marginalization to which they are subject: "Insofar as American Indians have been taken apart as peoples and reinvented as discourse, the referent of the category 'Indian' is a matter of much dispute. The premise of this essay is that, first of all, this condition of disputation is an effect of the 'Othering' province of the category itself" (88). Sequoya-Magdaleno's second argument is the ironic observation that the debate over "Indianness" is largely a consequence of historical engagements by Native people and communities with U.S. strategies of acculturation and regulation. This is not to say that Native people are responsible for the stereotyping of "Indians," but that U.S. coloniz-ing strategies have seen the emergence of an administrative category of "Indian," validated by such measures as tribal blood-quantum, or what Sequoya-Magdaleno calls "administratively produced difference." This "difference" has been "inscribed as the standard of identity cohering American Indian diversity; strategic identity-in-difference is adopted as the political basis for nationalist claims to 'self-determination' and tribal 'sovereignty' " (88). Ironically, then, Native people find themselves repre-sented by a category that produces that very subject position of "Indian": the stereotype that is the product of colonialist discourses of "Othering" is projected as the representative Native subject of claims to sovereignty. Sequoya-Magdaleno's distinction between the process of *identification* that produces the category "Indian" and the *identity* that this category is assumed to represent offers a productive context in which to consider Gerald Vizenor's concept of "postindian" identity formation.

Identities are always based on stories in Vizenor's work, so the reinvention of Native American Indian people as discourse, conceptual-ized by Jana Sequoya-Magdaleno, is the basis of Vizenor's treatment of identity issues. Some stories are "terminal creeds," such as the stories told by the colonizing forces of U.S. culture, which position Native people as "Vanishing Americans" and other romantic confections. Other stories embody a "survivance hermeneutic," Vizenor's term for the hybrid of survival and resistance (survivance) that is enacted, and continually reenacted, in the performance of meaning. In the collection of inter-views with A. Robert Lee published as *Postindian Conversations*, Vizenor describes "Indians" as "simulations of an absence" (161). In the absence of ontologically "real" persons that conform to the stereotype of Indians circulating in the hegemonic U.S. culture, Native American people simulate those images. Vizenor deliberately evokes Jean Baudrillard's vocabulary of simulacra and simulation to situate these performances of "Indianness" as identities with no "authentic" origin in tribal cultures. The word "Indian" names then not people but a category of identity formation under conditions of ongoing U.S. cultural imperialism. In *Manifest Manners* (1994), Vizenor's ironic gaze deconstructs all the categories of "Indian" definition that we have seen herein: "nationalism, pan-tribalism, new tribalism, and reservation residence" (59). A sustained oppositional and ironic perspective on the vacant subject position of the "Indian" characterizes what Vizenor calls the "postindian": the subject who dares to play with and beyond the stereotype of Indian identity. He proclaims the fact that "postindians renounce the inventions and final vocabularies of manifest manners [and are] the advance of survivance hermeneutics" (167). What he means here is that the figure of the "postindian" represents resistance and survival; survival through the refusal of tragedy, resistance through the refusal of "victimry," and the refusal of all simulations of the "Indian" that represent false assimilation to, or acculturation in, the culture of U.S. dominance. The postindian at once exposes the ontological absence that is constitutive of stereotypes of the "Indian," but at the same time makes present a trace of what it is that is absent. Vizenor explains:

> Native American Indians are the originary storiers of this continent, and their stories of creation, sense of imagic presence, visionary memories, and tricky survivance are the eternal traces of native modernity. . . . Native stories are an imagic presence, the actual tease of human contingencies, but indians are immovable simulations, the tragic archives of dominance and victimry. Manifest manners favor the simulations of the indian traditionalist, an ironic primitive with no cultural antecedence. (ix–x)

This trace, or excess of meaning that exceeds the empty cultural category that is the "Indian," is revealed in what Vizenor calls, in the essay "Shadow Survivance" in *Manifest Manners*, the "postindian turns in literature." In the absence of the "Indian," the traces or shadows of tribal survivance appear, along with the potential for different kinds of identity. "The traces are shadows, shadows, shadows, memories, and visions in heard stories" (63). The repetition of the word "shadow" indicates the multiple and diverse nature of these residual traces of tribal meaning that exist outside the culture of dominance. In the stories of the postindian, as in the discourses of survivance, language functions performatively to actively organize knowledge of ourselves and our world; this discursive performance is participatory, multiple and never fixed, always already in creative transformation.

Vizenor's deconstructive hermeneutic discourse of survivance provides a powerful strategy for subverting monologic U.S. colonial structures of oppression. His figure of the postindian offers to take control of Native American Indian identity formations by actively though ironically and "trickily" (often in the guise of the tribal Anishinaabe trickster figure) playing with and subverting those stereotypical images. The postindian then adopts a position of presence in the tribal traces of meaning and being, rather than the absence that is the position in which Indians are placed by the discourses of colonial dominance. In the interview "Visionary Sovereignty" included in *Postindian Conversations* (1999), he comments:

> The indian is ironic, to be sure, and a conveyance of manifest manners. Natives must overturn the simulations of the indian and leave the treasons of that slave name to the arbiters of colonial authenticity. (156)

Vizenor offers a position, characterized by irony, from which tribal and non-tribal scholars of Native American literature can speak. This is a position of resistance to those colonizing images to which all of us are subject. By refusing to replicate disempowering and demeaning stereotypical discourses of the Indian, all scholars of Native American Indian literature can find a position from which to engage this body of literature.

In the introduction to *Ethnocriticism* (1992), Arnold Krupat offers two stark alternatives: "we must either imperialistically 'tell our own story' *as* the other's, or imperialistically speak *for* the other, violent translation or insidious ventriloquism, the only alternatives" (9). In response to this rather Manichean allegory of reading Native American literature, Krupat promotes a third space akin to Homi Bhabha's concept (in Rutherford 1990) of a cosmopolitan space that is located between imperialistic U.S. neocolonialism and tribal separatism. This would be a space of transculturality or what Helmbrecht Breinig calls "transdifference." The kind of cosmopolitanism that Krupat champions is quite distinct from liberal cosmopolitanisms that promote a universal humanistic ideology, which obscures the material conditions of inequality and absence of social justice between and among discrete ethnic groups. Instead, Krupat encourages the critic of Native American Indian literature to "seek to replace oppositional with dialogical models" (26) of scholarly interaction, to resist the dangerous essentialism of discourses of "victimry," stereotypical "Indian" images, and Native American tribal cultural separatism. In this respect, Krupat offers an approach that is similar to Greg Sarris's conversational strategy, outlined previously. In his later book *Red Matters* (2002), Krupat elaborates on this ethnocritical approach to develop what he calls "cosmopolitan comparativism," a kind of intercultural translation that negotiates between or among the three critical approaches presented in the chapter "Nationalism, Indigenism, Cosmopolitanism: Three Perspectives of Native American Literatures." This essay has received notable critical comment, suggesting that Krupat's formulation, while not receiving universal acclaim, has been very significant in shaping the ongoing debates about "Indianness" and cultural sovereignty. Krupat acknowledges that these categories are identity categories that have been used variously for both colonialist as well as anticolonialist causes and participate in complex cultural, social, and historical contexts. He defines these critical categories as follows:

> The nationalist grounds her criticism in the concept of the nation and uses tribal/national sovereignty, a legal and political category, to guide her examination of Native cultural production. The indigenist foregrounds what is instantiated as a pan-Indian geocentric epistemology, a knowledge different from that of dispersed Europeans and other wanderer-settlers. It is this Other knowledge that subtends the indigenist's critical perspective. The cosmopolitan is more nearly—to coin an oxymoron—a well-organized *bricoleur*. Aware that casual eclecticism can lead to critical and political irresponsibility, and doubting the flexibility of a true *ingénieur*'s systematicity, the cosmopolitan would cobble her criticism out of a variety of perspectival possibilities. (ix)

Appropriately, Krupat sets his discussion of cosmopolitanism against the claims to Native separatism made by scholars like Elizabeth Cook-Lynn and Craig Womack, who pursue the study of Native cultures within the context of developing and supporting tribal sovereignty. He complicates our understanding of what is meant by the terms "nation" and "culture," opening the scholarly conversation to include the multiple voices of different nationalisms and different cultures not for the purpose of appropriation or assimilation but to make possible what Greg Sarris describes as "enabling people to see and hear the ways various voices intersect and overlap, the ways they have been repressed or held down because of certain social and political circumstances, and the ways they can be talked about and explored" (1999, 5).

As Jace Weaver remarks in the first chapter of *Other Words: American Indian Literature, Law, and Culture* (2001), the negotiation of agreement about what constitutes "Indianness" is "a process rendered more dysfunctional by the fact that for many years, for its own colonialist reasons, the United States government intruded itself into the questions of definitions, an intrusion that still has a significant impact on Indian identity politics" (4). This, in conjunction with the kind of network of disciplinary and other relations that comprise the scholarly field of Native American and Indigenous studies, for which Weaver and Robert Warrior, among other powerful voices, have called, means that this issue of "Indianness" cannot be ignored by anyone involved in the field. Writers, readers, scholars, communities, everyone concerned with the achievement of social justice and the right to self-determination for Native people must make this question of "Indianness" in all its complex historical determination a question to which they devote significant attention.

Works Cited

Breinig, Helmbrecht. *Imaginary (Re-) Locations: Tradition, Modernity, and the Market in Contemporary Native American Literature and Culture*. Tübingen: Stauffenburg, 2003.

Churchill, Ward. "A Little Matter of Genocide: Native American Spirituality & New Age Hucksterism," *The Bloomsbury Review* (Sept–Oct 1988), rpt. in Ward Churchill, *Fantasies of the Master Race: Literature, Cinema and the Colonization of American Indians*. Monroe: Common Courage Press, 1992.

Cook-Lynn, Elizabeth. *Why I Can't Read Wallace Stegner and Other Essays: A Tribal Voice*. Madison: U of Wisconsin P, 1996.

———. "Who Stole Native American Studies?" *Wicazo Sa Review* 12.1 (Spring 1997): 9–28.

———. "Cosmopolitanism, Nationalism, the Third World, and First Nation Sovereignty." *Wicazo Sa Review* 9.2 (1993): 26–32.

Jaimes, M. Annette. "Federal Indian Identification Policy: A Usurpation of Indigenous Sovereignty in North America." *The State of Native America: Genocide, Colonization, and Resistance.* Ed. M. Annette Jaimes. Boston: South End Press, 1992. 123–38.

Krupat, Arnold. *Ethnocriticism: Ethnography, History, Literature.* Berkeley: U of California P, 1992.

———. *Red Matters: Native American Studies.* Philadelphia: U of Pennsylvania P, 2002.

Murray, David. "Representation and Cultural Sovereignty: Some Case Studies." *Native American Representations. First Encounters, Distorted Images, and Literary Appropriations.* Ed. Gretchen M. Bataille. Lincoln: U of Nebraska P, 2001. 80–99.

Pulitano, Elvira. *Towards a Native American Critical Theory.* Lincoln: U of Nebraska P, 2003.

Ramirez, Arthur. "Feminist Neo-Indigenism in Chicana Aztlán." *Studies in American Indian Literatures.* Series 2.7.4 (Winter 1995): 71–79.

Roppolo, Kimberly. "Towards a Tribal-Centered Reading of Native Literature: Using Indigenous Rhetoric(s) Instead of Literary Analysis." *Paradoxa* 15 (2001): 263–74.

Rose, Wendy. "The Great Pretenders: Further Reflections on Whiteshamanism." *The State of Native America: Genocide, Colonization, and Resistance.* Ed. M. Annette Jaimes. Boston: South End Press, 1992. 403–21.

Rutherford, Jonathan. "The Third Space: Interview with Homi Bhabha." *Identity, Community, Culture, Difference,* ed. Jonathan Rutherford. London: Lawrence and Wishart, 1990. 207–21.

Sarris, Greg. *Keeping Slug Woman Alive: A Holistic Approach to American Indian Texts.* Berkeley: U of California P, 1993.

Sequoya, Jana. "How(!) Is an Indian? A Contest of Stories." *New Voices in Native American Literary Criticism.* Ed. Arnold Krupat. Washington and London: Smithsonian Institution Press, 1993. 453–73.

Sequoya-Magdaleno, Jana. "Telling the *différance*: Representations of Identity in the Discourse of Indianness." *The Ethnic Canon: Histories, Institutions, and Interventions,* ed. David Palumbo-Liu. Minneapolis: U of Minnesota P, 1995. 88–116.

Shanley, Kathryn W. " 'Born from the Need to Say': Boundaries and Sovereignties in Native American Literary and Cultural Studies." *Paradoxa* 15 (2001a): 3–16.

———. "The Indians America Loves to Love and Read: American Indian Identity and Cultural Appropriation." *Native American Representations: First*

    Encounters, Distorted Images, and Literary Appropriations. Ed. Gretchen M. Bataille. Lincoln: U of Nebraska P, 2001b. 25–49.

Vizenor, Gerald. *Griever: An American Monkey King in China*. Normal and New York: Illinois State University / Fiction Collective, 1987.

———. *Manifest Manners: Postindian Warriors of Survivance*. Hanover: Wesleyan UP, 1994.

———, and A. Robert Lee. *Postindian Conversations*. Lincoln: U of Nebraska P, 1999.

Weaver, Jace. *Other Words: American Indian Literature, Law, and Culture*. Norman: U of Oklahoma P, 2001.

Womack, Craig. *Red on Red: Native American Literary Separatism*. Minneapolis: U of Minnesota P, 1999.

Questions about the Question of "Authenticity"

Notes on *Moʻolelo Hawaiʻi* and the Struggle for *Pono*

Paul Lyons

We know that we are a distinct people that was once protected by its own government. We know that once that government was removed there was nothing to prevent the Americans from defining us however they wished, and nothing to keep us Hawaiian except our own determination.

> —Jonathan Kamakawiwoʻole Osorio,
> "What ʻkine Hawaiian Are You?"

Democracy and "Authenticity" in Occupied Hawaiʻi

The democracy of colonies.
For the foreigner, romances
of "Aloha,"
For Hawaiians,
Dispossessions of empire.

> —Haunani-Kay Trask, "Dispossessions of Empire,"
> in *Night Is a Sharkskin Drum*

Mo'olelo Hawai'i (literature, stories, histories) by those with mo'okūauhau (Hawaiian genealogy) connecting them to the 'āina (land, environment) participates in an enduring social movement that asserts the distinctiveness of Hawaiians as a lāhui (race, peoplehood, nation) and that is implicitly or explicitly involved in the pursuit of pono (righteousness, justice, well-being), one dimension of which is a call for self-determination or ea (sovereignty, independence, life, breath).[1] From the nineteenth century to the present, mo'olelo and the arts (in particular, mele [song, poetry, chant] and hula [dance]) have played a vital role in the lāhui's struggle, in the face of U.S. noho hewa (wrongful occupation), to perpetuate its values and maintain its convictions about distinctiveness—convictions upon which political claims are arguably grounded. Virtually every politically engaged kānaka maoli (Hawaiian) writer asserts that kānaka maoli look at the world from a different vantage point than settlers, one secured by the vertical narrative of genealogy rather than the horizontal presentism of U.S. blood-quantum definitions. The struggle to nurture a distinct space of articulation—seen as central to a reintegrated lāhui-to-come—has marked kānaka maoli political and cultural expression since the illegal overthrow of the Kingdom in 1893.[2]

At that time Hawaiian difference was emphasized putatively by haole (foreigners, Caucasians); assumptions about kānaka fitness for self-rule provided "moral" justification for seizing the Islands. In one sense, then, it is both an irony and a fraught legacy of the history of U.S. Empire that, since the resurgence of nationalist claims in the 1970s, Hawaiians have had to engage civil and uncivil questions about the "authenticity" of the mo'olelo of kānaka maoli as a people from both inside and outside of the lāhui. (These questions resemble those about "authenticity" raised in relation to other indigenous peoples, but take forms specific to the political situation of Hawaiians inside and outside of the Islands on identity/authenticity issues for Hawaiians in the diaspora, who currently make up roughly forty percent of the lāhui, see Halualani [195–243].) In another sense, for the occupying power there is no irony in questioning Hawaiian claims to distinctiveness as politically meaningful. The ideology of U.S. Empire requires a delegitimatization of the "authenticity" of indigenous claims to special relation to fellow kānaka maoli and 'āina through genealogy; U.S. law divides Hawaiian culture (decontextualized aspects of which the state invests in for militouristic purposes) from political claims, without regard for the consent of those "democratically" included. Empires (in seeming opposition to colonial systems with dual systems and center/periphery models) seek to fully incorporate lands, offering the encapsulated indigenes the right to join and prove loyalty by identifying with the occupying force as its borders expand: settler scholarship narrates this as not only for Hawaiian good, but as understood to be such by Hawaiians. However, the remarkable extent of Hawaiian resistance following the overthrow and occupation, including *kū'ē* petitions by different Hawaiian political parties that collected the signatures of nearly every adult Hawaiian, has been fully documented by Noenoe Silva (1998, 2004). This *kū'ē* (protest, resistance), which delayed annexation, was occluded within settler scholarship, little of which had any regard for Hawaiian perspectives as recorded in the extensive Hawaiian-language archive (including roughly one million pages of newspapers). From annexation through the Statehood Drive, U.S. public discourse mystified the events surrounding the overthrow, ultimately coming to romanticize Hawai'i as a realized example of what the United States as a whole (cleansed of black/white tensions) aspired to be: a multicultural nation united by democratic principles. As a University of Hawai'i scholar wrote in 1955, "neo-Hawaiians" were "outstanding proof of the power of American ideals to build citizens even on islands far from the continental coast" (quoted in Day 237).

After decades of these processes, post-statehood institutions promoted the belief that "Kānaka 'Ōiwi [Native Hawaiians] had become too racially mixed, too acculturated and assimilated" to be constituted as a distinct entity: "the only place to find a Hawaiian was in the ground" (Tengan and White 392). Today, this view is espoused by writers like Ken Conklin, who argues that Hawaiians are "fully assimilated, happily intermarried, living and working side by side with everyone else. They are everyone else" (quoted in Osorio 2001, 377). Alani Apio dramatizes how such assimilationist ideology interpellates and divides Hawaiians from each other in his play *Kāmau A'e* (1998), in which the protagonist says, "We're too much of everybody and everything else . . . We may learn Hawaiian but we think *american*" (67). His uncompromising cousin's response is to " 'oki" him from "Ka 'Ohana" (sever him from his family [68]). Likewise, Thurston Twigg-Smith, descendent of Lorrin Thurston, who was instrumental in the overthrow, argues against the legitimacy of "a class of people called 'Hawaiians' " because "percentage Hawaiians . . . have no historical origin other than having been created by federal and state statutes" (2005). Such claims against Hawaiians as "authentically" distinguishable from non-Hawaiians argue that there can

be no collective "self" to claim land, "self-determination," or "entitlements" to government funding.[3]

This chapter, written by a non-Hawaiian and concerned with clarifying tendencies in "authenticity" discourse for other non-Hawaiians,
emphasizes that, given what continues to be at stake, there is a marked difference between questions about "authenticity" brought by non-
Hawaiians and questions about "authenticity" raised among sectors of
the Hawaiian community. For non-Hawaiians, I argue, questions broa-
ched about the "authenticity" of aspects of Hawaiian history and culture
as objective tend to be as politically irresponsible and narrowly objec-
tifying as they are philosophically incoherent. Such questions are generally bad objects, category mistakes, confusions about the possibility of
disinterested scholarship within the political/epistemological economies
of Empire, in which fear and desire about what "authenticity" might
entitle are anxiously mixed. Media obsession with literary identity hoaxes
indexes the split between a desire for literary "reservations" and a need
to read indigenous claims as fiction. To pursue this line, I question the
question of "authenticity" itself by briefly exploring why, how, where
(when and under what political conditions) and for whom (and under
what institutional auspices), and with what effect (to whose benefit or
detriment or at what cost) questions of "authenticity" arise.

This suggests that to the extent that "authenticity" and "indigeneity" are today linked in what is inherently a contest over representation—aside from nostalgic senses in which authenticity might be
longed for—it should be acknowledged that the terms have multiple,
non-intersecting, and context-bound forms and functions, and that they
are valuable primarily as a way of discussing the articulations of voices
within social movements (on "articulation" theory see Clifford, 97–98).
I thus note differences in the ways that questions of "authenticity" are
raised *about* Hawaiians by non-Hawaiians become scenes of contesta-
tion *between* Hawaiians and non-Hawaiians, and are engaged *within* the
lāhui. Most Hawaiian scholars who address the topic regard questions
about "authenticity" as effects of occupation that could be legitimately
discussed only in contexts in which Hawaiian epistemological categories and language were placed on an equal footing with the cultural
knowledges and practices of the occupiers. Were such a public sphere to
be achieved, Laiana Wong argues, "authenticity" as currently conceived
"might become a non-issue, or one that is discussed solely as an academic exercise" (112). To show that Hawaiians never stopped desiring

spheres that prioritized Hawaiian values, I mark assertions of *lāhui* over the last century, and suggest that stories and *mele* have always been one defense Hawaiians mobilized against harmful aspects of the question of the question of "authenticity" (see Osorio 1992; Basham; Stillman).

It is important to foreground in this respect the urgency with which nineteenth- and early-twentieth-century Hawaiians recognized the challenges to distinctness that would be faced by future generations of Hawaiians. These writers address the *hanauna* (generations) with a resolute sense that genealogy weaves together *kūpuna* (ancestors, elders) with descendants through whom the *lāhui* lives. They saw that remaining connected to Hawaiian knowledges was critical to the *lāhui*'s survival. The myriad ways in which the materials gathered enable Hawaiian cultural revitalization today are testimonies both to the *mana* of the stories and the foresight of artist-patriots. Among the invaluable materials perpetuated in the *moʻolelo* are *oli* (chants), *moʻolelo* of *wahi pana* (legendary places), names of winds, accounts of cultural practices, and *ʻōlelo noʻeau* (proverbs) from a period before settler institutions dispersed materials and interrupted the living stream of Hawaiian thought.[4] As Amy Kuʻuleialoha Stillman demonstrates, "Re-membering" knowledges, and recognizing how "the fabric from which . . . fragments were torn [by settler scholarship] lies virtually intact," is today a vigorous "act of advocacy" (201).

Providing an archive in the process of retelling popular stories was the express aim of scholars like S. N. Haleʻole, who wrote in his preface to *Laieikawai* (a newspaper serial printed in book form in 1864) that he aimed to "hoikeike . . . i na mea kahiko a keia lahui kanaka, me ka aua mai hoi mai ka nalowale loa ana o kekahi o na moolelo punihei a lakou" ("depict . . . ancient customs of the people [Hawaiians/the nation] for fear lest otherwise we lose some of their favorite traditions" (342–43). The author-collectors of these stories differentiated their audience as Hawaiians and interested "foreigners." In his *kanaenae* (dedication, supplicating chant, preface) to both "Moolelo Hawaii o Pakaa a me Ku-a-Pakaa" ("The Hawaiian Story of Pakaa and Ku-a-Pakaa") and "Moolelo Hawaii no Kalapana," Moses Nakuina addresses "ka iwi o kuu iwi a me ke koko o kuu koko, ke kupa, ka oiwi ponoi o ka aina, Aloha oukou" ("bones of my bones, blood of my blood, natives, the true children of the aina, Aloha to you all" (Nakuina). In 1906, Piʻilani Kaluaikoʻolau likewise opens *Ka Moolelo Oiaio o Kaluaikoolau* (*The True Story of Kaluaikoolau*) with a *kanaenae* addressed to "oʻu Oiwi o ka pupuu hookahi; aloha na kini o ka ewe, ka iʻo, ka iwi a me ke koko o ka iwikuamoo hookahi" ("Aloha to my people of the same womb; aloha to the multitudes of the same lineage, the flesh, the bone and the flood of the same family" [3]). The message of these scholar-patriots was clear: so long as the stories and the language lived in the hearts of "ke kanaka i ke aloha ʻaina" (those who loved the land), the *lāhui* would live as well. That message echoes today: "To me those newspapers [in which the stories appeared] are direct ancestors of this journal," claimed Māhealani Dudoit, founding editor of *ʻŌiwi: A Native Hawaiian Journal*, whose achievement of a venue for Hawaiian expression will be touched on in my conclusion.

Forms and Functions of the Question of Authenticity

> Identity (who we think we are) is the foundation on which Native Cultural Studies is based. No other question is as important to us, and no other question is so seriously contested by others.
>
> —Jonathan Kamakawiwoʻole Osorio,
> "What ʻkine Hawaiian Are You?"

The first thing that non-Hawaiians who question the authenticity of aspects of Hawaiian self-representation should realize is that, however much they avow disinterested concern with accuracy, as the product of the ongoing U.S. occupation, and with the legacy of skewed settler histories, researches *about* Hawaiians are always already situated in the political realm; there are inherent senses in which the project of indigeneity forms against that which aims to extinguish its political meaning (Sissons 13). Whether charges of inauthenticity intend to do so, they are thus intrinsically deployable in both the court of public opinion and court itself against Hawaiian benefits or struggles for recognition (see Trask 1993, 161–78; and Guenther et al.). The implication tends to be that since Hawaiians do not practice their cultures exactly as they once did, they are no longer what they claim to be and thus their claims are groundless. Arguments by non-Hawaiians seeking to destabilize the "authenticity" of Hawaiian cultural definitions resonate against these contexts, and contribute to a hypochondric suspicion about invocations of tradition as part of the living narrative of indigenous people. Some confusion must be produced in fourth-grade students who read *in Hawaiian* the words of William Pila Wilson, a non-Hawaiian long committed to Hawaiian language revitalization, questioning the "authenticity" of the *lāhui*. In a pamphlet for Hawaiian immersion schools, Wilson poses the question, "He aha kēia mea he lāhui kānaka ʻōiwi? A he loaʻa anei kō Hawaiʻi nei lāhui kānaka ʻōiwi, ʻaʻole paha?" ("What is this thing, the Native Hawaiian nation? Does Hawaiʻi really have a native people or not?" [87, my translation]). Wilson answers his question by saying that Hawaiʻi has indigenous birds and plants, but that since Hawaiians migrated from different places, and intermarried, an "authentic" *lāhui* cannot be constituted. (For a critique of how Wilson's pamphlet appropriates the authority to define "authenticity," see Warner 85–86; and on non-Hawaiian appropriation of Hawaiian identity see Hall.)

In a more typical charge of "inauthenticity," Scott Whitney claimed in *Honolulu Magazine* that "Everyone thinks the word ʻohana expresses an ancient Hawaiian value. Not so. It turns out we made it up." Whitney presented this invention as representative of how "our public version of Hawaiian culture is a shared fiction, and an arbitrary story that depends on who the narrator is." The mistake occurred, Whitney argues, because Hawaiian activists of the 1970s "had to learn to be Hawaiian" and fooled themselves "into thinking that a modern value [was] really an ancient one" (2001a, 42, 43, 45). Among the respondents to Whitney's claim were Davianna Pomaikaʻi McGregor, who argued that while activists of the 1970s adapted the ʻohana concept for political ends, ʻohana was not a twentieth-century invention. Other scholars provided numerous examples of nineteenth-century uses of the word, including dictionary entries, along with cognates of ʻohana in other Polynesian languages. While apologizing for not checking old dictionaries carefully, Whitney maintained his view that many contemporary Hawaiian concepts today amount to "New Age mush" (2001b, 22), cleansed of the harsh practices of pre-missionary Hawaiʻi. That practices were discarded or modified during the century in which Hawaiians entered the global system as an internationally recognized nation with multiple treaties, for Whitney signifies irrevocable cultural rupture.

This reasoning—by which "authentic" indigeneity must be premodern, primitive, and unself-conscious (see Jolly) or a repressive, constricting eco-indigeneity (Sissons), requiring the replication of prior and stabilized entities—tilts progressive intellectuals, consciously or not, against indigenous claims. "The return to ʻauthenticity,ʻ " Masao Miyoshi argues, "is a closed route. There is nothing of the sort extant any longer in *much of the world*. How then to balance the transnationalization of economy and politics with the survival of local culture and history—without mummifying them with tourism and in museums—is the crucial question" (747, emphasis added). "Authenticity" here implies the purity of peoples to whom tourism (self-conscious performance of culture) has not come. In Miyoshi's borderless world, postcolonial globalism accelerates colonial modernity's smashing of the "aura" of an "authenticity" whose culture at best avoids existing as stuffed remnants that haunt museums. Peoples classifiable as "authentic" are (once only) like the objects of "First Contact trips" (the name of a tour company, one of whose excursionists recently described his adventures for readers of *The New Yorker*). Within this economy of "authenticity," the "romantic nationalist" appears, like the tourist promoter (though with different investments), the perpetrator of culture charade.

In only seeming opposition to this logic are destabilizations of "authenticity" offered by proponents of the idea that tradition is always self-conscious invention: since genuine cultures evolve and are never self-identical to what they were at a previous moment, they are either not actually "authentic," or else everything is always "authentic" in the sense that "authenticity" refers to whatever people actually do. "Authenticity" seen through this lens becomes either an empty (tautological) category, or one in which claims to "authentic" tradition could only be strategic essentialism. While "invention of tradition" arguments refigure Edward Sapir's (1924) notion that all genuine traditions are spurious, it is notable that in Oceania such arguments emerged in historical competition with indigenous activist-scholarship. Only when Oceanians invoked cultural categories in political contexts did non-indigenous scholars feel it incumbent on them to expose movement viewpoints as constructs.

Not surprisingly, "invention of tradition" arguments are challenged by Hawaiian scholar-activists and become public battlegrounds. That the arguments involve seemingly non-intersecting rhetorics is beside the point, which for Hawaiians is primarily about helping the *lāhui* in the present, and about maintaining Hawaiian relations, and Hawaiian authority over Hawaiian definitions.[5] Given this history, it ought to be axiomatic that when non-indigenous scholars pronounce on the "authenticity" of indigenous practices their reasons for doing so will be as worthy of consideration as their cultural insights. The desire to "help" in such matters, No'eau Warner argues, will not prove an adequate reason for entering into such discussions if the terms of involvement are not defined by those the non-Hawaiian "claim[s] to want to help" (79).

In contrast with logics that consign "authenticity" to unself-conscious primitivity or tautology, for Hawaiian scholars "authenticity" rarely resides in single truths that exclude other truths, and instead affirms shareable principles that benefit the *lāhui*. A given *moʻolelo* is "a fragment of a story" whose teller "recognizes that he is not saying everything there is to say about the subject" (Osorio 2002, 250). Nor is invention seen as cultural rupture: rather, it is "necessary for survival and does not render the product inauthentic" (McGregor 12). It is not a question of whether such processes occur, but of minding for whom and for what they claim place. Within the Hawaiian community, that is, there are rigorous disagreements about culture in which questions about "authenticity" or "accuracy" surface around aspects of memory and practice, with some more committed to (and better situated to maintain) literal and direct transmission from *kumu* (teachers) and *kūpuna* within families. However, in these discussions—in which non-Hawaiian contributions may be found valuable—the stakes are different, and the procedures for doing scholarship differ from those of outside investigators of "authenticity." In-community debates implicitly or explicitly function in the opposite direction of settler-colonial scholarship. Where the former tends toward the politically deconstructive and culturally debunking, in-community Hawaiian debates about "authenticity" tend toward construction, toward clarifying both the sources and poetics of contemporary practices within the *lāhui*.

A case in point is the touchstone *moʻolelo* of *ʻōlelo Hawaiʻi* (Hawaiian language), recognized as integral to expressing Hawaiian consciousness and ways-of-seeing. U.S. settlers involved in the overthrow banned Hawaiian as a medium of instruction in 1896, teachers punished students for speaking Hawaiian in school, and the number of native speakers rapidly declined; Hawaiian was "almost completely wiped out" as a living language by the mid-twentieth century (NeSmith 69). With the scarcity of native speakers today, the revitalization of the language involves linguistic and educational activism and, as Laiana Wong describes, "legitimate concerns have been raised about the authenticity of the product being promoted throughout the community as 'Hawaiian' " (94), given that most Hawaiian speakers today have learned Hawaiian as a second language from second-language speakers. As in many similar revitalization efforts, the politics of usage (prescriptivist/traditionalist versus flexible/adaptive) are as vigorously argued as the nature and purpose of the debate are agreed upon. What are prized are "clearly discernable link[s] to traditions" (Wong 98), however rigidly defined, that meet community needs. For NeSmith, who distinguishes sharply between Traditional and Neo-Hawaiian, and urges commitment to the former, the Hawaiian that *Kānaka Maoli* acquire will be less important than its use to substantively help Hawaiians to "maintain their distinct identity as one people" (75).

"Authenticity" in such arguments, in other words, relates to a broader, decolonization movement (on this context of Hawaiian literary production see Trask 1999); it resonates with efforts around Oceania in which, as Fijian scholar-poet Pio Manoa put it, "authentic" expression must "become the voice of the people feeling in a new language" (quoted in Hereniko). As in other locations, "authenticity" involves individual speech acts resonating within the emerging language spoken by a collective body living out the effects of a shared history. For Eduardo Galeano, "Our authentic collective identity is born out of the past and is nourished by it—our feet tread where others trod before us; the steps we take were prefigured—but this identity is not frozen into nostalgia . . . our identity resides in action and struggle" (121). In Hawaiian struggle, collective identity is a shared genealogical connection to the *'āina* and *lāhui* in which *being* resonates with (and recognizes itself in terms of) *doing*. To "be Hawaiian," Kaleikoa Ka'eo argues, is an "active verb, not a noun." *Being* active, in terms of interpreting, extending, and adapting the legacy, then, is less about being "shackled to mindless repetition" than about finding "a clue on your path toward liberation and right action" (Meyer 2003, 53).

Contemporary *Mo'olelo Hawai'i* and the Struggle for *Pono*

Art is the life that made that thing of paper or clay or stone.
It is the lives that the individual life is moving forward into another
stage of being.

—Māhealani Dudoit, "Carving a Hawaiian Aesthetic"

Lest we be lost
In someone else's story

—Imaikalani Kalahele, "Somewhere in the Swirl of History"

In *Native Lands and Foreign Desires*, Lilikalā Kameʻeleihiwa argues that "The question that arises continually for Hawaiians is and has been 'Pehea lā e pono ai?' that is, 'How is it that we shall be *pono?*' (10). While *pono* has a range of significations (goodness, uprightness, morality, moral qualities, correct or proper procedure, excellence, well-being, prosperity), Kameʻeleihiwa clarifies that the word is intimately bound up with land and sovereignty, so that loss of *pono* follows the loss of either. Noenoe Silva notes that *pono* refers to "justice" and "rights" as well. In this sense, the common and telling mistranslation of the state motto ("Ua mau ka ea o ka ʻāina i ka pono") as, "the life of the land is perpetuated in righteousness," drains the political valences of *pono*. When Kauikeaouli (Kamehameha III) wrote the motto, he clearly meant that the "sovereignty of Hawaiʻi was protected by *pono* behavior." Written for "Lā Hoʻihoʻi Ea" (restoration of sovereignty day), after the Paulet affair in 1843 (in which a British admiral seized the Hawaiian Islands without his government's permission), the motto weaves together multiple meanings of the word *ea*: the life-breath of the land is in being *pono*, protecting the rights of the people; *pono* authenticates productive relation between individual acts and the *lāhui* (see Kameʻeleihiwa, 184–85; Silva 2004, 37).

It can only be asserted here that even a cursory look at the historical *moʻolelo*—in particular those recorded in Hawaiian language newspapers that ran continuously from the 1840s to the 1940s—shows that Hawaiians, no matter how dispirited in the decades following annexation, never stopped connecting *pono* with justice and rights for the *lāhui*, and never stopped thinking of themselves as a distinct people connected to the *ʻāina*. A few examples must suffice. In 1927, an article written in *Ka Nupepa Kuokoa* asked,

> O ka ninau, aia kakou, ka lahui, mahea? Heaha ko kakou kulana ma loko o keia, ka aina i noho hanohano ia e ko kakou kupuna? Ma ko makou noonoo, aia kakou i lalo loa . . . ke nonoi nei ia oukou e hana like kakou no ka pono, pomaikai a holomua o ka lahui.
>
> We have a question: where are the Hawaiians? What is our position in this, the land where our ancestors lived nobly? In our thinking, we are very subordinate, and . . . we ask you to labor as we do for the righteousness and good fortune and progress for the race. (In Johnson 425)

In the 1940s, Alvin Kaleolani Isaacs wrote "E mau"—*mau* includes the senses of "unceasing, perpetual, persevering, enduring, steady,
constant"—a song picked up by later activists, that blended references
to Kauikeaouli's motto and Kalākaua's urge to Hawaiians to "Ho'oulu
lāhui" (increase the nation, make the nation grow):

> E mau ko kakou lahui, e ho'omau.
> E mau ko kakou 'olelo, e ho'omau.
> E mau ka hana pono o ka 'aina
> I mau ka ea o ka 'aina i ka pono.
> I ka pono—o ka 'aina.
> Ho'oulu ka pono o ka 'aina, e ho'oulu
> Ho'ola ka nani o ka 'aina, e ho'ola
> Ho'ola la, Ho'ola la, a ho'olaha
> I mau ka ea o ka 'aina i ka pono.
> I ka pono—o ka 'aina.
> Perpetuate our *lāhui*, persist
> Perpetuate our language, persist
> Continue the *pono* work of the land
> So that the sovereignty of the land is perpetuated through
>   *pono*.
> Through *pono*—of the land.
> Increase the *pono* of the *'āina*, nourish its growth
> The beauty of the land lives, nourish its life
> Let it live, let it live, spread this
> Perpetuation of the sovereignty of the land through
>   righteousness
> Through *pono*—of the land.

(My translation, text in Morales 38)

These lines were written at a time when Hawaiians were broadly repre-
sented as "happy-go-lucky 'ukulele strummers" or sullenly, self-destruc-
tively disengaged. Lawrence Fuchs's influential *Hawaii Pono* (1961)—a
book at once liberally rueful of Hawaiian demise and celebratory of U.S.
democratic achievement—argued that since the 1920s the "Hawaiians'
dominant response to the new and hostile environment of the Islands
was withdrawal into the past" (68)—a past Fuchs determined to be an
"unreal past in which fact and fiction were often blurred" (75). Never-

theless, Fuchs acknowledged that Hawaiians remained race consciousness and practiced core values: Hawaiian candidates in the 1930s used the slogan "Nana i ka 'ili" ("Look for the skin") (80), and even "Hawaiians who resented the overthrow of the monarchy by American haoles might welcome and feed a *malihini* haole stranger for weeks" (85).

This mix of "racial" pride and futility blend dramatically in the public sphere with the "Hawaiian Renaissance." Irked by newspaper articles stereotyping Hawaiians, John Dominis Holt, in "On Being Hawaiian" (1964), wrote one of its founding documents. Holt conceded that, in the face of a "haole culture" that they found "a farce," many of his generation "cavorted or smoldered in their bitterness," but then celebrated a "vast awakening among us Hawaiians" that "whether we agree or not we want to run our own show—at long last—as an ethnic and political conglomerate on our own terms" (8). Holt stresses his belief in Hawaiians' "right to win back our lands, those belonging to us, as 'reservations' 'belong' to our Indian brothers and sisters" (9). For Holt, whose works include the landmark novel *Waimea Summer*, Hawaiian writing involves "fusing the aesthetic image of the past with the present" while prioritizing "the land itself" (13).[6] Holt argued that while Hawaiians in the 1940s and 1950s felt "psychologically captive to the spirit of the past," young Hawaiians sensed "as only Hawaiians can sense this particular thing, that a greatness, something intangible yet powerful and enduring belonged to our people. . . . We are links to the ancients" (17). To this generation links with the past guided political activism. "We are talking about Aloha 'Aina 'Ohana," singer-activist George Helm said in a speech to the State House, "and if you cannot understand it, go and do your homework." As Harry Kunuhi Mitchell wrote in "Mele o Kahoolawe," the people were "Pa'a pu ka mana'o / No ka pono o ka 'aina" ("Together in one thought / to bring prosperity to the land") (in Morales 71, 86–87).

What this sketch suggests is that perhaps a better way to ask what is "authentic" about a Hawaiian expression is how it relates to the struggle to find what is *pono* for the *lāhui*. To the degree that this involves Hawaiians reactivating lines of connection, and solidifying a *lāhui* that was never ceded to the occupiers, it is a collective coming to terms with how the legacy of Hawaiian knowledge and ways-of-knowing resonates in the present. "Authenticity" is arrived at collectively and contextually; it is not a checklist of qualities, but rearticulations of qualities in relation to a movement seen as diverse and as "breathing in the many aromas of influence" (Meyer 2001, 128). "Although it is tempting to offer universalisms that would portray Kanaka ʻŌiwi as one people and one mind," Manulani Meyer writes, "to do so would ignore the multiple realities within the group" (2003, 85). This is the point emphasized in ʻŌiwi, a remarkable print-media expression of *lāhui*. As founding editor Māhealani Dudoit recalls, the journal was conceived of with "two key words" in mind—*moʻokūauhau* and *kuleana* (responsibility, privilege)— and has been guided by a need to clarify "our kuleana today within the moʻokuauhau of our people" ("Kūkākūkā" 1). While the journal's editorial dialogues do not engage specific legal/political issues, ʻŌiwi (native) assumes discursive sovereignty and exists to gather "the literary, artistic, and scholarly work of the ʻōiwi, the Native People of Hawaiʻi, to express the endurance and vitality of the nation" (back cover to issue 1).

Dudoit's vision of a journal open to all forms of Hawaiian expression, that would reach out to different segments of the Hawaiian community, has been realized in three issues (1998, 2002, 2003) with such success that it clearly answers a community's call. ʻŌiwi publishes works in Hawaiian, Hawaii Creole English, and English, often combining all three, displaying the trilinguality of much of contemporary Hawaiian writing; it gathers poems, stories, personal essays, biography, translated documents, testimony at legislative hearings, art work in various media, *pule* (prayers), such as Kanalu Young's "Pule no ka ea" (Prayer for Sovereignty) or *kanikau* (death chants), profiles of notable Hawaiians, and much else. The heterogeneity of *moʻolelo* suggests a project that attends less to laws of genre than to the larger social and movement contexts within which individual works of *kānaka maoli* expression take form.

In design, organization, and content, ʻŌiwi attempts to translate traditional practices "into the language of today" (Dudoit 22), often adapting oral and visual conventions to journal format. The issues start with *oli* (chant), and works are generally prefaced by a note from the author, introducing contributors to their audience (or to each other); a regular contribution is an editorial "talk-story," expressing various thoughts within the editorial *hui* (group, collective). Several of the issues have included essays by graphic artists on "Native Hawaiian Design." Graphic designer for the second issue ʻAlika McNicoll explores ways in which aspects of Hawaiian protocol inform design asking, "What would an approach look like that uses Hawaiian cultural sensibilities perceptually and conceptually different from one guided by Western sensibilities" (11). For Kamaka Kanekoa, graphic designer of the third issue, visual symbols are important in forming meaning, and one aspect of design is "the marriage of opposites or complementary pairs exhibited in the concept of pono" (9). New technologies allow a diversifying of "our communicative systems and create new forms of visual language based on our traditional knowledge of ʻōlelo and kākau' " (12).

The selection processes that animate the journal are well suggested in dialogues among ʻŌiwi's *hui*. Current editor Kuʻualoha Hoʻomanawa-nui describes the journal's work as "opening a community dialogue in a new way. We are Hawaiians talking to other Hawaiians" ("Huliau" 1). Kimo Armitage invites community participation with the words, "show us your own unique, valid Hawaiian perspective and we'll try to take care of you in the next issue. You're Hawaiian and what you say counts. There is power in your voice" ("Huliau" 6). For Michael Pule-loa, " ʻŌiwi offers Hawaiian people a chance to represent themselves in print. It's our hale, a house that we have built. You know when you read ʻŌiwi that you will find a real definition of what it means to be Hawaiian today and what it meant to be Hawaiian in the past. It also allows visitors the chance to find our hale and learn about who we really are. And it offers Hawaiian readers an opportunity to learn so much about themselves and about other Hawaiians, to see our diversity and our commonalities" ("Huliau" 10). Clearly, looking for *an* "authentic" Hawaiian voice within the journal would go against the spirit of open-ness and community inclusiveness that it fosters, yet the editorial *hui* agree that Hawaiian voices count as Hawaiian voices, and that stories Hawaiians tell about their lives move in alliance with a will—call it "authentic"—to *hoʻoulu lāhui*. What counts, as Noʻeau Warner argues about language revitalization, is that *moʻolelo* be "perpetuated among its own people, in its own context and environment" as part of "what can help make Hawaiians whole again" (77).

Notes

1. Hawaiian definitions in this chapter are checked against Elbert and Pukuʻi's *Hawaiian Dictionary*, to which readers should refer for additional resonances to invoked terms. *Lāhui*, for instance, is also a stative verb: "to assemble, gather together, the act of being together." "Literature" is not a Hawaiian category; *moʻolelo*, the word the dictionary provides, refers as well to history, tradition, essay, article, path, or minutes from a meeting, among other

meanings. Likewise, as Kuʻualoha Hoʻomanawanui notes, the word for poem, *mele*, refers as well to song, anthem, chant (of various kinds). Except where noted, I have used translations provided in bilingual editions, following the use of diacritical marks in those editions. *Mahalo* to Kahealani Clark for several references, and to Noenoe Silva and Laiana Wong, *kumu* (teachers, sources) whose class discussions have informed my ideas about authenticity and the importance of *moʻolelo*.

2. The multiple orders of sovereignty claims today (see Kauanui 2005b) all maintain the illegality of the 1893 overthrow of the Hawaiian Kingdom, a fact acknowledged in "Apology to Native Hawaiians on Behalf of the United States for the Overthrow of the Kingdom of Hawaiʻi" (Public Law 103–150). All express continuity of spirit with the nationalist *mele lāhui* (anti-annexation songs) of the 1890s (see Stillman and Basham, whose work most specifically explores continuities and transformations in the meaning of the term *lāhui*).

3. Hawaiian so-called entitlements (some eighty-five statutes) are under persistent legal attack by proponents of a "color blind" society, whose funding comes in part from right-wing Conservative groups; riding on the back of threats to legal dissolution of Hawaiian "distinctness" as a *lāhui*, the Akaka Bill (Native Hawaiian Government Reorganization Bill) has emerged as a stopgap measure. For those who oppose it, this bill would for the first time offer Hawaiian consent to the ongoing U.S. occupation of Hawaiian lands (see Kauanui 2005 and Kaʻeo 2005).

4. On the politically invested ways in which an orientalist settler scholarship refigures *moʻolelo*—distancing them from living practice by converting them into "legend" that can be appropriated by state tourism—see Bacchilega.

5. For a critical overview of the Joycelyn Linnekin–Trask debate, in which Linnekin argued that the concept of *malama ʻaina* (take care of the land), among others, was a contemporary construct, see Tobin, who emphasizes the importance of outsiders positioning themselves "relative to a Nationalist movement. We are not free to choose the location from which we write" (168).

6. For complementary definitions see Dudoit; Hoʻomanawanui; Trask 1999.

Works Cited

Apio, Alani. *Kāmau Aʻe*. Kailua, HI: A. Apio, 1998.

Bacchilega, Cristina. *Legendary Hawaiʻi and the Politics of Place: Tradition, Translation, and Tourism*. Philadelpha: U of Pennsylvania P, 2007.

Basham, J. Leilani. *He Puke Mele Lāhui: Nā Mele Kūpaʻa, Nā Mele Kūʻē a me nā Mele Aloha o nā Kānaka Maoli*. M.A. Thesis, University of Hawaiʻi, 2002.

Clifford, James. "Valuing the Pacific: An Interview with James Clifford." *Remembrances of Pacific Pasts: An Invitation to Remake History*. Ed. Robert Borofsky. Honolulu: U of Hawai'i P. 92–99.

Day, A. Grove. *Hawaii and Its People*. Honolulu: Mutual, 1993.

Dudoit, D. Māhealani. "Carving a Hawaiian Aesthetic." *'Ōiwi: A Native Hawaiian Journal* 1 (1998): 20–26.

Fuchs, Lawrence. *Hawaii Pono: A Social History*. New York: Harcourt, Brace, 1961.

Galeano, Eduardo. *We Say No: Chronicles, 1963–1991*. New York: Norton, 1992.

Guenther, Mathias, et al. "Discussion: The Concept of Indigeneity." *Social Anthropology* 14 (2006): 1, 17–32.

Hale'ole, S. N. *The Hawaiian Romance of Laieikawai*. Trans. M. Beckwith. Washington, DC: U.S. Bureau of American Ethnology, 1919.

Hall, Lisa Kahaleole. " 'Hawaiian at Heart' and Other Fictions." *The Contemporary Pacific* 17.2 (2005): 404–13.

Halualani, Rona Tomiko. *In the Name of Hawaiians: Native Identities & Cultural Politics*. Minneapolis: U of Minnesota P, 2002.

"He kūkākūkā 'ana, A Discussion." *'Ōiwi: A Native Hawaiian Journal* 1 (1998): 1–8.

Hereniko, Vilisoni. "Interdisciplinary Approaches in Pacific Studies: Understanding the Fiji Coup of 19 May 2000." *The Contemporary Pacific* 15.1 (2003): 75–90.

Ho'omanawanui, Ku'ualoha. "He Lei Ho'oheno no nā Kau a Kau: Language, Performance, and Form in Hawaiian Poetry." *The Contemporary Pacific* 17. 1 (2005): 29–81.

Holt, John Dominis. "On Being Hawaiian." Honolulu: Topgallant, 1974.

"Huliau" [Editor's Note]. *'Ōiwi: A Native Hawaiian Journal* 2 (2002): 1–10.

Johnson, Rubellite Kawena. *Kukini 'Aha'ilono: Over a Century of Native Hawaiian Life and Thought from the Native Hawaiian Language Newspapers of 1834 to 1948*. Honolulu: Topgallant Press, 1976.

Jolly, Margaret. "Spectres of Inauthenticity." *The Contemporary Pacific* 4.1 (1992): 49–72.

Ka'eo, Kaleikoa, panel discussion. "We Are Satisfied with the Stones: The Perils of the Akaka Bill." Kamakakūokalani Center, Honolulu, 14 October 2005.

Kalahele, Imaikalani. *Kalahele*. Honolulu: Kalamaku Press, 2002.

Kaluaiko'olau, Pi'ilani. *The True Story of Kaluaikoolau*. Trans. F. Frazier. Honolulu: U of Hawai'i P, 2001.

Kame'eleihiwa, Lilikalā. *Native Land and Foreign Desires: Pehea Lā e Pono Ai?* Honolulu: Bishop Musuem Press, 1992.

Kanekoa, Kamaka. "Graphic Artist's Note: Native Hawaiian Design—The Conveyance of Meaning through the Context of Culture." *'Ōiwi: A Native Hawaiian Journal* 3 (2003): 8–12.

Kauanui, J. Kehaulani. "Precarious Positions: Native Hawaiians and U.S. Federal Recognition." *The Contemporary Pacific* 17.1 (2005a): 1–27.

———. "The Multiplicity of Hawaiian Sovereignty Claims and the Struggle for Meaningful Autonomy." *Comparative American Studies* 3.3 (2005b): 283–300.

McGregor, Davianna Pomaikaʻi. " ʻOhana Answers." *Honolulu Magazine* 36.5 (2001): 12.

Meyer, Manulani Aluli. *Hoʻoulu, Our Time of Becoming: Hawaiian Epistemology and Early Writings.* Honolulu: ʻAi Pohaku Press, 2003.

———. "Our Own Liberation: Reflections on Hawaiian Epistemology." *The Contemporary Pacific* 13.1 (2001): 124–48.

Miyoshi, Masao. "A Borderless World? From Colonialism to Transnationalism and the Decline of the Nation State." *Critical Inquiry* 19.2 (1993): 726–51.

Morales, Rodney, ed. *Hoʻihoʻi Hou: A Tribute to George Helm & Kimo Mitchell.* Honolulu: Bamboo Ridge Press, 1984.

Nakuina, Moses. *The Wind Gourd of Laʻamaomao.* Trans. E. T. Mookini and S. Nakoa. Honolulu: Kalamaku Press, 1992.

NeSmith, Keʻao. "Tutu's Hawaiian and the Emergence of a Neo-Hawaiian Language." *ʻŌiwi: A Native Hawaiian Journal* 3 (2003): 68–77.

Osorio, Jonathan Kamakawiwoʻole. "Songs of Our Natural Selves: The Enduring Voice of Nature in Hawaiian Music." *Papers from the 8th Pacific History Association Conference.* Ed. D. Rubenstein. Mangilao, Guam: U of Guam P and Micronesian Area Research Center, 1992. 429–32.

———. "What ʻkine Hawaiian Are You?: A Moʻolelo about Nationhood, Race, History, and the Contemporary Sovereignty Movement in Hawaiʻi." *The Contemporary Pacific* 13.2 (2001): 359–79.

———. *Dismembering Lāhui: A History of the Hawaiian Nation to 1887.* Honolulu: U of Hawaiʻi P, 2002.

Pukui, Mary Kawena, and Sam. H. Elbert. *Hawaiian Dictionary.* Honolulu: U of Hawaiʻi P, 1986.

Sapir, Edward. "Culture, Genuine and Spurious." *The American Journal of Sociology* 29.4 (1924): 401–429.

Silva, Noenoe. *Aloha Betrayed: Native Hawaiian Resistance to American Colonialism.* Durham, NC: Duke UP, 2004.

———. "Kānaka Maoli Resistance to Annexation." *ʻŌiwi: A Native Hawaiian Journal* 1 (1998): 45–70.

Sissons, Jeffrey. *First Peoples: Indigenous Cultures and Their Futures.* London: Reaktion Books, 2005.

Stillman, Amy Kuʻuleialoha. "Re-Membering the History of Hawaiian Hula." *Cultural Memory: History and Identity in the Postcolonial Pacific.* Ed. Jeannette Marie Mageo. Honolulu: U of Hawaiʻi P, 2001. 187–202.

Tengan, Ty Kawika, and Geoff White. "Disappearing Worlds: Anthropology and Cultural Studies in Hawai'i and the Pacific." *The Contemporary Pacific* 12.3 (2001): 381–416.

———. "Of the People Who Love the Land: Vernacular History in the Poetry of Modern Hawaiian Hula." *Amerasia Journal* 28.3 (2002): 85–108.

Tobin, Jeffrey. "Cultural Construction and Native Nationalism: Report from the Hawaiian Front." *Asia/Pacific as Space of Cultural Production.* Ed. Rob Wilson and Arif Dirlik. Durham and London: Duke UP, 1995. 147–69.

Trask, Haunani-Kay. *From a Native Daughter: Colonialism and Sovereignty in Hawai'i.* Monroe, ME: Common Courage Press, 1993.

———. "Writing in Captivity: Poetry in a Time of Decolonization." *Inside Out: Literature, Cultural Politics, and Identity in the New Pacific.* Ed. R. Wilson and V. Hereniko. Lanham, MD: Rowman & Littlefield, 1999. 17–26.

———. *Night Is a Sharkskin Drum.* Honolulu: U of Hawai'i P, 2002.

Twigg-Smith, Thurston. "Akaka Bill Supporters Ignore Key Questions." *Honolulu Advertiser* (Letter to Editor), 26 August 2005.

Warner, No'eau. "*Kuleana*: The Right, Responsibility, and Authority of Indigenous Peoples to Speak and Make Decisions for Themselves in Language and Cultural Revitalization." *Anthropology and Education Quarterly* 30.1 (1999): 68–93.

Whitney, Scott. "Inventing 'Ohana." *Honolulu Magazine* 36.3 (2001a): 42–45.

———. " 'Ohana Troubles." *Honolulu Magazine* 36.5 (2001b): 22.

Wilson, William Pila. "He Lāhui Kanaka 'Ōiwi Anei kō Hawai'i Nei?" Hilo: Hale Kako'o, 1999.

Wong, Laiana. "Authenticity and the Revitalization of Hawaiian." *Anthropology & Education Quaterly* 30.1 (1999): 94–115.

2

Cycles of Selfhood, Cycles of Nationhood in Native American Literatures

Authenticity, Identity, Community, Sovereignty

David L. Moore

Over the past generation, an ancient notion has been emerging that underneath the many narratives of identity politics in Native American literatures, a driving energy that animates those stories and poems, either by its presence or its absence, is tribal sovereignty. Explicitly or implicitly, notions of tribal sovereignty and American nationhood have pushed against and around each other in battles, in the courts and Congress, and in daily life on the land and in the cities. That dance is American history, and its narration takes sometimes equally opposing forms, depending on one's perspective across or apart from the so-called frontier. Contemporary criticism and pedagogy around Native literatures have reached a saturation point in focusing so much on secondary identity issues that finally the prior sovereignty issues that always have shaped indigenous (and American) identity are crystallizing out of the mix. Questions of why colonial issues in the literature are secondary and why indigenous sovereignty issues are primary emerge when Native stories suggest narrative dynamics that do not merely reflect or deflect colonial power. Addressing those indigenous dynamics is the heart of an ethics of criticism and of pedagogy that a growing presence of Native scholars such as Elizabeth Cook-Lynn, Robert Warrior, Craig Womack, and others are helping to articulate. They are steering critics away from recycling the colonial gaze.

Since Native American literary criticism began in earnest in the early 1970s, the call has been to find a mode of criticism that is based in indigenous texts and contexts rather than in Eurocentric modes. Perhaps this effort is toward an indigenous perspective, but Elizabeth Cook-Lynn's statement names the impossibilities: "The frank truth is that I don't know very many poets who say, 'I speak for my people.' It is not only unwise; it is probably impossible, and it is very surely arrogant . . ." (quoted in Weaver 1997, 42). If Native writers cannot, then certainly non-Native academics cannot speak for Native people! Then what are we about here? Very simply: foregrounding and interpreting Native voices. Certainly a non-Indian critic can read a Native perspective and try to articulate a hermeneutics of meaning and a poetics of structure, though he or she can never speak for that perspective. Such a critic clearly must have an experiential, that is, contextual, relation to the Native American community and its ethos, which is expressed in the text. As described in the 1985 Lethbridge conference on "The Native in Literature" (see Thomas King et al.), the effort to speak and listen across and to and from cultural difference is ultimately impossible and at the same time absolutely necessary.

Native American writers have been beating the drum of a particular circle dance of the individual in the group for centuries. They start from the perspective of a besieged tribal sovereignty, and their narratives frequently tell either the loss or the reaffirmation, the past or the uncertain future, of Native nationhood. Tribal sovereignty, in turn, is the historical and legal, some will say spiritual, foundation of three central issues, the questions of authenticity, identity, and community, that cycle on each other in many forms in Native writing. Sovereignty emerges through many of these texts as the political principle underlying narratives of community, and through community into the other questions of authenticity and identity. Cycles of selfhood become cycles of nationhood around these four standards. In Native stories since contact, authenticity becomes the question of what is an Indian and what is America. Identity becomes the question of how an individual does or doesn't fit into definitions of the "authentic" Indian versus white culture. And community becomes the question of where other Indians place the individual on that spectrum, as well as where or how Indian nations fit into the larger nation.

Larger questions that govern authenticity, identity, and community emerge as issues of the static or dynamic qualities of culture and the permeability of cultural boundaries. Native stories express that permeability in many ways, not the least of which is a crossing of genre in numerous texts, combining ethnography, history, and autobiography in poetry and prose. Specific writers in their historical circumstances take various approaches to those three key questions, plus tribal sovereignty as the fourth issue, the ground on which authenticity, identity, and community grow and change. As an example of permeable narrative, Acoma poet Simon Ortiz's generous lines include in retrospect even such historic tragedies as the Sand Creek Massacre of 1865 as a part of this cyclic process: "That dream / shall have a name / after all, / and it will not be vengeful / but wealthy with love / and compassion / and knowledge. / And it will rise / in this heart / which is our America" (*from Sand Creek*, n.p.). Ortiz envisions the losses at Sand Creek as only a part of the story. At the heart of that dream of America, by Ortiz's formulations, is tribal sovereignty, an extreme test of America's dream of *e pluribus unum*.

A key dynamic of this process is how the "questions" of Native identity and authenticity, key to so much of contemporary Native literature, leads to sovereignty and community not as "answers" in the literature, but how these four terms—authenticity, identity, community, and sovereignty—map different modes of reading Native texts, each looking for and recognizing a different narrative, and each with its own political resonances. Authenticity tends toward the anthropological, identity toward the psychological, community toward the historical, and sovereignty toward the political. Each drawing on the mythical and the geographical, they separately interpret Native narratives with sometimes unfortunate resonances that undermine the stories' own purposes for Native survivance. Instead, authenticity cannot be understood outside the changing contexts of identity, community, and sovereignty. These contexts generate a definition of authenticity within American Indian societies different from the "terminal creeds" of specular social sciences. Indian writers thus reshape "authenticity" as a flexible and resilient process of translation and adaptation to change.

Authenticity as Translation

Although they are intricately entwined, each of the four terms asks separate questions as lenses of analysis. Reading for authenticity asks, "what
is Indian about this text," generally pursuing an analysis that locates
criteria of Indianness in an ethnographic past. Thus Jerald Ramsey suggests "literary ethnography" as the rubric for Native literary studies.
Or Arnold Krupat carefully analyzes the "bicultural composite com-
positions" of Indian autobiography to delineate precisely what is and
what is not "Indian" about the text (1985, 31). H. David Brumble
explores constructions of the self in Native autobiography, comparing,
like Krupat, the real with the less-real Indian subjectivity in the text, as
group oriented rather than individualistic, respectively, and suggesting
that "self-written autobiography is at least the subject's *own* fiction, the
subject's own conception of the self, and so it must always be authentic
in this sense at least" (11). Jace Weaver has coined a descriptive phrase
for this kind of analysis, as a "gymnastics of authenticity." Similarly,
Susan Bernardin points out that Native writers as well as critics, Native
and non-Native, have all too frequently been embroiled in what she
calls "the authenticity game." The reason for dismissing the question of
authenticity is that it eclipses other compelling questions and dynamics.
As we have seen, a focus on authenticity tends to remain caught in a
colonial relation to Native texts, at times because of the positionality
of the critic as much as of the text. The Native voice of the text is relegated to that static, "authentic" past, solidifying the critic's position in a
specular, retrospective present. Insofar as authenticity—which remains a
premium—is defined only as pure or precolonial, such a focus excludes
post-contact indigenous cultures from that prized quality.

In a very different view of culture and authenticity, Diné philoso-
pher Marilyn Notah Verney writes of a continuing "authentic being" of
her cultural lifeways in contrast to "the inauthentic ways of the dominant society" (137). This comparative turn pushes authenticity toward
something beyond the description of ethnographic and psychological,
or group and individual, authenticity. She identifies an ethical principle
underlying the various forms authenticity may take. Writing of a "metaphysics of respect" (135), Verney affirms a processual, active dynamic of
authenticity in its conversational, interactive ground:

Once ideas are written down, in black and white, those ideas
become objects, something to be studied and taken apart. This process

of writing separates our being in the world, and we can lose touch and become isolated from all our relations. To be effectively taught in an academic classroom, American Indian philosophy must be taught orally. . . . Our philosophy can retain its meaning by making connection with those who are willing to listen to our oral teachings. (138)

For Verney, authenticity is neither bound by nor set in time. Echoing David Abram's comparisons of orality and literacy that in turn draw on Walter Ong, authenticity in Verney's Diné context is relational and alive, indeed communal, and thus ongoing in Indian communities, as well as in Indian classrooms. It does not reside in language printed on a page and thus frozen in time. Authentic relationality and vitality are built originally on relations between the speaker and her own language as oral, not written, embodied in the mouth and ear rather than projected permanently onto a page.

Now we arrive at the beginning: Acoma writer Simon Ortiz's discussion of "cultural authenticity in nationalism" forecasts Verney's vivifying claim. In his 1981 essay, "Towards a National Indian Literature: Cultural Authenticity in Nationalism," Ortiz links authenticity to identity as he articulates a further linked dynamic of community in Native narratives. He announces that authenticity is adaptable, deriving from the community effort to translate experience, ancient or modern, into a community aesthetic, into community terms. For Ortiz, a Southwestern author of poetry, fiction, and essays, authenticity arises out of people's mouths, pens, typewriters, and computers: "the indigenous peoples of the Americas have taken the languages of the colonialists and used them for their own purposes" (10). He merges authenticity with the act of translation into the discourse of First Nations: "the creative ability of Indian people to gather in many forms of the socio-political-colonizing force which beset them and to make those forms meaningful in their own terms" (8). One example Ortiz uses in his essay presents the "joyous and vigorous sight to behold" of his Uncle Dzeerlai "prancing and dipping" and "expressing his vitality from within the hold of our Acqumeh Indian world" on specific fiesta days that are "celebrations on Catholic Saints' days" (7). Presaging Verney's "making connection with those who are willing to listen to our oral teachings" as a dynamic factor of authentic expression, Ortiz cites another example of being "Acqumeh and Indian . . . in the truest and most authentic sense" during a different commemorative event each September, "coming exactly upon the route that Juan de Onate's soldiers took when they razed Acqu in the winter of 1598." On this occasion, Uncle Dzeerlai portrays a clown version of Santiago, "the patron saint of the Spanish soldiers . . . dressed in ostentatious finery . . . the hobby horse steed stuck between his legs" (8). An authentic Acoma representation of a pivotal four-hundred-year-old colonial experience reduces colonial power by translating it into a caricature. The ostensible victor's history is reduced to ridicule while affirming Acoma lifeways. Claiming representation of that history and of that enemy "for their own purposes" works both to sustain the Acoma culture and to strengthen its dynamics of exchange and change.

A recent Northwestern example of such authenticity in a very different tone and context might be a musical track on one of several CDs by the award-winning Black Lodge Singers, a drumming and singing group from the Blackfeet Reservation in Montana. In a children's pow-wow song, the lyrics, sung over a driving drumbeat, begin and repeat, "Is it a bird? No! Is it a plane? No! Oh my gosh it's Mighty Mouse—hey hey ya hey ya!"

Authentic translation into Native and tribal terms remains the goal, but Ortiz does not depict that goal as facile. In an interview published two decades after his 1981 essay, he confronts the difficulty of cross-cultural terminology and language use throughout the colonial era.

> I think one of the things about Native American intellectualism and writing is that we have often been caught in a real dilemma, sort of a forced choice about what to do in terms of the language to use. So we end up very early on, starting five hundred years ago, going along with the colonizer, the Spanish conquistador first and then other Europeans. As a means of survival, we were forced to acquiesce. Yet, it's a choice that people did make. And so to some degree, repercussions of that continue which really undermine our sense of wholeness. Not that there isn't a way in which one can still be whole and express oneself in terms of one's integrity—cultural, spiritual, or physical integrity—with this other language. But it's got to be a real choice; it's got to be a real choice. (Purdy and Hausman 3)

Once a choice is made, then the chosen language becomes "meaningful in their own terms" for Native speakers and writers within the specific history.

It may clarify the dynamics of that difficult choice to invoke Bakhtinian terms, whereby we recognize that Ortiz is affirming Native entry into the precarious heteroglossia of European languages. For Ortiz, the historical fact that European tongues formulated a particular language use, with dominating linguistic paradigms, does not eclipse the historical fact that Native tongues have reformulated that language use and those paradigms as well. The Bakhtinian theory of polyglossia indeed marks an invitation for voices to join and alter the chorus, to make the choice that Ortiz describes. The polyglossic and permeable structures of language itself open those doors to authentic translation, and Native writers and many of their communities have made the strategic choice to enter in. Ortiz thus allows for a level of agency and invention, of flexibility and adaptation in his literary approach to authentic indigenous national identity and individual artistic expression.

Such a robust definition of authenticity introduces a different sense of temporality that contrasts with a prevalent static view of Native cultures. In the static view, a singular Native culture, in order to remain authentic, must camp forever in the eighteenth, seventeenth, or sixteenth century, or even leap back to the Stone Age, the ultimate petrified source of the stereotypically perturbing "stoic Indian." Again, the real Indian must be the precolonial Indian. This static view of one Indian past, as dramatically exciting—and unthreatening—as a diorama or a *tableau vivant*, is necessary to reinforce the liberal sense of perpetual progress in American culture, which must appear ever changing, ever youthful, ever individualistic, liberated and "free" of the past, ever free of responsibility to community, ever committed to an economy of "growth" and ready to "light out for the territories." The ground of that American culture remains Indian land.

Ignoring its own past, America does not view its authentic self as contemporary with Benjamin Franklin, yet it views "authentic" American Indians just so, just as European hobbyists do as well. True Americans or Europeans need not wear powdered wigs, yet true Indians must wear feathers. In fact America insists on looking at Indians with Franklin's eyes, or James Fenimore Cooper's. Colonial eyes, open only to religious conversion or later ethnographic objectification of Native subjects, have remained ignorant of Simon Ortiz's translation dynamic by ossifying authenticity into a time-bound past. You are either Indian or modern. In the mid-1990s, one of my own close friends from high school in New York City said to me over lunch on the upper West Side, "Why don't they just give up that Indian stuff and become Americans?"

Apparently, you can't be both. You are either Indian or American. Indian or educated. You can't be both. You are either Indian or Christian, or Indian or white. You can't be both. Most painfully, many Indian youth, against the material realities of exchange in their own Indian families, are warped into believing these either/or expectations in the mainstream for Indian authenticity. They thus feel that to succeed they have to reject "the past"—as their own Indianness—in order to live in the white man's world, or they have to remain losers as uneducated Indians.[1] Identity becomes linked to victimhood, to a wooden authenticity, a dead past, and the ensuing identity crisis leads to reservations' highest teen suicide rates in the country. Vanishing sometimes seems like the only way.

If Indian youth are to unlearn the impossible authenticity-as-past imposed on them by a dominant culture that would fantasize and thus engineer their "vanishment," it is Native writers who show them how, through laughter and perseverance. In an intriguing reversal of the indefatigable vanishing Indian stereotype, some Native writers have argued that Americans already have become more Native than they care to admit. Non-Native Americans are the vanishing breed! Authentic America is Native today!—according to this reading, in its federated and bicameral constitution, in its agriculture, in some of its architecture, even in its gradual gestures toward democratic equality for women and minorities. Indeed, as I explore elsewhere, this reversal becomes the ironic fold structuring much of Native humor. Individual whites might "play Indian" to fulfill their romantic quest for authenticity, but meanwhile, back at the ranch, their political economy and their body politic have already been shaped inexorably by the original cultures of this land. America is great, according to this narrative of interactive authenticity, because of its Indian heritage, because of what Indians gave and are giving America today.

The idea of a redefined authenticity, that acculturation works both ways and that the colonials have been and can be influenced if not transformed, is a notion with much wider circulation among the colonized than the colonizers. Choctaw author and playwright Leanne Howe, for instance, in "The Story of America: A Tribalography," writes, "Native stories are power. They create people. They author tribes. America is a tribal creation story, a tribalography. . . . our stories made the immigrants Americans nevertheless" (29). Howe and others assert that America itself is a Native story. This transformative power of language is the very choice of translation that Ortiz invokes in his redefinition of authenticity, "to make those forms meaningful in their own terms."

Identity as Change

If we have learned from Native American authors that authenticity is the ability to translate experience into one's own terms, that formulation assumes in the phrase "one's own terms" a knowledge of self, a "one's own," an identity. Across cultures, that self-identity may be ever changing in cycles of selfhood and otherness, of interaction and interpenetration with the world and the body. Love and curiosity, as well as fear and security, drive such cycles toward a sense of integrity within cultural forms. To survive and thrive, the self must have developed a perceiving eye, it must have accumulated a symbolic vocabulary to describe its perceptions, and, crucially, it must have decided on a set of values by which to discriminate among those symbols to match its perceptions to the world as closely as it can. That set could be called identity, closely tied to authenticity. To whatever extent necessary, it must become the author of its world. Thus behind Simon Ortiz's notion of authenticity as translation stands a notion of an identity with the authority to translate. Authenticity is a kind of authority. By Ortiz's definition, the modern authentic possesses authority to cross discursive communities, to translate colonial experience into indigenous language and vice versa. An authentic author expresses an identity, however static or fluid, and storytelling, whether literate or oral, explores the massaging or bruising interplay of identities.

Thus we return to another of the basic questions driving Native literature. Following closely the common binary logic of authenticity as temporal or racial—past or present? Indian or white?—a mode of reading for "identity" asks, as Chickasaw scholar and writer Louis Owens opens his study of the Native American novel, "What is an Indian?" (3). He explains, "The recovering or rearticulation of an identity, a process dependent upon a rediscovered sense of place as well as community, becomes . . . a truly enormous undertaking. This attempt is at the center of American Indian fiction" (5). Even with the "rediscovered sense . . . of community," Owens's focus on identity leads in turn to descriptions of "the dilemma of the mixedblood, the liminal 'breed' seemingly trapped between Indian and white worlds" (40) as "the dominant theme in novels by Indian authors" (40).

> For, in spite of the fact that Indian authors write from very
> diverse tribal and cultural backgrounds, there is to a remark-
> able degree a shared consciousness and identifiable worldview
> reflected in novels by American Indian authors, a conscious-
> ness and worldview defined primarily by a quest for identity:
> What does it mean to be "Indian"—or mixedblood—in
> contemporary America? (20)

As he equates "Indian" here with "mixedblood," the full weight of history
leans on Owens's dualistic critical construction, where the binary logic
of power in colonial and capitalistic dichotomies traps both narratives
and criticism, writers and readers, in this dilemma of the mixedblood.
By this logic, the descriptive force of dialectical materialism comes to
bear most intimately on the bodies, even the genetic codes, of Indian
characters. It is a narrative vortex that swallows Indian lives.

Native writers since the beginning of colonialism have offered a
counter-narrative to this dominant theme and structure that Owens identifies: if identity is the dialectical text, tribal sovereignty, through tribal
community, remains a dialogical context. Yet the analysis that Owens
offers is tragically mesmerized by the dialectical trap, the continuous
back and forth between only two options. For example, in *Mixedblood
Messages* when he has described James Welch's research for the historical
novel *Fools Crow*, Owens writes that authenticity questions are enough
to drive a critic or a novelist crazy:

> Are we not caught up in a Borges-like maze of contradictory
> signifiers when an Indian author must go to white writings
> about Indians to find out who he or she is or where he or
> she comes from and then "write back" against the dominant
> culture? To write "authentically" the "Indian" author must
> consult constructions of "Indianness" by the dominant non-
> Indian culture that has always controlled printed discourse.
> It is enough to drive one mad. (19)

This is the madness of material dialectics, the ceaseless swinging of the
pendulum of duality between Indian and white, aligned tragically with
past and present. What a number of authors do with this reductive
formulation is to blur the racial and temporal boundaries, at times to
elude them altogether in redefinitions of what it means to "write 'authen-

tically.'" Yet authenticity in Owens seems equated with antiquity, if when only written records remain, such authenticity is available only via non-Indian writers of those records.

Native writers, including Owens, raise strategic questions of aesthetics, ethics, and politics: whether art can elude, transcend, deconstruct, ignore, resist, or revise such material history. When issues on the Indian streets of reservations and cities are reduced to a competition between tradition and methamphetamines, or only slightly more benignly between grandma's storytelling and the seductive violence of video games, the literary efforts of Indian writers seem far from turning the tide of Indian suicides. The patterns of resilience and "survivance" documented in Native literature remain far from political leverage, but they are part of a cultural resurgence, and they form the long echo of a drumbeat toward pluralism that recent political and legal discourse of tribal sovereignty continues.

Louis Owens's further discussion of identity is important here for its retrospective focus on authenticity and its suggestion of a transcultural trick. Although he describes writers moving beyond "ethnonostalgia," the temporal structure of his binary analysis tends to reify that regretful yearning for the past. Owens refers to "the dilemma of identity and authenticity which, while common to inhabitants of the modern Western world, is particularly intense for Native Americans and, especially, mixedbloods" (11). Owens's own conflicted experience as a novelist and critic surfaces in his subtle analysis, worth quoting here at length.

> Native American writing represents an attempt to recover identity and authenticity by invoking and incorporating the world found within the oral tradition—the reality of myth and ceremony—an authorless "original" literature. . . . In every case, however, the Native American novelist plays off of and moves beyond (and challenges the reader to likewise move beyond) this faint trace of "Rousseauist" ethnonostalgia—most common to Euramerican treatments of Native American Indians—toward an affirmation of a syncretic, dynamic, adaptive identity in contemporary America. (1992, 11-12)

Thus Owens frames the key question of Native identity in terms of a dilemma between oral and literary traditions, while he gestures toward a wider field where an "adaptive identity" might find "syncretic, dynamic" possibilities for survivance. In that direction, Owens contrasts Native American fiction with the postmodern and deconstructionist focus on a fragmented self. Owens sees in Native literary efforts an affirmation of traditional "eternal . . . elements" against modern "fragmentation and chaos" (19–20). His map of the literary conflict bears resemblance to the historical conflict zone known as the frontier. Thus he provides a metaphysical corollary to colonial history, even catching cosmic "eternal and immutable elements" or philosophical negotiations of history in the frontier binary. One effect is to reify nostalgia. However, Owens's study then moves on to invoke Gerald Vizenor's trickster survivance in a wider field of possibilities, linking trickster discourse to those "eternal and immutable" values. Yet Owens still insists on "the frontier" as a useful descriptor, against postmodern chaos in his dual system of an oral past against a literary present (1998, 25–26).

Owens's efforts at redefinition correspond with those of Tewa anthropologist Alfonso Ortiz, whose essay, "Indian/White Relations: A View from the Other Side of the 'Frontier,'" delineated more than a dozen specific revisions to historical discourse that need to take place in rewriting American Indian and Indian history. Including revaluations of "civilization," "wilderness," "frontier," "religion," "government," and "leadership," among other warped categories of mainstream historical discourse, Ortiz lands on a basic human identity, re-representing Indians as "multidimensional and fully sentient human beings" (10). He presents this basic perspective as the fundamental shift necessary toward a history beyond stereotypes. The specific material historical revisions Ortiz offers from his "Other Side of the 'Frontier'" fill in the ideological gaps that would swallow Owens's more rhetorical moves from the same direction.

While Owens is careful not to minimize the historic force of the frontier and its oppositional paradigms, he also is careful in his discussion to balance individual and group dynamics in Native identity formations, as he alludes to a "communal, authorless, and identity-conferring source" (1992, 11–12). Unlike Simon Ortiz, Owens locates that source of identity in an authentic past. His terms evoke one of the most useful discussions of identity yet articulated, useful especially because of the harsh lessons of duality that it may offer.

Toward a wider field of choices for young American Indians, and perhaps for other Americans, James Clifford describes indigenous identity as "a nexus of relations and transactions" that offer strategic options unavailable to Owens's maddening dualisms. In his chapter "Identity in

Mashpee," Clifford tries to understand what is behind the elder Mash-pees' claim ("No one is going to tell us we're not Indian"), when the courts turned down their petition for federal recognition in the 1970s. Looking across the frontier at different structures for narrating identity under colonial history, Clifford explains,

> Stories of cultural contact and change have been structured by a pervasive dichotomy: absorption by the other *or* resistance to the other. A fear of lost identity, a Puritan taboo on mixing beliefs and bodies, hangs over the process. Yet what if identity is conceived not as a boundary to be maintained but as a nexus of relations and transactions actively engaging a subject? The story or stories of interaction must then be more complex, less linear and teleological. What changes when the subject of "history" is no longer Western? How do stories of contact, resistance, and assimilation appear from the standpoint of groups in which exchange rather than identity is the fundamental value to be sustained? (344)

Clifford juxtaposes dualistic and non-dualistic systems of thought: on the one hand a "pervasive dichotomy" battling over absorption or resistance, and on the other hand a "nexus of relations" vivified by exchange. Not surprisingly, dialectical thinking would interpret this juxtaposition as merely another dualism, as dichotomy versus nexus. As I have said (in the essay "Decolonializing Criticism: Reading Dialectics and Dialogics in Native American Literatures"), dialectics cannot read dialogics. Alternatively, dialogical thinking, a "nexus of relations and transactions," would read the juxtaposition not in oppositional terms, not as a nexus opposed to a dichotomy, but as a wider field of triangulations embracing smaller dichotomies, a field "in which exchange rather than identity is the fundamental value to be sustained" (344). Here the field of relations or exchange itself has value. Community itself, the changing and exchanging interrelationships that generate kinship, "is the fundamental value to be sustained" (344). Identity then takes on a larger scope. The individual is not set against the group, precisely because "individual versus group" (344) are dualistic terms of a different, dialectical system.

Part of the potency of Clifford's analysis is that it does not naïvely dream away dualisms; it encircles them. It makes visible some viable alternatives to tragic oppositionality. Certainly the colonial experience, like much of historical narration, has been driven largely by oppressive dualities. Certainly various Native orators, writers, and storytellers, like non-Native writers and historians act and react, speak and respond in both dualistic and multifaceted, dialogical forms. If by the seeming necessities of day and night, life and death, male and female, white and Indian, dualities of this kind often drive the way we all experience the world, Indian writers tend to write their stories in dialogical terms that enlarge that experience. The material forces of oppositionality remain on Clifford's map, and they often launch the plot of Native narratives. If the historical hierarchies of race, class, and gender manipulate those dualisms, strategies for political action, for identity construction, and thus for narration, are not limited to absorption or resistance. Instead, the actual triangulations of each oppositional moment offer relations and exchanges that redefine the possibilities for survival.

Discussions of Native American autobiography and indigenous constructions of the self have clarified some of these dynamics linking identity and community. Notably, Arnold Krupat argues, that selfhood represented in Native autobiographies "most typically is not constituted by the achievement of a distinctive, special voice that separates it from others, but, rather, by the achievement of a particular placement in relation to the many voices without which it could not exist. . . . Indian autobiographies are quite literally dialogic" (1989, 133). Such cultural construction of personal interrelationships and "a particular placement" in a system of interpellations eventually navigates across cultural contacts and conflicts as well.

For example, where the ingrained frontier dualisms would erect barriers between white and Indian as between educated and uneducated, many American Indians have triangulated those options by being both Indian and educated (as well as both Indian and white). Less obvious examples might be a twentieth- or twenty-first-century Inuit choice of a snowmobile over a dog sled, or a Lakota dancer's choice of an RV camper trailer over a tipi on the summer powwow circuit. Although binary thinking must identify Indian with the primitive, and white with the technological, an Inuit hunter or a Lakota dancer sees a way to triangulate those oppositional categories, to sustain distinct culture and community while adopting technological innovations of the global industrial economy. In the 1820s, steel pots and tomahawks exchanged in the fur trade did not make Cheyenne women or men question their Cheyenne identity. In the sixteenth, seventeenth, and eighteenth centuries, the introduction of the horse along the length of the Western

Hemisphere did not make Indians any less Indian in anyone's eyes. Many tribal mythologies incorporate the horse into the origin stories of their communal identity.

Less comfortable examples of exchange today might include Native American individuals, tribes, or corporations who do not live up to the "noble" side of a noble savage stereotype: when some go to court in land disputes and do not fulfill idealized roles as communal ecologists; or when some invite hazardous industrial waste sites and technologies on to the reservation to boost their local economies; or when some develop high-tech businesses with federal defense contracts. When binary thinking still lumps racial others with lower classes, thus Indians with poverty, the new economy of gaming casinos on a few luckily situated reservations, and the enormous wealth they provide for a few tribes, again confuses dualistic categories that would relegate Indians to second- or third-class citizenship. Multiple frontier-boundary crossings and triangulations such as these begin to map a more complex field of relations than the "Puritan taboo on mixing beliefs and bodies" would allow. Eventually they evoke a different body politic, a new national identity.

This subversive refusal by dialogism to fit into the linguistic categories of the dominant dialectic invokes different ways of knowing the world, of using language, of perceiving and relating across cultures. A dialogical ethics translates into an aesthetics. The very exchange processes of identity formation that Native Americans have developed in infinite ways over the last five hundred years turn into flexible narrative structures. We thus find in identity maps a link between indigenous ethics and aesthetics. The ways that Native narratives structure identity on a field of authenticity, community, and tribal sovereignty authorize an aesthetics with ethical ramifications for readers of that literature. For a people inculcated in the abusive effects of others' inability to think beyond expansionist dualisms, expression of a different aesthetic becomes survival.[2]

As we see especially in the last two generations of Native writers, such as Momaday, Silko, Welch, Young Bear, and Vizenor, a variable Native aesthetic resonates with various modernist and postmodernist projects. Gerald Vizenor, for a prime example, invokes Jean-François Lyotard's definition of postmodernism "as incredulity toward metanarratives," when he affirms his own literary endeavors as "postindian":

> The postmodern turn in literature and cultural studies is
> an invitation to the ruins of representation; the invitation

> uncovers traces of tribal survivance, trickster discourse, and
> the remanence of intransitive shadows. (1993, 7)

Prevailing historical and anthropological representations of Indians, as
Vizenor asserts, are "terminal creeds" that project only the end of Indians
that were always already European projections anyway. Those representations therefore are "ruins." Vizenor's skepticism of "the aesthetic remains
of reason in the literature of dominance" and of "the paracolonial pretensions that precede a tribal referent" casts off those ruins of representation,
in favor of "an invitation to tribal survivance" (7).

Part of the popularity of contemporary American Indian writing
among its wide non-Indian readership may be attributable to this parallel across such vastly different roots of similar expression as modernist, postmodernist, and ethnic literatures. That celebratory modernist
skepticism of "clear and distinct representation" echoes Marilyn Notah
Verney's Diné philosophy of language that we discussed in relation to
authenticity, where, "This process of writing separates our being in the
world, and we can lose touch and become isolated from all our relations"
(138). When centuries of representations of Indians would reduce them
to "the vanishing American," Native artists become directly invested in
"responding, searching, thinking, inventing, and writing" in ways that
make visible indigenous forces of survivance that are irreducible to definitive Euro-American erasures. The material ethics of cultural survival
trigger a grounded aesthetics, as Owens puts it, "toward an affirmation
of a syncretic, dynamic, adaptive identity in contemporary America."
Artistic creation maps identity formation, and vice versa. Native aesthetics, drawing on the ethical ground of authenticity, identity, community,
and sovereignty, generates narrative structures in poetry and fiction that
drive the modernist aesthetic into the "irreducible" field where both
myth and history begin.

Community as Animism

In complementary contrast to Owens's assertion that novels by American
Indian authors are "defined primarily by a quest for identity," Cherokee
critic Jace Weaver affirms "community" as the key to Native literature.
Because they so interweave, it really is unnecessary to insist on pri-
ority for either one or the other. In his 1997 study, *That the People
Might Live: Native American Literature and Native American Community*,

Weaver concocts a neologism, "communitism," combining "community" and "activism," to describe literature that "has a proactive commitment to Native community, including what I term the 'wider community' of Creation itself" (xiii). Weaver sees Indian writers' rhetorical activism on behalf of Indian community as definitive of their literature.

> I would contend that the single thing that most defines Indian literatures relates to this sense of community and commitment to it. . . . In communities that have too often been fractured and rendered dysfunctional by the effects of more than 500 years of colonialism, to promote communitist values means to participate in the healing of the grief and sense of exile felt by Native communities and the pained individuals in them. It is, to borrow from Homi K. Bhabha, "community" envisaged as a project—at once a vision and a construction—that takes you "beyond" yourself in order to return, in a spirit of revision and reconstruction, to the political *conditions* of the present. (43)

Weaver gets at an undergirding worldview and politic of Native literatures in "this sense of community and commitment to it." It is difficult to summon any Indian writer whose impulse for writing does not engage "the healing of the grief and sense of exile felt by Native communities" over "more than 500 years of colonialism." The agonies of authenticity and identity described by Krupat, Brumble, Ortiz, and Owens take place on this often uncertain and slippery stage of Native community.

I have suggested that not only is healing of Indian community a goal and a context of Indian writing, but that certain epistemological dynamics of Indian community form the very method, content, and structure of many Native narratives. From Apess to Alexie, from Winnemucca to Silko, discursive elaborations of community values permeate the meaning and the manner of narration. If there is a key dynamic, it is not only commitment to community, but a kind of commitment *of* community in the way stories are told. As may be true of literary endeavors in general, Native texts strive to generate fellow feeling. The very manner of writing Native stories creates community across disjunctive frontier boundaries that have tried to limit Indian lives.

Contours of thought generated by indigenous kinship values build the stories that American Indians tell themselves and the invaders. In a 1994 essay on "Decolonializing Criticism" I proposed that readers of Native literatures need to follow the lead of Native writers into the dialogical structures in many Native stories. Readers then would take a community-based approach if they are to do justice to Native texts, since those texts are so woven with community dynamics and needs. Drawing on James Clifford's discussion, cited earlier, of "Identity in Mashpee" characterized by a "nexus of relations," I distinguished between dialectics and dialogics as ways of reading Native literatures.

To recap, dialogics follow the voices of community context, whereas dialectics are prone to colonial binaries of frontier thinking. From James Fenimore Cooper to Zane Grey, the dialectical logic of imperial nostalgia erases the vanishing Indian under the advancing frontier. Even critical analyses that reduce Native narratives to dialectics risk repeating the dualistic traps of history. Yet analyses that explicate Native narratives via dialogics not only clarify complexities but also begin to explain historical and cultural strategies of survivance in Indian stories. From John Rollin Ridge to Simon Ortiz to Gerald Vizenor, a dialogic of exchange and adaptation affirms Indian lives in the future of America.

A dialogical perspective, while not denying the power of specific dialectical interactions and dominations, incorporates multiple dialectics to recognize a more complex field where crisscrossing dialectics layer and act. Within that dialogical field, individuals and communities may play either immanent or transcendent games, deconstructing dialectic oppositions or materially transcending them on the larger field. This ability to play beyond the historical script of opposition is perhaps the secret engine of community, where for instance Salish individuals caught between Indian and white or traditional and Christian or indigenous and technological may choose to both undercut (immanent strategy) and to flip outside (transcendent strategy) of those standard oppositions and to be technological *and* traditional *and* Christian *and* Indian—all as ways of affirming membership in a complex community.

A less technical and more direct explanation of dialogics might point to animism. The animistic perspective is one compelling direction moving positively beyond my 1994 discussion of decolonializing criticism and into traditional perspectives. On a dialogical field, as on an animistic field, everything has a voice. Everything participates mutually in perception and communication. Objects are subjects. Trees, stones, animals, places have their own consciousness. That point is at the core of indigenous links to the land. As Meskwaki poet and novelist Ray A. Young Bear writes of the value of the ground,

My maternal grandmother used to say it was crucial we have a place of our own. Listening intently, I learned that our lives were dependent upon a plethora of animistic factors immersed in ethereal realities. Basically, she instructed that the very ground on which we all stood, Grandmother Earth, was the embodiment of a former Supernatural being. She was all of nature, this Grandmother: She was the foundation for rivers, lakes, fields and forests; she provided homes and sustenance for insects, birds, reptiles, fish, animals, and human beings. She held everything together, including the clouds, stars, sun, and moon. Our sole obligation, my grandmother instructed, in having been created in the first place by the Holy Grandfather, is to maintain the Principal Religion of the Earthlodge clans. (xii)

At the core of kinship, of community, in the heart of Native epistemology is what Young Bear calls animism, "the tribal domain where animism and supernaturalism prevailed" (250). "Listening intently" to what Young Bear prefers to call "ethereal realities" is what animates a Native redefinition of community on the land, and hence of tribal sovereignty.

The notion of animism, as with dialogism, is thus a sense that everyone can speak—that they are animate and conscious. Dialectics tends to reduce "the other" to a projection of or reaction to the self, an antithesis. Thesis against antithesis becomes self against non-self. In contrast, animism tends to see and listen to the other as a self in its own right, as an alterity, an other as a self, not merely as a non-self. When you link this notion of mutual animated subjectivity with Young Bear's "Philosophy of Insignificance,"[3] along with the terms introduced by James Clifford, the individual in a system of authenticity-identity-community-sovereignty becomes the relatively insignificant nexus in a system of relations all animated by ethereal significance.

Thus the founding two-dimensional frontier dialectics of white/ Indian or civilization/wilderness or culture/nature or even mind/matter—built on dualisms deep in the linguistic and ideological structures of Western cultures—are all the more inadequate to tell the stories of the last five hundred years. Although many on "both sides" of the racial divide have been tragically persuaded by those dualistic reductions imposed by colonial imperatives, dialogical reading opens up generations of conversations, sometimes tragically cut off, sometimes ignored, sometimes quietly prevalent, sometimes comically surprising, that have crossed the colonial divide from so many angles. Those crossings begin to map a different sense of community.

Before we all dance in the circle together, however, we need to be more alert to ongoing issues of power still polarizing the colonial divide. Although non-Native readers often sentimentalize and lament a single sense of Native community as some naïve pantheistic kinship system, they rarely register how such a reduction to a prelapsarian paradise serves America's need to infantilize the Indian. National bookstore chains now feature literature and history sections on "Native America," while Indian oral stories often remain catalogued and thus reduced in "Children's Literature." The "Great White Father" continues to infantilize the Indian body on disputed land, now that racist demonizing has become unpolitic. In fact, Native communities, built on stories even as they build new stories, have always been complex, often conflicted systems of tradition and innovation, poverty and vitality, vision and shortsightedness, wisdom and corruption, dispossession and renovation. Out of this complexity spring the gossip and legends, the jokes and the literature that reaffirm implicitly and explicitly an underlying tribal community characterized by internal tensions.

Thus those communities and their cultures are always changing, where "authenticity" develops and changes with community. As Laguna writer Leslie Silko suggests,

> I tend to align myself with the tougher-minded people. The folks at home will say, "If it's important, if it has relevance, it will stay regardless of whether it's on video tape, taped, or written down." It's only the western Europeans who have this inflated pompous notion that every word, everything that's said or done is real important, and it's got to live on and on forever. . . . The people at home who say the story will either live or die are just being honest and truthful. (Barnes 89)

According to Silko, attachment to purity, "everything that's said or done is real important," derives from an illogic that equates authenticity to the past, "and it's got to live on and on forever." Instead, a certain tough human humility in the face of more-than-human forces finds ways to survive beyond expected change. It is neither fatalism nor resignation that sees change coming, but a resilient realism of community facing change together. While the atavistic equation of authenticity and past history implicates discussions of identity, the community is there in the very embrace of those questions.

Weaver's focus on communitism affirms how Native texts serve to sustain and heal the community contexts out of which they emerge. However, what this present essay recognizes also is that many Native writers are and were conceiving not only of Native community, but of American national identity, American community, as well—frequently from a dialogic, non-dualistic, non-frontier worldview. Their work to heal their own communities takes on the ineluctable challenge of healing America itself. Extending Weaver's communitism, Native writers from William Apess to Sherman Alexie have often linked their Native national communities to the American nation—not always in desperate terms of passively being engulfed or assimilated by the "mainstream" but in resistantly exchanging cultural strengths and reinventing American community. Such redefinitions of authenticity and identity interacting with community comprise key moments in the cycle that plays out in Native stories.

Strategies of indigenous writers to form larger communities need be neither a sentimental retreat to romantic homogenization nor a naïve surrender to co-optation. They extend community exchange into a pluralistic society as both a pragmatic and a visionary prospect. In the eighteenth century, the Iroquois suggestion to the colonists that they join together in a "Covenant Chain" as a more efficient trading partner with the Iroquois Confederacy offers a major historical example of this process of extending community without surrendering identity.[4]

Sovereignty as Sacrifice

Louis Owens spoke to the link between community and identity, describing Native writers working at the "rearticulation of an identity, a process dependent upon a rediscovered sense of place as well as community." James Ruppert, in dialogue with Paula Gunn Allen, Leslie Silko, Geary Hobson, and Jack D. Forbes, speaks of a "greater self in the communal" as an indigenous value that bridges the conceptual divide between individual and group: "This path to identity is an active one where the individual works with others to define a place and existence for himself or herself" (28). This process of rebuilding grounded, communal identity leads us to further discussion of the underlying term, sovereignty. I use this term in the context of its current political leverage as a force toward the goal of Indian community on the local level, and as a term for literary dynamics in Native texts: the energy, the will of the people. Far more, and less, than "self-government," sovereignty, in diverse usage, is a value of "the people first." It becomes a feeling, a spirit, a quality—of good humor, open-heartedness, and generosity combined with courage to sacrifice for the community. It thus forms a logic of sacrifice for the people in their place on the land. "My land is where my people lie buried." Their sacrifice makes the land sovereign as sacred.

If reading for authenticity tends to follow an ethnohistorical and cultural dialectic between present and past, and if reading for identity tends to follow a parallel socio-psychological and ideological dialectic between European and Native, then reading for sovereignty as the basis for community maps a dialogic field among all of the aforementioned.

Wilma Mankiller's autobiography usefully divides into what may seem to a Euro-American view like a three-part syllogism that might neatly summarize this sequence: "roots, turmoil, balance," where "roots" comprise the thesis; "turmoil" provides the antithesis; and "balance" synthesizes the two. However, historically and legally that linear sequence does not describe the story of Wilma Mankiller, nor of the Cherokees, nor of other Indian nations, because that "balance" is not a synthesis of "roots" and "turmoil." Instead, in the dawning light of "inherent powers" and "stories in the blood," that balance is a cyclic return to the ground of sovereignty that always already existed in the field of relations. If authenticity questions are about Native roots, and identity questions are about the turmoil of those roots being laid bare, then questions of sovereignty and community remain the ground in which to replant that tree and to try to balance that turmoil. In Native stories, sovereignty is that field, the community politic and textual context from which Native narratives of roots and turmoil draw life.

Thus scholarly polemics about Native stories, if the scholars focus on authenticity or identity as the goal, the "meaning," of the narrative, can remain suspended between the horns of a colonial dilemma. Locked in the limiting logic of either/or narration that have structured discussions of authenticity and identity, marching to the death beat of dualism, such critiques often miss the narrative energy that survives the terminal creeds. However, when scholarship and classrooms include sovereignty issues, "teaching the conflicts" can conceive of ways to move through colonial oppositions to more complex issues such as internal struggles or the specific dynamics of cross-cultural exchange. Engaging the fuller field of terms, while deconstructing colonial terms, a ground theory is part of a process of constructing a usable past and future for both Native and non-Native readers. Teachers and scholars of the literature who eclipse textual issues of complex sovereignty and community in favor of more reductive and polarized identity issues run the risk of lingering within, even perpetuating, colonial relations, where identity is patently a question of colonial discourses while sovereignty engages Native discourses.

To underscore the fuller spectrum of sovereignty issues is not to underestimate the carefully nuanced descriptions of identity questions in the fiction, the poetry, the autobiography and other non-fiction, nor in the criticism. Instead it is to recognize community politics and culture as contexts shaping those issues of identity as much as colonial history shapes them.

Prior to its historical, political, and legal meanings in Indian country, sovereignty, in its varied usage by Native storytellers, conveys a nest of qualities, a spirit, born from and giving birth to community, identity, and authenticity. It evokes a rich spectrum of virtues or powers that may take dramatic or quiet expression, including loyalty, memory, dedication, perseverance, generosity, courage, confidence, humor, hope, reverence, respect, and humility. Infinitely inventive combinations interweave and play with this set of qualities in Native American societies and personalities. The quality of sovereignty gives Indian people a reason to live, a reason to be strong beyond their individual selves, a wider, deeper fulfillment of self in service to the whole. From formal, ritual, and ceremonial settings to informal, social, and everyday ones, these vital qualities of open-hearted strength are there to sustain Indian lives and maintain resilience under generations of difficulty. Certainly such qualities borne of sovereignty bear the impersonal buffeting of common losses, large and small, but these qualities are also under sustained assault—as is legal sovereignty itself—by deliberate oppositional powers in the designs of colonial history and in the insidious forces of internal erosions. The result today is a driving tension between economic and psychological depression, on the one hand, and political and cultural regeneration, on the other. For centuries the narrative of this tension and its incremental resolutions has been what Gerald Vizenor calls "stories in the blood" against the "terminal creeds" of Western history. To read those stories is to read the stories of sovereignty.

Due to the primary importance, and perhaps the ineffability, of the term, we need refocused study of tribal sovereignty for those readers of Native literatures who are unfamiliar with this cultural, political, legal, and historical issue. I recognize Robert Warrior's approach, to "use the term 'sovereignty' in a rather undefined way" because "a definition of sovereignty should emerge from the experience of communities rather than in academic discourse" (51). The challenge for the academy is to respond to, rather than impose, definitions of sovereignty expressed in the literature.

Rennard Strickland offers a useful metaphor for contemporary tribal sovereignty: "imagine the eagle as the sovereign and each arrow held in the claws as the embodiment of the attributes of sovereignty. . . . What arrows does it still hold? . . . we see the tribal eagle with few of the arrows of sovereignty in place, but nonetheless still a sovereign, free-flying and powerful" (247). Strickland goes on to discuss the history and legal concepts of tribal sovereignty: "The roots of Native Americans' sovereignty and the laws of her sovereign nations stretch back long before the black robes or the blue coats came and built their courthouses and guardhouses" (251). Strickland puts sovereignty into perspective not only in terms of pre-Columbian time, but equally in terms of a certain timelessness. Sovereignty in Strickland's rendering becomes both an individual and a communal force for clarity of purpose in service to a society, a nation.

Joseph P. Kalt and Joseph W. Singer put the issue of sovereignty in one contemporary perspective in a 2004 publication of the Harvard Project on American Indian Economic Development:

> The last three decades have witnessed a remarkable resurgence of the Indian nations in the United States. After centuries of turmoil, oppression, attempted subjugation, and economic deprivation, the Indian nations have asserted their rights and identities, have built and rebuilt political systems in order to implement self-rule, and have begun to overcome what once seemed to be insurmountable problems of poverty and social disarray. The foundation of this resurgence has been the exercise of self-government by the more than 560 federally recognized tribes in the U.S. (1)

Although Kalt and Singer set self-government as the foundation of this political and cultural resurgence, the question remains whether such historic revitalization is founded on less definitive events in Indian communities. Leaving the elusive dimensions of that originary question aside, there is no historical doubt that the new politics of what some call tribal sovereignty has grown volcanically in the last generation, grounded in the Indian Self-Determination Act of 1975. That act followed the political, cultural, and literary resurgence of Indian cultures in the sixties. So before Kalt and Singer's "last three decades," where did tribal sovereignty come from? What is the origin of this power of Native nations and voices to define—represent—and govern themselves?

Looking back a generation earlier in *The Nations Within: The Past and Future of American Indian Sovereignty*, Vine Deloria Jr. and Clifford M. Lytle discuss "a vast reservoir of inherent powers" as they came clear in the legislative unfolding of the 1934 Indian Reorganization Act:

> "Powers of Indian Tribes" was issued on October 25, 1934, and was some thirty-two pages in length, hardly a casual commentary on the wording of the statute [IRA]. The opinion adopted the theory that "those powers which are lawfully vested in an Indian tribe are not, in general, delegated powers granted by express acts of Congress, but rather inherent powers of a limited sovereignty which has never been extinguished." The theory of tribal political powers was that Indian tribes had at one time been fully sovereign and that in embracing a relationship with the United States they had, from time to time, allowed some of those powers to be changed, modified, or surrendered. They had, however, a vast reservoir of inherent powers, which any political entity had. . . . (158)

This legal formulation of "inherent powers" summons up legalistic, humanistic values that evoke Emerson's transcendentalism and Jefferson's "unalienable rights." As a foundation of American law, it is a Platonic, certainly abstract, one may even say nearly metaphysical or mystical, substratum extending across colonial history.

Simon Ortiz suggests such a spiritual foundation in his 1981 essay, cited earlier. He focuses on sovereignty as "nationalism" underneath the identity narratives. In a move that resolves any linear tendencies in analyses of authenticity, identity, and community, Ortiz invokes what may be called an "authentic humanism":

> it is not the oral tradition as transmitted from ages past alone which is the inspiration and source for contemporary Indian literature. It is also because of the acknowledgement by Indian writers of a responsibility to advocate for their people's self-government, sovereignty, and control of land and natural resources; and to look also at racism, political and economic oppression, sexism, supremacism, and the needless and wasteful exploitation of land and people, especially in the U.S., that Indian literature is developing a character of nationalism which indeed it should have. It is this character which will prove to be the heart and fibre and story of an America which has heretofore too often feared its deepest and most honest emotions of love and compassion. It is this story, wealthy in being without an illusion of dominant power and capitalistic abundance, that is the most authentic. (12)

With disarming probity, Ortiz is suggesting that ongoing colonial dominance is a mask that fears its own "deepest and most honest emotions of love and compassion." Such a human context would welcome his argument, by which authenticity is sovereignty and sovereignty is authenticity. The "illusion of dominant power" would recognize multiple centers of power, a pluralism that we might look to as a federation of domestic *in*dependent nations. He indicates that what is authentic Indian culture and identity is precisely the very human process of putting experience into Indian terms that make sense to Indian peoples. In his formulation, authenticity equals humanity, as humans tell stories to make sense of their world. Yet they must remain sovereign to tell their own stories. The impulse to national identity and sovereignty is itself authenticity, and thus Native storytelling is all about that impulse, that drum.

Notes

1. See Duran and Duran (1995); and O'Nell (1996) on the "empty center" of some contemporary American Indian cultures.
2. Thanks to conversations with Kathryn Shanley for this clarification.

3. See my discussion of Young Bear's philosophy of insignificance in Moore (1997, 322–30).

4. See Venables (1992).

Works Cited

Abram, David. *The Spell of the Sensuous: Perception and Language in a More-Than-Human World*. New York: Vintage, 1996.

Bakhtin, M. M. *The Dialogic Imagination: Four Essays*. Ed. Michael Holquist. Trans. Caryl Emerson and Michael Holquist. Austin: U of Texas P, 1981.

Barnes, Kim. "A Leslie Marmon Silko Interview." *Journal of Ethnic Studies* 13.4 (1986): 83–105.

Bernardin, Susan. "The Authenticity Game: 'Getting Real' in Contemporary American Indian Literature." *True West: Authenticity and the American West*. Ed. William R. Handley and Nathaniel Lewis. Lincoln: U of Nebraska P, 2004. 155–75.

Brumble, H. David. *American Indian Autobiography*. Berkeley: U of California P, 1988.

Clifford, James. *The Predicament of Culture*. Cambridge, MA: Harvard UP, 1988.

Deloria, Vine, Jr., and Clifford M. Lytle. *The Nations Within: The Past and Future of American Indian Sovereignty*. Austin: U of Texas P, 1984.

Duran, Eduardo, and Bonnie Duran. *Native American Postcolonial Psychology*. Albany: State U of New York P, 1995.

Howe, Leanne. "The Story of America: A Tribalography." *Clearing a Path: Theorizing the Past in Native American Studies*. Ed. Nancy Solomon. New York: Routledge, 2002. 29–48.

Kalt, Joseph P., and Joseph W. Singer. *Myths and Realities of Tribal Sovereignty: The Law and Economics of Indian Self-Rule*. Cambridge, MA: HPAIE, 2004.

King, Thomas, Cheryl Calver, and Helen Hoy, eds. *The Native in Literature*. Oakville, Ontario: ECW Press, 1987.

Krupat, Arnold. *For Those Who Come After: A Study of Native American Autobiography*. Berkeley: U of California P, 1985.

———. "Monologue and Dialogue in Native American Autobiography." *The Voice in the Margin: Native American Literature and the Canon*. Berkeley: U of California P, 1989. 132–201.

Mankiller, Wilma, and Michael Wallis. *Mankiller: A Chief and Her People*. New York: St. Martin's Press, 1999.

Moore, David L. "Decolonializing Criticism: Reading Dialectics and Dialogics in Native American Literatures." *Studies in American Indian Literatures* 6.4 (Winter 1994): 7–35.

———. "Ray A. Young Bear." *Dictionary of Literary Biography Vol. 175 Native American Writers of the United States*. Ed. Kenneth M. Roemer. Detroit: Gale Research, 1997. 322–30.

O'Nell, Theresa DeLeane. *Disciplined Hearts: History, Identity, and Depression in an American Indian Community*. Berkeley: U of California P, 1996.

Ong, Walter. *Orality and Literacy: The Technologizing of the Word*. London: Methuen, 1982.

Ortiz, Alfonso. "Indian/White Relations: A View from the Other Side of the 'Frontier.' " *Indians in American History*. Ed. Frederick E. Hoxie. Arlington Heights, IL: Harlan Davidson, 1988. 1–16.

Ortiz, Simon. *from Sand Creek*. 1981; rpt. Tucson: Arizona UP, 2000.

———. "Towards a National Indian Literature: Cultural Authenticity in Nationalism." *MELUS* 8.2 (Summer 1981): 7–12.

Owens, Louis. *Mixedblood Messages: Literature, Film, Family, Place*. Norman: U of Oklahoma P, 1998.

———. *Other Destinies: Understanding the American Indian Novel*. Norman: U of Oklahoma P, 1992.

Purdy, John, and Blake Hausman. "A Conversation with Simon Ortiz." *Studies in American Indian Literatures* 12.4 (Winter 2000): 1–14.

Ruppert, James. *Mediation in Contemporary Native American Fiction*. Norman: U of Oklahoma P, 1995.

Strickland, Rennard. "The Eagle's Empire: Sovereignty, Survival, and Self-Governance in Native American Law and Constitutionalism." *Studying Native America: Problems and Prospects*. Ed. Russell Thornton. Madison: Wisconsin UP, 1998. 247–70.

Venables, Robert W. "The Founding Fathers: Choosing to Be the Romans." *Indian Roots of American Democracy*. Ed. Jose Barreiro. Ithaca, NY: Akwe:kon Press, Cornell UP, 1992. 67–106.

Verney, Marilyn Notah. "On Authenticity." *American Indian Thought*. Ed. Anne Waters. Oxford: Blackwell, 2004. 133–39.

Vizenor, Gerald. "The Ruins of Representation: Shadow Survivance and the Literature of Dominance." *American Indian Quarterly* 17.1 (Winter 1993): 7–24.

Warrior, Robert. " 'Temporary Visibility': Deloria on Sovereignty and AIM." *Native American Perspectives on Literature and History*. Ed. Alan R. Velie. Norman: U of Oklahoma P, 1994. 51–62.

Weaver, Jace. *That the People Might Live: Native American Literature and Native American Community*. New York: Oxford UP, 1997.

———. *Other Words: American Indian Literature, Law, and Culture*. Norman: U of Oklahoma P, 2001.

Womack, Craig. *Red on Red: Native American Literary Separatism*. Minneapolis: U of Minnesota P, 1999.

Young Bear, Ray A. *Remnants of the First Earth*. New York: Grove Press, 1996.

3

"Back when I used to be Indian"

Native American Authenticity and Postcolonial Discourse

Lee Schweninger

In this chapter I argue that borrowing from postcolonial studies in order to theorize issues of authenticity can help readers of Native American literature understand and address similar concerns in the United States. More specifically, I argue that notions and characterizations of the "authentic Indian" by mainstream or dominant American culture present problems similar to those addressed by postcolonial scholars in other contexts, and thus postcolonial theory offers a way into discussions of Native American literatures as scholars and Indian authors confront and challenge generalized conceptions of authenticity or in some cases (perhaps inadvertently) themselves perpetuate myths of the authentic. As long ago as 1994 Arnold Krupat cites the authors of *The Empire Writes Back* in an essay to argue that Native American literature could "usefully be theorized as postcolonial literature" (169). Despite this hopeful beginning, twelve years later Eric Cheyfitz can lament in his 2006 essay "The (Post)Colonial Construction of Indian Country" that "postcolonial studies have virtually ignored American Indian communities." He argues for the importance of theorizing postcoloniality, however, maintaining that "we might understand this indigenous (post)colonialism as emphasizing a practical or political . . . postcolonialism" (4). Similarly, in an essay on indigeneity in the Caribbean, Peter Hulme writes that issues of identity and indigeneity have too long been ignored. And further, Hulme urges that "indigeneity is an avowal of ethnic distinctiveness and national sovereignty based on the historical claim to be in some sense the descendants of the earliest inhabitants of a particular place. These are unfashionable claims, and their terms can all easily be put under erasure by cultural criticism; but they cannot—and should not—be ignored" (295). Thus, at the same time that I point out the problematics of "authenticity" and suggest how a sense of authenticity maps itself onto identity, I acknowledge the importance of an identifiable identity in very real and significant situations.

Investigating the issue of who can speak for whom, Linda Alcoff notes that "certain privileged locations are discursively dangerous. In particular, the practice of privileged persons speaking for or on behalf of less privileged persons has actually resulted (in many cases) in increasing or reinforcing the oppression of the group spoken for" (7). I am aware of the dangers involved in speaking *for* others myself in the present context, for to do so is to participate "in the construction of their subject-positions" (9). Yet ultimately, as Alcoff concludes, we must continue "the important discussion going on today about how to develop strategies for a more equitable, just distribution of the ability to speak and be heard." According to Alcoff, speaking *for* should ultimately "enable the empowerment of oppressed peoples" (29). In my context here, I wish to suggest the dangers involved in—and the usefulness of—attempting to find, invent, or somehow locate an "authentic" Indian. I wish to suggest how the very real Makah whaling controversy and how literary works by Native American writers (primarily, for my purposes here, the poetry of Mark Turcotte) force us to formulate and rethink issues of authentication or authenticity.

It has become a truism of Native American literary scholarship that Native American people have endured the imposition of the mainstream's essentializing and stereotyping of Indians (beginning with the term "Indios" itself) and that contemporary Native American writers have challenged that mainstream imposition of the "Indian" upon tribal people, literary characters, screen actors, and essentially any real or imagined people of Native American descent. Anishinaabe writer Gerald Vizenor writes that the "name *Indian* is a convenient word, to be sure, but it is an invented name that does not come from any native language, and does not describe or contain any aspects of traditional tribal experience and literature. . . . The American Indian has come to mean *Indianness*, the conditions that indicate the once-despised tribes and, at the same time, the extreme notions of an exotic outsider; these conditions are advocated as *real* cultures in the world" (1995, 1). In a similar vein, Jana Sequoya-Magdaleno has argued that an "administratively produced difference is . . . culturally inscribed as the standard of identity cohering American Indian diversity" (1995, 88). Yet as writers and critics challenge such attempts at authenticating, they at the same time run the risk of essentializing Native American experience, culture, or people themselves. In the context of Australian Aboriginal writing, for instance, Gareth Griffiths points out in his essay "The Myth of Authenticity" the "difficult and ambivalent position which the Aboriginal writer is forced to occupy in the complex task of simultaneously recuperating the traditional and contesting the profile of identity for Aboriginal peoples in contemporary Australian political and cultural space" (74). Native Americans are in a very similar position, even to the extent that the term "Indian" is as problematical as "Aboriginal." In reference to Native Americans, Gerald Vizenor points out that the "word Indian, and most other tribal names, are simulations in the literature of dominance" (1994, 10–11). It is thus important to be aware that the terms "Indian" and "Native American" are merely glosses, necessary fictions, but necessary in that to avoid them altogether could well prohibit productive discussion.

Compounding the problem of identity and authenticity is the market itself. As Amal Amireh and Lisa Majaj suggest—in a different but applicable context—in their introduction to the collection *Going Global*, "Third World women's texts became welcomed for their 'authenticity,' and Third World women were admitted into Western feminist circles because they were 'authentic insiders' who could speak for or criticize their cultures from a knowing position. . . . But the focus on authenticity has not been unproblematical. Not only were Third World women construed as representatives of their culture, they were often viewed as if they *were* their cultures" (9). Although Amireh and Majaj do not write in the context of literary North America, one can make the same point about Native North American literatures. On the back cover of a HarperPerennial edition of Louise Erdrich's novel *Tracks*, for instance, one can read that "Ms. Erdrich's novels, regional in the best sense, are 'about' the experience of Native Americans the way Toni Morrison's are about black people." Or one reads this from the *Chicago Sun-Times* on the revised paperback edition of Erdrich's *Love Medicine*: a "novel that stares more broadly at many of the truths of Native American life in this country than any fiction I've read." Such blurbs, according to Krupat, "usually represent a loose way of expressing longing for some presumptive aboriginal authenticity or wisdom" (172). In such a context, Erdrich is thus made spokesperson for some pristine, genuine Native America, and she thereby becomes the authority and is necessarily "authentic." That "authenticity" is in large measure presumably what sells, or certainly helps to sell, her books.

Jana Sequoya argues that as "an effect of the discourse of authenticity encoded in the thesis—revival (of essential Indianness), the antithesis—invention (of a spurious identity), denies to those of native American descent the conditions of modern identity-formation celebrated as freedom by the general citizenry throughout the history of the United States" (1993, 282). Again postcolonial studies help us theorize just such an issue. In reference to the South African film *The Gods Must Be Crazy* (1980) about an African man's unsought encounter with "the West," for example, Griffiths writes that the "implication is that the indigene sheds authenticity the moment he or she leaves the reserve to claim a position in the wider community" (85, n.1). In these contexts the indigene, "aboriginal," or "bushman," is authentic only in "place," and that place is prescribed by the larger, external, colonizing mainstream culture.

Although perhaps difficult to define, these prescriptions of authenticity that the colonizer imposes can have very real consequences. In her essay "How(!) Is an Indian? A Contest of Stories, Round 2" (2000), Sequoya acknowledges the importance of "authenticity" at the same time that she points out the very problematical issues involved: "Although the future of the authentic Indian is a figment of the popular imagination, it nevertheless has real consequences for contemporary American Indian people" (284). Her examples of these real consequences are Collier's 1934 Reorganization Act, which required Native Americans to become enrolled members of a specific acknowledged tribe and the 1990 "Indian Arts and Crafts Act" which required that Native artists be enrolled tribal members in order to have their art sold as "genuinely" Indian (282–84). Another more recent example of the "real consequences" was (and continues to be) the issue confronting the curators of the National Museum of the American Indian as they made their decisions concerning what would indeed be "Indian" and therefore deserving of a place in the public display spaces in the museum on the Smithsonian Mall in Washington, DC.

We can see how issues of authenticity become of crucial importance in the first of two extended examples: the Makah whale hunt controversy. Decisions as to whether or not the tribe would be allowed to hunt were based in part on the status of the tribe's whaling tradition; that is, on whether or not a Makah was authentically a whaler. According to an NOAA Fisheries revised opinion at the 1997 International Whaling Commission meeting in Monaco, for example, the issue of self-esteem was allowed as a permissible rationale for hunting. The committee found that "subsistence hunting includes far more than physical survival. It is a way of life that includes historical practices and is the cultural 'glue' that holds the Tribe together" (Blow 8). Interestingly, there was much division within the tribe itself concerning whether or not the Makahs needed to turn to whaling to regain or even continue their identity. But despite opposition from within and outside the tribe, in May 1999 the Makah Tribe of Washington State reinstituted the long-dormant tradition of whale hunting by killing a gray whale. Despite the fact of the successful hunt, the ongoing controversy demonstrates that it remains next to impossible to essentialize Native Americans even within a single tribe. First of all, proponents argue correctly that treaty rights recognize the hunting tradition and guarantee the right of the Makahs to whale. Tribal proponents of whaling continue to argue also "that the cultural needs and traditions of the Makah outweigh political and moral objections" (Walker n.p.). They insist on the fact of an ongoing tradition, even though in a variety of ways, the Makahs reinvented the "tradition" of whaling itself after several generations of its dormancy. As the whaling crew members themselves are proud to relate, they had to do historical, archival research in order to build their canoe, design their harpoons, and reinstall the ceremonial practices surrounding the hunt. One of the actual hunters, Micah McCarty, says he feels the need to resist the white man's culture and believes that the whale hunt, somehow, will keep it away: "bringing this whale back into the culture," he says, "will save us from being swallowed up" (quoted in Blow 8). In these ways, the "authentic" Makah is a whaler, and tribal members thus argue that to deny the people the right to hunt gray whales would simply be another instance of the colonial power denying a colonized people the right to live their traditional lives. What these proponents do not articulate is that there is an irony inherent in their claiming those treaty rights at the same time that they assert the importance of tradition. That is, the very concept of the "traditional Makah" is compromised in the face of contact with European colonizers in that the very contact necessitates a treaty guaranteeing "traditional" rights at the same time it makes manifest the very fact of cultural change.

At the same time that some tribal members formulate arguments to demonstrate how the authentic Makah is a whaler, however, it must be acknowledged that many Makah families never were whalers, and that furthermore, in contrast to proponents, some Makah opponents to whaling argue that whaling is not and need not be a fundamental part of a Makah's identity, especially given the fact that until 1999, no living Makah had ever whaled. Tribal elder Alberta Thompson, for example, paraphrases a Quileute tribal member who argues that one does not have to "kill a whale to keep [the] tradition[s]. We know our traditions, we know what we've done in the past, we know what we're doing now, and we can pass all of this on to our children." Even though she opposes whale hunting as a means of authenticating oneself, however, Thompson does acknowledge the concept and importance of an identifiable tribe and tribal identity: when the tribe "get[s] split in half," she says, "we're weak. We have a hard time judging what's right and wrong" ("A Makah Elder Speaks" n.p.). In an essay for the *Seattle Times*, Lynda Mapes writes about the controversy, quoting a Makah elder, Lawrence Moss, who argues that the "family doesn't need whaling to tell them they are Makah. I don't need a whale killed to be any more Makah than I have been my entire life" (Mapes n.p.). In this sense, then, people from within the same tribe and thus equally and authentically "Makah" counter the assertions by another group of Makahs, people who attempt to define the authentic Makah as a whaler.

In her essay "Tools for a Cross-Cultural Feminist Ethics," Greta Gaard argues that in the "case of the Makah, the whale hunting practices of a certain elite group of men have been conflated with the practices and substituted for the identity of an entire culture. Indeed, the dominant group of the Makah may be seen as using a form of strategic essentialism to achieve their goals" (2001, 17). At least intuitively aware of the strategic essentialism, or this attempt to establish a tribal identity through whaling, Chickasaw writer Linda Hogan argues that instead of whaling, the Makahs would do better to consider a tradition even older than whaling, that of listening to those who argue for the importance of balance, the old tribal women elders, the "true and deep wellspring of a culture" (Hogan; see Gaard 2000, 98). In her book coauthored with Brenda Peterson, *Sightings: The Gray Whales' Mysterious Journey* (2001), Hogan reiterates her point about the importance of listening to tribal elders, writing that in "their location at the end of the continent, a people are trying to lay claim to an older world and its complex of ceremony, but which people? It may very well be the silenced older women" (154). Whichever identity any particular Makah individual adopts, however, it will necessarily exclude the alternative identity, and it is in this sense that the intra- and intertribal controversy over Makah whaling makes the problem of establishing authenticity clear.

My point in referring to the controversy over Makah whaling is not to argue for or against the legality, morality, or traditional status of the whale hunt, but rather in this context to suggest that issues of authenticity (whether fashioned by economic, cultural, or other motives) are at the very center of important political situations faced by the people who may or may not be considered Native American, or in this case traditional Makah. Indeed, in granting the Makahs their treaty right, in deciding to allow the Makahs their quota of whales, the International Whaling Commission considered the tradition and authenticity of a whaling culture. In such a decision-making context, authenticity, cultural identity, and a sense of a tribal affiliation are obviously just as crucial and significant as they are difficult to determine in the first place.

In literature, issues of authenticity are equally central (even though the consequences might be less immediately profound), especially in contexts ranging from subject matter to marketing, to instituting or perpetuating stereotypes among both the non-Indian population and also among Indian readers themselves. Issues of authenticity in literature can thus eventually find their way into a people's understanding of who they are and thus influence their own sense of identity. Certainly it is helpful to understand that through the study of literature we can recognize that the "authentic" Native American book (novel, collection of poems, memoir) is at the center of literary and cultural production. Crow Creek Sioux writer and critic Elizabeth Cook-Lynn makes the very relevant point that the academic discipline of American Indian studies has the potential to become "one of the useful mechanisms for the deconstruction of colonization not only in academia but in society as well" (22). It is thus important to point out that issues of appropriation and authentication have been at the forefront of much Native American writing at least since the late 1960s and the beginning of what Kenneth Lincoln has identified as the Native American Renaissance. Indeed, Krupat argues that "Native American written literature today may be seen as very much engaged in [the] project of anti-imperial translation" (170). We could, of course, trace this issue back as far as published Native writing in the United States. Pequot writer William Apess (1798–1839), for instance, confronts the issue of identity and authenticity when he asks his readers how an Indian is different from a person of European descent in his essay "An Indian's Looking-Glass for the White Man" (1833): "I am not talking about the skin but about principles. I would ask if there cannot be as good feelings and principles under a red skin as there can be under a white" (156). In his groundbreaking book *Custer Died for Your Sins* (1969), Vine Deloria Jr. repeatedly calls into question issues of authenticity, both by spoofing the concept of "plight" and by making a facetious but significant point about the stereotyping of Native Americans: "Our foremost plight is our transparency. People can tell just by looking at us what we want, what should be done to help us, how we feel, and what a 'real' Indian is really like. . . . Because people can see right through us, it becomes impossible to tell truth from fiction or fact from mythology. Experts paint us as they would like us to be. Often we paint ourselves as we wish we were or as we might have been" (1–2). As this passage makes clear, Deloria is aware of the complexity of the authenticity issue: to a certain extent Native Americans accept the fiction of "Indianness" imposed upon them by the dominant culture. Carried to its extreme, the authentic Indian becomes a non-Indian creation.

According to the authors of *The Empire Writes Back*, "One of the major acts of abrogation in post-colonial literature is a rejection of the process by which 'authenticity' is granted to the categories of experience authorized by the center at the expense of those relegated to the margins of empire" (Ashcroft et al. 91). The insight of Ashcroft and his coauthors sheds light on similar issues in Native American literature. In the essay "Mapping the Mixedblood," for example, Louis Owens (Choctaw-Cherokee) articulates the problem of authenticity, of "Indianness," that many contemporary Native American authors face: "Euramerica remains involved in an unceasing ideological struggle to confine Native Americas with an essentialized territory defined by the authoritative utterance 'Indian.' Native Americans, however, continue to resist this ideology of containment and to insist upon the freedom to reimagine themselves within a fluid, always shifting frontier space" (27). Also aware of the dangers both of essentializing and of "Indians" seeking the "authentic Indian," Gerald Vizenor maintains that there is a distinction between the dominant impositions and the tribal literature: "postindian warriors," as he calls them, "create new tribal presence in stories. . . . the simulations of survivance." In *Manifest Manners*, Vizenor writes that the "Indian was an occidental invention that became a bankable simulation; the word has no referent in tribal languages or cultures. The postindian is the absence of the invention, and the end of representation in literature; the closure of that evasive melancholy of dominance. Manifest manners are the simulations of bourgeois decadence and melancholy" (11). In this sense Vizenor moves away from the dominant culture's impositions, but at the same time, like Makah elder Alberta Thompson, he acknowledges the importance of tribal identity, an identity maintained despite and separate from those dominant impositions.

In the context of literature and the importance of authenticity, then, I turn to my second detailed example, the poetry of Turtle Mountain Chippewa writer Mark Turcotte. Turcotte asks probing questions about authenticity, rejecting the process (to use Ashcroft's phrasing) through which authenticity is granted. With the "Back When" section of the collection *Exploding Chippewas* (2002), the poet inquires into the nature of identity, mixed-blood status, and authenticity. In this "Back When" series, Turcotte presents the speaker's autobiography, from his first reaching for the light and his mother's "weeping breast" to the scene of his mother's deathbed in the poem "Orbit" (5, 26). Each poem in the series, a snapshot of the speaker's life, begins with the same line, "Back when I used to be Indian," yet in the second and subsequent lines the speaker shifts to the present tense: "Back when I used to be Indian / I am reaching toward the light . . ." or "Back when I used to be Indian / I am scratching it all down . . ." (5, 11).

The shift in tense from the first line to the following lines immediately raises questions concerning authenticity. Most immediately, perhaps, the shift suggests both an acknowledgment of "Indianness" and at the same instant a denial of the same. If the signifier "Indian" has any validity whatsoever in the opening line, if it suggests any sort of connection with cultural practices and beliefs, for example, or if it serves as an ethnic marker in any way, it is not generally thought of as something one is and then suddenly is not, or something one was yet is no longer. To acknowledge "Indianness" in the opening line thus constitutes a statement on the speaker's part of being Indian in what is to follow. But even within the one line itself, Turcotte denies the reader such an easy duality. That is, the implication is that if the speaker was an "Indian" "back when," then the speaker is an Indian in the present as well. Being

Indian is not a profession one can simply discard or resign from. Or is it? That is precisely what the speaker seems to do. Indeed, as if to emphasize the shift in status (as well as tense), every second line in the series begins with an assertion of the state of being, and in the present tense: "I am . . .". It is as if the speaker is establishing a new identity, yet at the same time the speaker of these poems frustrates any easy identity with stereotypical Indianness. The fact of the past tense juxtaposed with the present in the next line (and throughout the remainder of the poem) suggests a rejection or a refutation of Indianness, as if to say, even if it were once so, it is so no longer. The speaker acknowledges his "Indianness" but implies by the notion of "back when" that he is not Indian, even though the poem itself exists as a statement about being Indian, but being Indian on the speaker's own terms.

This shift in tense thus suggests a sort of colonial/postcolonial dynamic with identity. The notion of *back when I was part of the colony that named me "Indian"* stands in contrast to the present (post)colonial state in the present tense. As Krupat points out, "there is not yet a 'post-' to American Indian colonial status" (169). Even if there were a "post-" in the colonial status, there is of course an irony inherent in colonialism in that the effects of colonization are not easily overcome. Turcotte's poems suggest some of the difficulties in any attempt to find an authentic self in the face of colonialism. A colonized people, he suggests, feel the effects of the colonization long, long after contact whether or not the colonizer retains political or military control in any literal sense.

The repeated opening line of the poems is also a way for Turcotte to challenge the dominant culture's attempts to identify the authentic subject through stereotypes. In the poem "Battlefield," for example, he frustrates any easy association of Indian with hair color or complexion:

> Back when I used to be Indian
> I am standing outside the
> Pool hall with my sister.
> She, strawberry blond . . . (8)

In this poem the speaker confronts and exposes the reader who might want to classify the authentic Indian as one with black hair. Similarly, in the poem "Twist" he challenges another stereotype when he portrays his "white" friends rather than himself as drunkards. In the poem he describes a drinking spree with a group of white men, and in the middle section, Turcotte seems to undercut the stereotype of the drunken Indian by depicting the white boys as the drunks. They are the ones drunk enough to vomit and crawl around on their knees. But the speaker also recalls that on the drive back from his and his friends' outing, at the edge of a farmer's field, a deer comes onto the road in front of them:

> A deer staggers into our headlights,
> an arrow through its neck. The blade
> in my pocket dances against
> my hip, digs in, begins to whisper
> to my mixed
> up blood. (12)

The allusion to what might be considered stereotypically "Indian" in this instance is immediately undercut by the context of white drunks and the reference to a young mixed-blood's "mixed up blood." Modern day bow hunting aside, the disjuncture of the boys driving an automobile and the deer shot with an arrow (along with some perhaps ancestral whisper of the dancing knife for the gutting) refuses to let the reader be comfortable with any specific association of Indianness and, in this case, deer hunting, drinking, or gutting and cleaning.

In the poem "Visitation," Turcotte makes a similar move or "twist" when the speaker juxtaposes a night-time vision of a buffalo with a Tonka toy truck:

> Across the room a buffalo snorts,
> nudges the yellow Tonka truck
> with its nose. (7)

The image of a buffalo (potentially a stereotypical evocation of Plains Indian culture) is challenged (even denied) by the image of that buffalo nudging a post-contact (late twentieth-century) toy truck, and the image forces the reader to consider the effects of colonization, especially in that the near extermination of buffalo was one of the means by which the colonizer attempted to control (or exterminate) the Plains peoples. The poem also suggests the irony inherent in the fact of the toy truck itself, a replica of a real earthmover and thus a symbol of loss of land: the very literal moving of dirt in a dump truck, of course, but also the taking of land that was the buffaloes' and the Plains Indians'.

Once the speaker uses the signifier "Indian" in the opening line, he need not offer anything else in the poems that identifies him as "Indian." In the course of the series as a whole, the speaker describes his birth, childhood, adolescence, adulthood, marriage, fatherhood, and finally the death of his mother. Any attempt to impose an "Indian" identity on the speaker other than from that first line is thus just that, an imposition. The poems are not about being Indian in any conventional, traditional, stereotypical, or "authentic" sense. In fact, in the moment in (past) time that Turcotte allows his speaker to be "Indian," he subverts the conceptual framework. He does this by first switching tenses and thereby denying "Indianness" in the present, or in "real" time, then by not offering anything identifiably (anything that the mainstream non-Indian reader might see as) "Indian" in the subsequent lines of the poem. He thus subverts the only possible allusions to what an implied reader might understand as "authentically" Indian.

There is an exception to this motif, however. In the poem "Burn," the speaker does identify himself, in that he is identified by another, as Indian. He is on the dance floor at a bar, "Back when I used to be Indian / I am crushing the dance floor," when a white girl moves toward him and hisses: "*go go Geronimo.*" The first-person speaker stops dancing, and switches to the grammatical third person, almost as if the speaker is simultaneously himself and not himself; he is forced to see himself as Other. The speaker is himself looking at "Geronimo" who is in a sense also the speaker himself:

> I stop.
> All silence he sits beside the fire
> at the center of the floor, hands stirring
> through the ashes, mouth moving in the shape
> of my name. I turn to reach toward him,
> take one step, feel my skin begin
> to flame away. (15)

The switch from first to third person suggests that in response to the words spoken by the white girl, the dancer—who again has (and has not) identified himself as Indian—is somehow outside himself, distanced from himself. The perhaps authentic stoic, silent man, sitting at a fire, is set in sharp contrast to the dancing man crushing the floor. The silent man is also set in sharp contrast to the first-person narrator who reaches toward this form of the self as he witnesses it turn to ash. If there is an "Indian" self there, an authentic Indian, in name or in body, he is not anything the dancer (from the grammatical first person) can grasp onto or identify with. He is nothing that can be classified as authentic.

In the sense of authenticity, the white woman's words, spoken from an essentializing and stereotyping (and racist, "go go Geronimo") mind-set, serve to threaten and compromise the dancer's sense of self and self-confidence achieved through dancing. According to Ashcroft et al., "[l]anguage is a power because words construct reality. The assumption by the powerless is that words are the signifiers of a pre-given reality, a reality and a truth which is only located at the centre" (1989, 81). By speaking the words, "*go go Geronimo*," the white girl—at the cultural and power center by virtue of her whiteness—imposes a reality upon the dancer that simultaneously (falsely) identifies but thus (effectively) disenfranchises the actual dancer as it refers to and embodies the colonizer's "authentic" Indian. She identifies him according to what she might understand as an authentic Indian. The Geronimo to whom she refers is undoubtedly the "white" construction of the turn-of-the-century Geronimo, famous for his resistance, and in this reduction of Indian to the one well-known image, she denies the speaker of the poem, the actual man on the dance floor, any sense of self for himself.

Although the issue of authenticity is perhaps most obvious in the "Back When" series, in poems in the "Exploding Chippewas" section of the collection Turcotte further challenges the authenticating stereotypes imposed upon "Indians" in the efforts of the colonizer to calibrate and identify an authentic Indian. As he identifies it, he calls the effort into question with the poem "In the Dream-All-Night Laundromat":

> The old man . . .
> is dreaming again that he is
> the young Indian boy he once
> saw in a movie . . . (64)

The old man never was that Indian boy. Indeed, outside the movie industry, that young Indian boy never existed. The juxtaposition—of the Hollywood image of a boy and the dreamer, an old man, drunk and on the verge of death in the all-night Laundromat—suggests not only the fallacy of mainstream attempts to present an "authentic" Indian but the damage such attempts do to those upon whom the stereotype is imposed. In this sense, we come back to Jana Sequoya's important point that, although "the figure of the authentic Indian is a figment of the popular imagination, it nevertheless has real consequences for contemporary American Indian people" (284). Most immediately in the context of this poem, the consequence is that the old man sits in a Laundromat and lives a life in direct and absolute contrast to the filmic Indian boy warrior, the young Indian man seducing the white farmer's daughter (from another movie) or even the "Indian man he never once / saw in a movie" who stands over John Wayne and breaks the cowboy's spine. The effect of the imaginary authentic Indian is thus to delimit and deny the actual human being, and in the case of this poem, conscribe him to an ignoble death in an all-night Laundromat.

As Turcotte's poetry and as the Makah whaling controversy suggest, issues of authenticity remain at the center of Native American life and art. The issue is of fundamental importance both because the authentic Indian is a construct imposed from the outside and because that construct nevertheless has important ramifications in the cultural and political realms of Native American life. A recent blatant and chilling example of the political import of authenticity is the controversy concerning Cherokee scholar Ward Churchill, (former) ethnic studies professor at the University of Colorado. In an effort to get him fired in the aftermath of his comments concerning the September 2001 attacks on the World Trade Center towers, a conservative group questioned the "professor's ethnic ancestry" (Smallwood). In this attempt to set severe limits on academic freedom and freedom of speech, this group invented an authentic Cherokee to meet their needs and then to claim that Churchill does not fit by established standards of authenticity. Natsu Saito, Churchill's wife and spokesperson in this instance, points out that such means are "spurious" and that "the federal government has used criteria other than bloodlines to recognize people as American Indians, including 'self-identification and recognition by the community' " (Smallwood). That is to say, authenticity is much more complex than can be accounted for by the absurdly unreliable information provided by Ancestry.com (the website used by reporters for a major Colorado newspaper). Clearly, the creation of the authentic in this instance is in service to an effort to delimit and deny particular rights to a man whose ancestry has, of course, nothing to do with his controversial statements or his scholarly publication record, but is indeed a possible way to get him fired since he is in other ways protected by the First Amendment. Were his tribal credentials found to be inauthentic, imply his detractors, the whole body of his scholarship and thus his professorial legitimacy could be called into question. As reported by Interim Chancellor Phil DiStefano at the University of Colorado, in his response to a faculty committee's report, "Questions raised about Professor Churchill's possible misrepresentation of his ethnicity in order to gain employment advantage were reviewed, resulting in a finding of no action warranted" (DiStefano). Nevertheless, in June 2006 DiStefano announced his intent to dismiss Churchill from his faculty position for allegations of research misconduct, and in July of 2007 the Board of Regents voted to fire him.

It is my hope that the discussion presented here will help us better recognize and be prepared to challenge the colonial enterprise of fabricating "authentic" or "inauthentic Indians" and the use of that fabrication to limit a person's social, cultural, or career options, to deprive an individual or a group of appropriate rights and privileges. Ashcroft and his colleagues write that the "problem with claims to cultural authenticity is that they often become entangled in an essentialist cultural position in which fixed practices become iconized as authentically indigenous and others are excluded" (2000, 21). It is just such essentialist positions, whether imposed from the outside or from within, which inspire or which are used to justify exclusion or failure to include; it is just such positions that demand the most careful scrutiny. The Makah whaling controversy, the case against Ward Churchill, and Mark Turcotte's poetry all give evidence of the potential use and misuse by the power center of conceptions of authenticity. It is my hope that the interrogation of stereotypes and attempts to authenticate can help promote yet further discussion of how such efforts to set limits manifest themselves in colonial contexts and are in need of being contested vociferously and repeatedly.

Works Cited

Alcoff, Linda. "The Problem of Speaking for Others." *Cultural Critique* 20.1 (1991–1992): 5–32.

Amireh, Amal, and Lisa Suhair Majaj, eds. "Introduction." *Going Global: The Transnational Reception of Third World Women Writers*. New York: Garland Publishing, 2000. 1–25.

Apess, William. "An Indian's Looking-Glass for the White Man." *On Our Own Ground: The Complete Writings of William Apess*. Ed. Barry O'Connell. Amherst: U of Massachusetts P, 1992. 155–61.

Ashcroft, Bill, Gareth Griffiths, and Helen Tiffin. *The Empire Writes Back: Theory and Practice in Post-Colonial Literatures*. New York: Routledge, 1989.

Ashcroft, Bill, Gareth Griffiths, and Helen Tiffin, eds. *Post-Colonial Studies: The Key Concepts*. New York: Routledge, 2000.

Blow, Richard. "The Great American Whale Hunt." *Mother Jones* September/October 1998. http://www.motherjones.com/cgi-bin/print_article

Cheyfitz, Eric. "The (Post)Colonial Construction of Indian Country: U.S. American Indian Literatures and Federal Indian Law." *The Columbia Guide to American Indian Literatures of the United States Since 1945*. Ed. Eric Cheyfitz. New York: Columbia UP, 2006. 3–124.

Cook-Lynn, Elizabeth. "Who Stole Native American Studies?" *Wicazo Sa Review* 12 (Spring 1997): 9–28.

Deloria, Vine, Jr. *Custer Died for Your Sins: An Indian Manifesto*. New York: Macmillan, 1969.

DiStefano, Phil. "Recommendation of Interim Chancellor Phil DiStefano with Regard to Investigation of Research Misconduct." 26 June 2006. http://www.colorado.edu/news/reports/churchill/distefano062606.html

Erdrich, Louise. *Love Medicine*. New and Expanded Edition. New York: HarperPerennial, 1993.

———. *Tracks*. New York: HarperPerennial, 2004.

Gaard, Greta. "Strategies for a Cross-Cultural Ecofeminist Ethics: Interrogating Tradition, Preserving Nature." *Bucknell Review* 44.1 (2000): 82–101.'"

———. "Tools for a Cross-Cultural Feminist Ethics: Exploring Ethical Contexts and Contents in the Makah Whale Hunt." *Hypatia: A Journal of Feminist Philosophy* 16.1 (Winter 2001): 1–26.'"

Griffiths, Gareth. "The Myth of Authenticity: Representations, Discourse, and Social Practice." *De-Scribing Empire: Post-Colonialism and Textuality*. Ed. Chris Tiffin and Alan Lawson. New York: Routledge, 1994. 70–85.

Hogan, Linda. "Silencing Tribal Grandmothers: Traditions, Old Values at Heart of Makah's Clash Over Whaling." *Seattle Times* 15 December 1996. B9.

Hulme, Peter. "Survival and Invention: Indigeneity in the Caribbean." *Postcolonial Discourses: An Anthology*. Ed. Gregory Castle. Oxford: Blackwell Publishers, 2001. 294–308.

Krupat, Arnold. "Postcoloniality and Native American Literature." *The Yale Journal of Criticism* 7.1 (Spring 1994): 163–80.

Lincoln, Kenneth. *Native American Renaissance*. Berkeley: U of California P, 1983.

"A Makah Elder Speaks: An Interview with Alberta Thompson." *Earth First: The Radical Environmental Journal* 19.4 (1999). http://www.earthfirstjournal.org/efj/ feature.cfmID=30&issue=v19n4

Mapes, Lynda V. "Some Makahs Oppose Whale Hunt." *Seattle Times* 1998. http://www.orchahome.de/makah.htm

Peterson, Brenda, and Linda Hogan. *Sightings: The Gray Whales' Mysterious Journey*. Washington, DC: National Geographic, 2001.

Owens, Louis. "Mapping the Mixedblood." *Mixedblood Messages: Literature, Film, Family, Place*. Norman: U of Oklahoma P, 1998. 25–41.

Sequoya, Jana. "How(!) Is an Indian? A Contest of Stories, Round 2." *New Voices in Native American Literary Criticism*. Ed. Arnold Krupat. Washington: Smithsonian Institution Press, 1993. 453–73.

Sequoya-Magdaleno, Jana. "How(!) Is an Indian? A Contest of Stories, Round 2." *Postcolonial Theory and the United States: Race, Ethnicity, and Literature*. Eds. Amritjit Singh and Peter Schmidt. Jackson: U of Mississippi P, 2000. 279–99.

Sequoya-Magdaleno, Jana. "Telling the *différance*: Representations of Identity in the Discourse of Indianness." *The Ethnic Canon: Histories, Institutions, and Interventions*. Ed. David Palumbo-Lui. Minneapolis: U of Minnesota P, 1995. 88–116.

Smallwood, Scott. "Controversy Over Colorado Professor Grows to Include Questions About His Tenure and Heritage." *The Chronicle of Higher Education* 18 February 2005. http://chronicle.com/

Turcotte, Mark. *Exploding Chippewas*. Evanston: Triquarterly Books, Northwestern UP, 2002.

Vizenor, Gerald. *Manifest Manners: Postindian Warriors of Survivance*. Hanover: UP of New England, 1994.

———. "Introduction." *Native American Literature: A Brief Introduction and Anthology*. New York: HarperCollins, 1995. 1–15.

Walker, Peter. "The Makah Whale Hunt: Politics Meets Tradition." The Humane Society of the United States. http:www.hsus.org/ace/11740

4

The X-Blood Files

Whose Story? Whose Indian?

Malea Powell

This is a story.

This is the kind of story that needs to begin with the storyteller, with a statement about her present past, so that you know something about the constellation of other stories that prompt this telling. Or, as my elders would say—this is who I am; this is how I heard it.

Because this is a story about blood and appropriate behavior, I want to be clear about who I am. I am a mixed blood, a descendant of the peoples now called the Miami Indian Nation of the State of Indiana (more commonly called "Indiana Miamis") and the Miami Nation of Oklahoma. I have relatives in both places, but I am not enrolled.[1] The first documented contact between Miami peoples and Europeans happened about 1654. We were living in an area northwest of what is now Green Bay, Wisconsin—far from our traditional homelands, a rough triangle of land and rivers beginning in what is now Chicago and widening to points near present-day Cincinnati, Ohio and Evansville, Indiana. So, about 350 years ago, when French explorers Radisson and Grosseilliers came upon a village they estimated at containing around twenty thousand inhabitant Native peoples, they reported what they thought they saw—twenty thousand Miamis. But even in 1654, Miami culture was already "hybrid," an accumulation of borrowings and adaptations from extensive pan-tribal contact married to our own practices of beliefs—but then this can be said of almost *any* culture at any period in history, can't it? It is, however, especially true of Miamis.

During the first three centuries of intense colonial exploration and settlement in "the Old Northwest," the Miami Confederacy was one of the largest confederacies of Native peoples on the continent.[2] Our alliances with our indigenous neighbors established ways of relating to "others" that paved the way for our seventeenth-century alliances with the French, which led to the creation of a *metís* society of tribal peoples who acted as intermediaries in the development of the complicated trade and political relationships we needed to have with the French, Spanish, English, and (later) American colonists invading our homelands. Because Miamis controlled the rivers and portages that provided important transportation routes through the densely wooded terrain of Indiana and Eastern Ohio, our contact with European and American explorers, hunters, and traders was a strategic necessity. It's through alliance, persistence, and adaptation that we have survived—after the Treaty of Greenville (1795), after the fall of Prophetstown (1811), after the treaty making that followed the War of 1812, after the treaties that ceded larger and larger portions of Miami-held lands and eventually removed half of the tribe (1846) to Kansas then Oklahoma, after the illegal termination of the Indiana Miamis' federal status (1890s), after all of it, we survived.[3] In the words of Floyd Leonard, Principal Chief of the Oklahoma Miamis, "of course, traditions changed as time changed," but, as Lora Siders (elder of the Indiana Miamis) reminded us, "basically we're still the same" (141, 193).

In my mind as I write this, I keep hearing the narrator in that Sherman Alexie story, "Witness, Secret of Not"; he says, "One Indian doesn't tell another what to do. We just watch things happen and then make comments" (216). As the editor of *Studies in American Indian Literatures* since 2001, I've been watching a lot of things happen here in American Indian Studies, especially in that corner of the field where we study literatures and writing, and I feel like I have a close-up view of what Native literary studies looks like at this particular moment in time. Additionally, as a scholar in Rhetoric and in American studies, I've been able to see the extent to which Native studies can, and should, "play" well in other interdisciplinary fields, and how understandings of Native literatures and Native writing might change those other fields as well. In other words, I've had the opportunity to see and hear some pretty interesting, and pretty disturbing, things and, well, I've got some things to say about what I've seen and heard. The story that follows, then, is offered as commentary, as a series of observations that might lead us to a way of imagining the possibilities for twenty-first-century Native scholars and for scholars of Native writing and literatures. Yes, I know that those two categories present distinct, but sometimes overlapping, problems and predicaments; however, I think the actual people who inhabit those categories (and their overlaps) depend on one another much more than we have considered to date, so I'll take the chance of keeping both categories alive in this story.

In the past decade, Native scholars and scholarship in Native studies have grown increasingly concerned with definitions of, and claims to, Indianness. Gerald Vizenor's fiction and critical work frequently raises the questions of Indian identity through the "crossblood," marking the ironic presence of real Indian peoples as absence in the dominant cultural narratives of America, and citing the reimagining of those narratives with the presence, in spirit or in fact, of Nanaabozho, the Woodlands trickster.[4] As Vizenor often points out, humor and irony can be powerful tools in dismantling the oppressive narratives of manifest manners and their singular insistence on the beaded and feathered, stoic and wise, disappearing problem—"the *indian*."[5] Though some would write the tale of the Native intellectual with the same singularity and woe present in manifest manners, Vizenor, and I, prefer to see the ironic instances of our presence in the academy. These instances are persistent, not only in that all academic and intellectual work in this country is literally enacted on Native ground, but also in the chicaneries of publication and disciplinary separation that often embroil us in seemingly incidental imperial complicities.

An example in the form of a signifying chain—and since I started with Vizenor, I'll continue with him—an honoring of sorts to some advice he gave me one summer in Berkeley: "we must always tease the manners." Vizenor's *Fugitive Poses: Native American Indian Scenes of Absence and Presence* is part of the University of Nebraska Press's Abraham Lincoln Lecture Series publications. The series "aims to reflect the principles that Abraham Lincoln championed: education, justice, tolerance, and union" (frontispiece). Lincoln, of course, was the president who ordered the Santee hangings in 1862 after their resistance to the dealings of an Indian agent whose swindling left them starving, an act that, coincidentally, made possible Charles Alexander Eastman's sojourn at both Dartmouth and Wounded Knee on the whim of Lincoln's decision to spare Christian converts, one of whom was Jacob Eastman, from execution. Charles Eastman's *The Soul of the Indian* (1916), which tropes W. E. B. Du Bois's *The Souls of Black Folks* (1903), is an interesting and problematic text. Interesting in that it is as much a negotiation of Eastman's own connection to the mythical *indian* as it is a piece of persuasion about the humanity and morality—the simple goodness—of this idealized and noble "Indian." Problematic in ways too numerous to engage here but significantly symbolized in the slippage between the implied plurality of Du Bois's title—soul*s* of folk*s*—and the equally implied singularity of Eastman's: one soul, one Indian, one way to be Indian? At any rate, the city of Lincoln, Nebraska is, of course, also named after Abraham Lincoln—it is home to the University of Nebraska and its university press, and it became my scholarly home just a year after I spent a vaporous July in Berkeley working with Vizenor in a workshop on American identities.

While it is easy to argue the coincidental here, I choose instead to see relationships—to people, to places, to the past, to the future—and in those relationships to map meaning. Not blame nor blamelessness, not right or wrong, but the relationship of people who live now to our ancestors, to the land, and to the events that unfolded on the land. For example, my current scholarly home signifies quite differently. This is not to say that my relationship with the university is "bad" or "good," only that it is informed by—and responsible to—this history and its consequences.

I began thinking seriously about the consequences of such relationships during a 1999 workshop sponsored by a now-defunct native cultural preservation group affiliated with the Museums at Prophetstown project. This workshop brought Eastern Woodlands elders and tradition-bearers together with local Native people and some non-Indian allies for a week of fellowship and learning. The workshop was followed by the Waapaashiki Peoples powwow, a traditional gathering of Native folks from the Wabash River area in present-day north central Indiana. In the midst of these activities, as I enjoyed the company of my friends and relatives and the glee that accompanied my beginner's luck with quillwork, I was also reading Devon Mihesuah's edited collection *Natives and Academics*. And I was finding an essay by Elizabeth Cook-Lynn to be especially troubling. In that essay, "American Indian Intellectualism and the New Indian Story," Cook-Lynn attacks a whole host of Native scholars she calls "urban mixed-bloods" for participating in work that she claims is "not generated from the inside of tribal cultural influence" because these scholars have been "removed from cultural influence through urbanization and academic professionalization . . . biology and intermarriage" (1998, 129). She points out that in the writings of "Gerald Vizenor, Louis Owens, Wendy Rose, Maurice Kenny, Michael Dorris, Diane Glancy, Betty Bell, Thomas King, Joe Bruchac and Paula Gunn Allen" there are "few useful expressions of resistance and opposition to the colonial history at the core of Indian/White relations" and that, in fact, "there is explicit and implicit accommodation to the colonialism of the 'West' " (1998, 124).

Though I am in hearty agreement with Cook-Lynn's urgings that we turn to "the life-affirming aesthetic of traditional stories, songs and rituals," I couldn't help but wonder, as I looked around at all the Native people participating in the Prophetstown workshop and dancing at the Waapaashiki powwow, whose stories, songs, and rituals "count" and whose do not in her anti-mixed-blood claims? Whose complicated histories and messy relationships to conquest and colonization simply become unimportant, unheard, absent in this narrative of who can, and who can't, "get it right"—the "it" being what Cook-Lynn calls "Native intellectualism" (135)? Each time I am at gatherings of Native people at home in Indiana, I clearly see the "tribalism" Cook-Lynn so rightly calls for; however, it's equally clear to me that Cook-Lynn's definitions *wouldn't* see that tribalism since the tribal nations in Indiana[6] are mixed-bloods (urban and rural), the *metís* who, in another essay, Cook-Lynn describes as people who "were and probably still are seen by native peoples as those who were *already converts* to the hostile and intruding culture simply through their marriage into it" (1996, 35). Here is where the real consequences of Native scholarship and its entanglements become crystal clear to me. It is one thing for Indian peoples to appear only as absence in that "American" tale—we know what that's about, that rhetoric of empire; it is, however, quite another thing for some Native peoples to be declared absent from the story that "we" Native intellectuals tell about ourselves. That's another kind of empire entirely.

It seems to me that the most important lesson that continued colonization of North America should have taught us is that internal colonization is the most insidious, the most effective, and pernicious method of our continued oppression. That Native peoples would believe the "blood" arguments of the colonizers is simply devastating—it has the potential to arithmetically erase the possibility of a Native future if we use it as our only measure of "Indianness." That this belief is reiterated, reworked, and imposed in the politics of Native studies in the academy is simply not acceptable. *We cannot afford to exclude one another.* More than half of the Indian people in this country do not live in reservation communities. Many tribes, like the Indiana and Oklahoma Miamis, are completely comprised of non-reservationed mixed-bloods who, nonetheless, think of themselves as Native peoples who participate in the cultural practices of their tribal nations. Some of those practices are certainly different from those of other tribal cultures—what counts as "tradition" and "Indian" for Cherokees, for instance, looks very different than what counts for Lakotas, for Hopis, for Oneidas. We all know this: we can't define these things for one another. If we respect indigenous sovereignty in the ways that our scholarship claims we do, then we must respect the authority of tribal communities to determine what is, and what is not, part of their culture; to decide who is, and who isn't, part of their community. Further, if we understand the genocidal effects of colonization and its subsequent diasporas for Native peoples, again, as our scholarship claims we do, then we can't afford not to pay attention to *all* the possible outcomes of those processes—detribalization, adoption, intermarriage, sterilization, and so forth—for the contemporary ancestors of those peoples who lived through colonization. In the American Indian studies community, we can't afford to believe in "one soul, one Indian," that idealized and always-disappearing myth, and we can't afford unconsciously to perpetuate those beliefs in our scholarly practices.

We would go far if we took the advice of other "third world" intellectuals like Chandra and Satya Mohanty and recognized, explicitly and implicitly in our intellectual endeavors, that the "colonized are not just the object of the colonizer's discourses but [are] the agents of a conflicted history, inhabiting and transforming a complex social and cultural world" (19). In doing so we might remember that the ultimate irony of the term "Native intellectuals," and in the forced presence of Indians in Euro-American educational settings, is that we don't have to accept a definition that includes the impositions of imperialism—we have earned the dominant cultural capital to define ourselves differently than Euro-American scholars might have defined us fifty years ago. We have fought for a place within an institution of dominant cultural power *in order* to do this—to write ourselves into a history that once depended on our exclusion, to reimagine Indianness in our own varying and multiplicitous tribal ways, to create and re-create ourselves as always already present on this continent. We understand their language now; we speak it and we understand its value.

> [I want the children] to learn all they can learn and be able to further the course of the Indian in the big world outside, . . . I think that [going to college] is the salvation of the tribe, of tribal heritage. We need people who are educated, who understand the world to keep the tribe in shape financially & spiritually." (Leonard 144)

If, as Cook-Lynn suggests, sovereignty is the word of the day, then we have to acknowledge that gaining mastery of those "master's tools" has allowed us to make some progress in legally, historically, and imaginatively insisting on ourselves. The "imaginative" work of Momaday and Ortiz, the legal/historical work of Deloria, even the critical work of Cook-Lynn, are significant and productive for *all* Native intellectuals—not just for Kiowas, Acomas, and Dakotas—because they made space for future generations of Native writers, teachers, activists, artists, and scholars. We have done what we had to do, and part of that entailed taking the tools of Euro-American cultural participation that were forced upon us and using them in our own ways to broadly advance Native sovereignty on multiple fronts—in quincentennial and mascot protests, land-use and treaty-rights legislation, tribally based K–16 curriculum and pedagogy, and more. Native scholars and writers have, to borrow a phrase from Joy Harjo and Gloria Bird, not only "reinvented the enemy's language";[7] we have reinvented the enemy's knowledge and forms of knowledge-making. That we have the luxury of university jobs and emeritus retirements, that we attend academic conferences, publish, critique, and disagree about those reinventions is proof of our success at using Euro-American tools to our own ends. The growing number of Native scholars, mixed-bloods included, are proof of *our* work at reimagining the "proper" relationship between Natives and academics—our very bodies represent the tensions and negotiations inherent in more than five hundred years of contact and colonization.

The "coincidence" of our entanglements within institutions of education in the United States doesn't simply equal "sellout" or "less Indian." We are not that simple and our decisions to participate in those institutions have not been that simple. As a field we have made these participations a space of agency in this "paracolonial" (not postcolonial) moment. What this space of scholarly agency offers us is another kind of language, a rhetoric, with which we can continue to articulate our critiques and instantiate our presence in a way that *can't be unheard* since it comes from the very belly of the beast—the institutions of Euro-American indoctrination—the place where dominant cultural knowledge is made. Clearly, those institutions aren't simply going to disappear; therefore, in taking seriously the consequences of our ironic entanglements with these paracolonial institutions, we can't afford to accept a narrow vision of who "we" are and where "we" come from. Nor can we afford to ignore our potential allies in those institutions, no matter their cultural heritage or ancestral backgrounds, if we want the field of Native studies to have the kind of revolutionary potential it can have inside and outside the walls of the university. My assumption here is that most Native scholars understand the necessity for scholarship to arise from and be tied intimately to the needs of Native communities.[8] This is not an easy task in the best of circumstances but an even less possible one given the "divide and conquer" strategies that currently occupy too much of our intellectual energies. At the end of her essay in Mihesuah's collection, Cook-Lynn relents a bit and suggests that perhaps the "urban mixed-blood" work she finds so objectionable "can be looked upon as a legitimate criticism of existing society, a realistic criticism of a system of untidy ethics written by a new generation of thinkers who are separated from a real Indian past, people who have no Native language to describe the future" (1998, 134).[9] She then questions her own relenting—"But where does it all end?"—and tries to convince readers that if *any* allowance is made for the differing historical and material circumstances of various tribal communities, we'll find ourselves on the slippery slope of not being able to judge "Indianness" (1998, 132). So, where *does* it all end? In the simple arithmetic of blood-quantum and intermarriage? In "real" and "less real" Indians? Or perhaps in a recognition that both "domination and resistance take place in a world which is multiply determined and mediated" (Mohanty and Mohanty)? Where does this story end—in our presence or our absence?

Ojibwa writer David Treuer's first novel, *Little*, opens with absence. "The grave we dug for my brother Little remained empty even after we filled it back in. And nobody was going to admit it" (3). Later, as Donovan, the abandoned child / adopted brother / narrator of much of this text, tells us, "That day, when the grass was still dead, we took the opportunity not to lie to ourselves, but to lie to everyone else. As we dug the hole, it was a relief to know that although we had nothing to put in it, on the outside we could show our determination. . . . Everyone came out of the house and stood around, pretending discomfort when the discomfort wasn't at his [Little's] death. It was at the why of his short, speechless life" (6–7). Little is, we learn, a mixed-blood—deformed, fearless, and nearly speechless (the only word he utters is "you"). He is the son of Celia, Donovan's adopted Native mother, and was conceived when Celia was raped by Father Gundesohn while she scrubbed the floor of the church—an act discovered by her mother, Jeanette, and avenged by packing the priest's mouth and nose with snow. Symbolically, Little is not afraid of water or of drowning; in one scene he jumps innocently off the top of the dam and into the river to catch a fish that the other children—Jackie and Donovan—have hooked and struggled with. In the whole of Treuer's novel—a text that narratively begins at the end with Little's grave and wends its way back through webs of history, relations, and colonization to suggest a "now" that is complicatedly mixed—we are eventually given the cause of Little's death—he has drowned two hundred feet off the ground in the town's water tower. Donovan tells us, "He jumped, that's all I can ever guess for sure. But think about it. Doesn't it make sense that the water supply was the best way for him to be in everything? Touching, filling, completing everything with holes in it. Now every person that got city water would be with him" (231). All that mixed-ness, the violence of conquest, of violation, the stubborn persistence of the handful of people left in Treuer's town. Poverty, their sense of history and relatedness—all of it in Little, and all of Little in "you."

In *Tribal Secrets: Recovering American Indian Intellectual Traditions* (1995), Robert Warrior (Osage) calls for Native scholars to engage in "intellectual sovereignty," "a cultural criticism that is grounded in American Indian experiences but which can draw on the insights and experiences of others who have faced similar struggles" (xxiii). Scott Lyons (Anishinaabe), in his 2000 essay "Rhetorical Sovereignty: What Do American Indians Want from Writing?" reminds us that "sovereignty is the guiding story in our pursuit of self-determination, the general strategy by which we aim to best recover our losses from the ravages of colonization: our lands, our languages, our cultures, our self-respect," and thus argues for "rhetorical sovereignty"—"the inherent right and ability of *peoples* to determine their own communicative needs and desires . . . to

decide for themselves the goals, modes, styles, and languages of public discourse" (449–50). One of the most critical things that rhetorical
sovereignty requires of us is "a radical rethinking of how and what we
teach as the written word at all levels of schooling, from preschool to
graduate curricula and beyond" (450). In *That the People Might Live:
Native American Literatures and Native American Community* (1997), Jace
Weaver (Cherokee) advocates "communitism"—"community + activism"
(xiii)—and he advises that in studying Native literatures, we must "define
literature broadly as the total written output of a people": a definition
that includes biographies, autobiographies, and tribal histories (ix).

What all of these scholarly "calls" have in common is a real sense
that Native knowledge, barely acknowledged for centuries, not only can
no longer be ignored within institutions of education on this continent, but can bring something powerful and radically important to those
institutions *and to our own communities.* Not only are Native scholars
refusing to be confined to a single discipline within the academy, we
have begun to insist upon the interconnections, the relationship—as
Lyons points out—between what we learn/teach in preschool and what
we learn/teach in graduate school, the relationships we share with others
who have survived the experiences of colonization. We have a lot to learn
from one another, but it seems to me that what we're all working for
has at least one outcome in common: a "useful expression of resistance
and opposition to colonial history" (Cook-Lynn 1998, 124). Even if we
weigh and define each of the words in that phrase differently, we *still*
have a lot to learn from one another. Our survival *still* depends upon
each other's survival. We are, after all, relatives; that is, if we believe the
teachings of our elders, our traditions. If we take them seriously then we
must treat one another as relatives, right? The end of Treuer's novel goes
like this: after all the mixing and drowning, all the bus-riding, car-liv-
ing, birthing and coffee-drinking. After all the near-myth references and
the not-so-urban, not-all-mixed-bloods untangle parts of their story and
leave other parts knotted in memory. After all of that, we find Donovan
at the fish hatchery, watching:

> The smallest of disruptions, nerves firing before the eye, . . . I
> saw a dart, a silver flash, secrets collapsed in empty balloons
> of tissue the size of a seed, of a kernel of corn. The eggs
> were hatching. A tail pushed another shell apart, shimmering
> shiny muscle never before used, its width less than a pencil

lead, a feather of cartilage. . . . I could see the heart, a red pulse the size of a single raspberry capsule. The spinal cord, hair-thick, was alive with the electricity of message. Another. Another. I couldn't keep track of them all. Soon there would be more and more. There would be too many to count, too many to know.

In his 1999 book *Red on Red: Native American Literary Separatism*, Craig Womack (Muskogee/Cherokee) writes:

> I say that tribal literatures are not some branch waiting to be grafted onto the main trunk. Tribal literatures are the *tree*, the oldest literatures in the Americas, the most American of American literatures. We *are* the canon. . . . Without Native American literature, *there is no American canon*. We should not allow ourselves, through the definitions we choose and the language we use, to ever assume we are outside[rs]. (7)

Throughout his text, Womack argues for what he calls a "kind of 'Red Stick' literary criticism," one that "emphasizes Native resistance movements against colonialism, confronts racism, discusses sovereignty and Native nationalism, seeks connections between literature and liberation struggles, and, finally, roots literature in land and culture" (11). Womack doesn't pull his methodology out of thin air; instead he roots it firmly in Muskogee history and in a particular group of "traditionalist Creeks" who in 1813–1814, "seeing their land invaded from all sides . . . had to come up with a radically different way of dealing with a threat that had hitherto not existed" (11–12). What they came up with was, in Womack's words, an "anticolonial movement, fuelled by religion and myth, . . . influenced by Shawnee ally Tecumseh's apocalyptic teachings and rooted in the Creek square grounds" (12). This movement applied the teachings of tradition "in radical new ways with attention given to analysis, criticism, and political reflection" (12). Womack advises that Native scholars begin with the anticolonial movements in our own particular tribal histories and theorize from there.

As exciting as these anticolonial possibilities might be, any desire to build a critical mass of Native scholars in universities may yet be undone, by the smorgasbord approach to departmental hiring, by increasing budget shortages, by the growing inroads being made against affirmative action hiring policies, and by our willingness to leave these imperfect but powerful institutions of dominant cultural instruction. Lyons admits that "without some turn in the current assault on affirmative action, I suspect all talk on rhetorical sovereignty will likely happen away from the university" (466), and he frequently cites tribal colleges as the real possibility for such revolutionary activities. Cook-Lynn, who credits affirmative action programs for her twenty-year presence in the academy, has been blunt in her assessment of the possibilities for Native scholars in universities. In the preface to her book *Why I Can't Read Wallace Stegner: A Tribal Voice*, Cook-Lynn writes of her initial hopes:

> For me it was never just a matter of getting a job and becoming part of the mainstream; instead, it was that the entire history of America, vis-à-vis the continent's indigenous population, had to be rewritten, and the place to do it was in the nation's colleges and universities. New narratives were required, I said. Tribal interests had to be maintained. Small wonder that I became so disillusioned. At the close of two decades, I'd had enough and left my tenured faculty position for the open hills and prairies of home. (1996, ix)

And though Cook-Lynn claims to "admire those American Indian scholars who have the courage to continue" (xi), elsewhere she writes:

> The university is a place where few Indians reside and where the few who are present are notable for their willingness to change tribal traditions to mainstream traditions of modernity, transcribing in English and imagining in art some principles of personal (not tribal) politics and expressing the Indian experience in assimilative and mainstream terms. (1998, 127–28)

Clearly, Cook-Lynn has changed her mind about the possibility of "new narratives" being produced by Native scholars. In her indictment of "hang around the university Indians," Cook-Lynn implies the argument—much speculated and gossiped about by Native scholars but rarely raised in print—maybe we should all just go home. So, what would happen if we all just went home? All of us. While the movement of Native scholars into other educational venues is a significant phenomenon, and I certainly would not want to argue that tribal colleges, community colleges, and public schools don't need Native teachers and administrators, I'm not all that crazy about the thought of all of us leaving all those white folks to their collective and enduring fantasies about Indians.

If, and this is the central "if" of my comments here, if what we are after is "Native intellectualism," or "intellectual sovereignty," or "rhetorical sovereignty," or "communitism," or "academic guerillas," or "Red Stick criticism," then we need to think carefully about the tactics we use when we define ourselves and the work that we do. What are our goals and responsibilities? Must they all be the same if we claim them as "Native"? Must *we* all be the same? What of our considerable and not inconsequential differences? We're more than ready to claim that the dominant culture doesn't know what to do with difference, *what will we do with difference*? Clearly, I don't think we should all go home, even though there are days, weeks, when nothing is more appealing than home, nothing less appealing than my life in the university despite the material privileges that I enjoy there. Clearly, I want to insist upon the presence of Native peoples in universities as not merely assimilation, acculturation, or coincidence; our presence is a necessary and vital counterpoint to the living history of these institutions that have for too long had the last word on Indians. And these universities are built on Native land—they are *our* places; they belong to us. What Cook-Lynn seems really to be asking of Native scholars is an important and defining question, one which mirrors Barbara Christian's old but not forgotten query—"[F]or whom are we doing what we are doing?" (77). Joy Harjo, in a 1996 interview with Robert Warrior, claims that the questions we ask now are the same ones we've been asking since the advent of Europeans on this continent: "Who are we? How are we? Who are our children? And what are we all becoming together?" (quoted in Weaver 164). While this is the end of my story, the varied and multiplicitous answers that we might collectively offer to Harjo can be the beginning of other kinds of stories—too many to count, too many to know.

Notes

1. Some of you will want to stop reading here, I know. I could go on at length about why I haven't tried to enroll, despite the fact that I have all the necessary documentation to fill out an enrollment application, and become a "card-carrying Indian," but that is much beyond the scope of this essay, which

will, I hope, at least make clear some of the consequences of our decisions—mine to tell this story, yours to decide whether or not to continue reading.

2. During the seventeenth and eighteenth centuries, the Miami Confederacy included at least the Weas, Piankashaws, Peorias, Illinis, Potowatomis, Shawnees, Delawares/Lenapes, as well as some Ojibwas, Hurons, and Ottawas.

3. Further historical information about the Miamis can be found in Rafert (1996).

4. See Vizenor's critical texts (1994, 1993).

5. See Vizenor (1998).

6. And, yes, there *are* tribal nations in Indiana, no matter the lore— Pokagon Potowatomis, Indiana Miamis, Weas, various Shawnee bands, Lenapes, and others.

7. See Harjo and Bird (1997), particularly their introduction to this edited collection.

8. For an eloquent, persuasive, and fairly comprehensive take on this, see Linda Tuhiwai Smith (1999).

9. The assumption that having Native language makes one "real" is a different, but related, variant of the blood-quantum argument. It overlooks two things: first, the deliberate devastation of Native languages as part of the plan of colonization; secondly, the resurgence and significance of Native language revitalization movements in the past decade. In overlooking these things (both well beyond the scope of this essay), this argument also holds Native people themselves accountable for the degradations of colonization and overlooks the historical realities of many tribal communities' long endurance in the face of colonization.

Works Cited

Alexie, Sherman. *The Lone Ranger and Tonto Fistfight in Heaven.* New York: Atlantic Monthly Press, 1993.

Cook-Lynn, Elizabeth. *Why I Can't Read Wallace Stegner and Other Essays: A Tribal Voice.* Madison: U of Wisconsin P, 1996.

———. "American Indian Intellectualism and the New Indian Story." Ed. Devon Mihesuah. *Natives and Academics: Researching and Writing about American Indians.* Lincoln: U of Nebraska P, 1998. 111–38.

Christian, Barbara. "The Race for Theory." *Feminist Studies* 14.1 (Spring 1988): 67–79.

Harjo, Joy, and Gloria Bird, eds. *Reinventing the Enemy's Language: Contemporary Native Women's Writings of North America.* New York: W.W. Norton & Co., 1997.

Leonard, Floyd. *Always a People: Oral Histories of Contemporary Woodlands Indians*. Ed. Rita Kohn and W. Lynwood Montell. Bloomington: Indiana UP, 1997. 138–45.

Lyons, Scott. "Rhetorical Sovereignty: What Do American Indians Want from Writing?" *College Composition and Communication* 51.3 (2000): 447–68.

Mohanty, Satya, and Chandra Mohanty. "Contradictions of Colonialism." Review of *Recasting Women: Essays in Colonial History*. Ed. Kum Kum Sangari and Sudesh Vaid. *The Women's Review of Books* 7.6 (March 1990): 19.

Rafert, Stewart. *The Miami Indians of Indiana: A Persistent People*. Indianapolis: Indiana Historical Society, 1996.

Siders, Lora Marks. "Lora Marks Siders." *Always a People: Oral Histories of Contemporary Woodlands Indians*. Ed. Rita Kohn and W. Lynwood Montell. Bloomington: Indiana UP, 1997. 190–96.

Smith, Linda Tuhiwai. *Decolonizing Methodologies*. London: Zed Books, 1999.

Treuer, David. *Little*. New York: Picador, 1995.

Vizenor, Gerald. *Narrative Chance: Postmodern Discourse on Native American Indian Literatures*. Norman: U of Oklahoma P, 1993.

———. *Manifest Manners: Postindian Warriors of Survivance*. Middletown, CT: Wesleyan UP, 1994.

———. *Fugitive Poses: Native American Indian Scenes of Absence and Presence*. Lincoln: U of Nebraska P, 1998.

Warrior, Robert. *Tribal Secrets: Recovering American Indian Intellectual Traditions*. Minneapolis: U of Minnesota P, 1995.

Weaver, Jace. *That the People Might Live: Native American Literatures and Native American Community*. New York: Oxford UP, 1997.

Womack, Craig. *Red on Red: Native American Literary Separatism*. Minneapolis: U of Minnesota P, 1999.

5

Modernism, Authenticity, and Indian Identity

Frank "Toronto" Prewett (1893–1962)

Joy Porter

Due to his Indian ancestry, the Canadian poet Frank James Prewett was nicknamed "Toronto" by the illustrious literary friends he met while recovering in England following his service in World War I. Those friends included Virginia Woolf, Siegfried Sassoon, Robert Graves, and the doyenne of the Bloomsbury set, the rich and generous Lady Ottoline Morrell. Each figure found Prewett's poetry important and his Indian identity both intriguing and meaningful. Woolf typeset Prewett's first book *Poems* (Hogarth Press), which appeared in 1921, and when the *Times Literary Supplement* favorably reviewed it, she remarked to Lytton Strachey in a letter, "The Literary Supplement, by the way, says that Prewett *is* a poet: perhaps a great one."[1] Graves was convinced of Prewett's literary importance. He edited Prewett's *Collected Poems*, published posthumously in 1964, and noted in the introduction, "Dedicated poets like Frank Prewett are few in any age; and lamentably so in this" (viii). Sassoon was sure Prewett was special from the moment he set eyes upon him. He told Graves, "Toronto is a great man, and will be a great writer,—greater than you or me, because of his simplicity of mind and freedom from intellectual prejudices" (quoted in Wilson 34). Like Lady Ottoline Morrell, Sassoon had a deep intellectual friendship with Prewett and supported him so that he might write creatively. He supplied him with travel money and cash for about five years while Morrell gave him gifts, hospitality and, eventually, an agricultural job on her country retreat, Garsington Manor in Oxfordshire. Both for a time fell in love with "Toronto" or were, at the very least, strongly sexually attracted to him. They made sure he was introduced to and moved within circles that included Leonard Woolf, W. B. Yeats, Thomas Hardy, Wilfred Owen, Edmund Blunden, T. E. Lawrence, Aldous Huxley, Mark Gertler, S. S. Koteliansky, and Dorothy Brett, the latter yet another Bloomsbury figure whose letters reveal some variety of romantic attachment with Prewett. Just after the war, Ottoline Morrell was so taken with Prewett that she wrote to Robert Graves determined to set up a "debating society and dining club with Frank Prewett, Masefield, Marsh, Lytton Strachey, [Karl] Liebknecht and Trotsky as honorary members" (quoted in O'Prey, 286).

Today Prewett is regularly claimed as part of the Native American literary canon and work from his second book of poetry *The Rural Scene* (1924) is frequently anthologized.[2] However, non-native critics have recently begun to stress that evidence for Prewett's Indian ancestry and background is in fact extremely slight, if it is present at all.[3] This chapter makes no intervention into the specifics of that debate, but does argue that what is most evident within Prewett's relationships and to a lesser extent in his work, is a set of themes that correspond to a modernist sensibility concerning things "authentically Indian." Whether we agree with Prewett's representation of himself as Indian or not, he nevertheless met a need within the sensibilities of the important literary figures he befriended: a need for the glamour and difference associated with the stereotype of things Indian.

Being Frank Prewett

Frank Prewett was born in Ontario in 1893 and his early descriptions of growing up on a large farm surrounded by corduroy roads and mixed Indian-white families are reminiscent of Ernest Hemingway's descriptions of his early experiences growing up at the wood's edge at Oak Park, Illinois.[4] The family moved to Toronto in 1900, but like Hemingway (who was born six years after Prewett in 1899), Prewett's formative experiences were of being close to wilderness and of being encouraged to share the strict conservative values of the Northeastern pioneer, including respect for strong religion, hard work, and self-determination. Throughout his life however, Prewett was to find little of value in the Old Testament Anglican sin-and-vengeance faith that had been drummed into him each day at the kitchen table by his grandfather.[5] Instead, and in particular after his experiences in World War I, Prewett chose to think of himself and to present himself in three main ways: as a poet, as an Indian, and as someone with a strong spiritual dimension.

Prewett's introduction to the British literary elite and his presentation of himself as an Indian were intimately linked. Having arrived at the front in 1916, he suffered spinal injury after being thrown from his horse in the Royal Artillery, returned to the front as an officer in the Royal Welsh Fusiliers, and was then diagnosed as suffering from neurasthenia, or shell shock, in 1918. He was then sent to Lennel, a country house near Coldstream in Scotland, to recover. Siegfried Sassoon arrived at Lennel soon after Prewett and first met "Toronto," who was seven years his junior, when Prewett was dressed in full "Indian" regalia including headdress. This was as part of a costume party organized as therapy for the Lennel patients. Sassoon retained an especially vivid memory of the evening, August 20, 1918, and told Ottoline Morrell,

> I wish you could have seen him one night when they all (except me!) dressed up. He was got up in red-Indian garb—the change was astonishing. The high cheekbones and wide-set eyes were quite startling and the lovely freedom of movement—a young brave . . .

Whether Prewett was Indian or not, he certainly looked the part, that is, he perfectly matched the non-Indian image of the exotic and compellingly attractive native warrior. He was five feet, nine inches tall when he enlisted, with hazel eyes, a dark complexion, deep-set eyes and, as so often remarked, high cheekbones. He had, as the Canadian writer Bruce Meyer puts it, a "Valentino" quality that was both striking and alluring. The artist Mark Gertler said of Prewett in 1921, "Women seem rather taken with him, goodness knows why . . ." and even toward the end of his life, when Vivienne Jenkins created his bust, she had to admit, "There was something about him to which you just could not help being drawn" (quoted in Prewett 1964, 3–4).[6]

A month after first meeting Prewett, Sassoon's attraction to him was, if anything, even stronger. He was determined that "Toronto" should be introduced to Ottoline and her crowd. He wrote on September 4, 1918:

> The nicest creature here is a young Canadian poet from Toronto who was in France a long time and only just escaped insanity owing to having a very sensitive and active brain, which rebelled against the horror and monotony. He is now quite well and is being discharged as unfit. He has a strong strain of red Indian which adds piquancy to his character as he is very proud of his Iroquois ancestry. I think he could write well as he has a keen educated insight into human things and a strong sense of humour.[7]

As this quotation shows, Sassoon was convinced that "Toronto" was Indian. Prewett himself consistently maintained that he was Indian, defended the point in public, and gave greater detail about it to those who were important to him. One of those who have questioned Prewett's Indianness is Bruce Meyer. He has noted Prewett's seeming inconsistency; how he told Lady Ottoline Morrell he was Sioux, Robert Graves and Sassoon that he was Iroquois, and Dorothy Brett that he was Mohawk. However, all of this could have been more or less true given that the Mohawk (Keepers of the Eastern Door) are part of the Iroquois Confederacy and in light of the fact of a long history of Sioux and Iroquois interaction. Although debated, it is commonly held that the Sioux were known to their Algonquian neighbors and enemies as the "little/treacherous snakes" relative to their "big snake" enemies the Iroquois and, like the Iroquois, the Sioux originally came from the east before they moved to the upper Mississippi region. Admittedly, Sioux and Iroquois relations have across time been characterized by war, but this does not preclude a simultaneous history of selective adoption and intermarriage, and either or both factors could have been part of Prewett's family history.[8] It is true that, as with so many who appear to invent an Indian heritage, Prewett does not seem to have provided anyone with details about his family in terms of a relationship with a named native community.[9] He made no reference, for example, to a specific Sioux affiliation with say, the Dakota, Nakota, or Lakota nations, or with any linguistically cognate tribe such as the Assiniboine, Hidatsa, Mandan, Winnebago, Iowa, Omaha, Ponca, Oto

Missouri, Kaw, Osage, or Quapaw.[10] However, this does not necessarily mean that Prewett's Indian heritage was invented; it may simply have been elided or obscured within his own family history in response to the larger reality of anti-Indian prejudice and the dominance of Anglo-Saxon Christianity. Meyer does admit that it is possible that Prewett's maternal grandmother could have been Iroquois, but also stresses the fact that Prewett's own relatives, especially his sister Olive, have strongly disagreed with the idea that their family tree had any native link. Again, myriad reasons may exist for such a family debate and it cannot be held as conclusive evidence that Prewett invented his ancestry. Although Meyer refers to the fact that another veteran of the war who had spent time in northern Ontario, Englishman Archibald Stansfeld Belaney (Grey Owl), hoodwinked the public into believing that he was an Indian in the excellent cause of 1920s Canadian conservation, in truth this has no direct bearing on Prewett's ethnic identity whatsoever (Meyer 8).[11]

The idea of the Indian warrior soldier was certainly a popular one at the time and the phenomenon of Indian men fighting in the Great War was attracting considerable public attention when Prewett met Sassoon. According to the authority on this topic, Russel Lawrence Barsh, in 1918 up to one-third of all adult Indian men were in uniform and the wartime American press revelled in the opportunity this presented to insert colorful imagery and romantic stereotypes into the story of the fight against tyranny in Europe. Barsh provides two telling examples of this stereotyping. One appeared in the *Literary Digest* in 1918 when a Cherokee in the 142nd Infantry was reported as explaining why he enlisted with the words "He kill um papoose and kill um squaw, so me Jess Fixon will find this Kaiser and stick um bayonet clear through. Ugh!" The second is President Wilson's oft-repeated story about the Indian doughboy who complained to his officers at boot camp, "Too much salute, not enough shoot." This appeared in the *Philadelphia Public Ledger* on September 25, 1918. Both quotations perpetuated an image of Indians that was completely at odds with the modern skills, including language skills, possessed by the great majority of those who served. Elsewhere, however, as Barsh notes, some newspapers modified the stereotype. The *Literary Digest*, also in 1918, admitted that Indian soldiers in camp "dress, eat, sleep, fight, play, work, and drill just the same as other soldiers," while the *New York Evening Herald* acknowledged that it was possible to spot "Apaches wearing wrist watches" at the front. Barsh points out that the popularity of the Indian soldier was due to the fact that his presence could be presented as both a validation of Allied legitimacy and as a vindication of U.S. expansionism and the assimilationist program that accompanied it. Overall, the war served to bring Indian and non-Indian worlds closer together. As Barsh notes: "Despite experiences with discrimination and problems arising from cultural differences, Indians generally came away from their service experience with more positive attitudes towards whites, a sense of entitlement to fair treatment, and an orientation towards Euro-American political values" (281). Barsh demonstrates that the newspaper stories about exceptional Indian valor on the front did in fact have a firm basis in truth, but he also notes that Indian bravery did not prevent Indian soldiers from being exposed to the same terrifying battle conditions as their fellow combatants. Like Prewett, they were as susceptible to trauma or, as it was then known, shell shock, as any other person who experienced the theater of war. There is no concrete reason to doubt that Sassoon could have and did meet an Indian soldier at Lennel in 1918, at a time when each man was recovering from the crippling psychological effects of combat.

As far as Sassoon was concerned, Prewett's attractiveness was intimately associated with stereotype, with a noble savage version of "Indianness" that harks back to the dime novel and captivity narrative. He described him to Edward Marsh as a "Canadian-French-Red Indian," and would later admit that his "intimacy with Toronto Prewett began with a strong sexual attraction," which in fact "horrified" Toronto when he recognized it (Sassoon 1981, 162). He wrote the following poem, prompted by that first meeting at the convalescent home at Lennel. That meeting had occurred at a time in their lives when both men were more or less at a breaking point, Prewett having just spent two years in the Ypres Salient and on service elsewhere and Sassoon having served since August 1914 and having had his statement against the continuation of the war read out in the House of Commons on July 30, 1917. His poem "Fancy Dress," published in the volume *Picture-Show* (1919), reads:

Fancy Dress

Some Brave, awake in you tonight,
Knocked at your heart; an eagle's flight
Stirred in the feather on your head.
Your wide-set Indian eyes, alright
Above high cheek-bones smeared with red,

Unveiled cragg'd centuries, and led
You, the snared wraith of bygone things—
Wild ancestries of trackless Kings—
Out of the past. . . . So men have felt
Strange anger move them as they knelt
Praying to gods serenely starred
In heavens where tomahawks are barred.[12]

It has been suggested that Sassoon's meeting at this point with Prewett helped him to accept the homosexual feelings that had caused him so much guilt and anguish in previous years. Prewett could not respond to Sassoon's desire for him, but thought very highly of him, stating in 1919, "I shall always feel with a conviction beyond argument that he is one of the best men on earth" (McPhail and Guest 172).[13] Interestingly, Sassoon's biographer Jean Wilson seems to have fallen for the same set of Indian myths as Sassoon. She writes of Prewett, "He claimed Iroquois ancestry, which might have been responsible for his striking high-cheek-boned face, and possibly for his keen insight into human nature" (504). Others of the Garsington set were always to remain less sure of Prewett's Indianness and, indeed, seemed not to care overmuch whether they were being hoodwinked or not. Mark Gertler wrote to Koteliansky on January 20, 1921:

Toronto is quite a nice young fellow. I could never make up my mind whether he is a fraud or genuine, but even if he is a fraud, he's a nice homely one. . . . Women seem rather taken with him, goodness knows why . . . I used to like going into Oxford with him and having a fling—that is to say a drinking bout, on which occasion he made an amusing companion. He could drink ever so much without getting drunk. (Gertler 197)

Whether Prewett was Indian or not, a discourse about Indianness was clearly something that he shared with those with whom he kept up important relationships. In 1920, after his attraction as far as Sassoon was concerned had waned and the relationship had settled into platonic friendship, Prewett was repatriated to Canada. From there, a country Prewett had by then decided was a literary wasteland, "Toronto" often wrote back to his patron in England, Lady Ottoline Morrell, with references either to Indian qualities or to Indians themselves.[14] He would joke about how good his manners were "considering my barbarous origins" and said he would have liked to have been able to send Ottoline's daughter Julian an Indian costume, but he was "unable to get an authentic one." One Indian figure on a Toronto streetcar particularly caught his attention, and he used the incident to highlight to Ottoline the gap between Indian stereotype and reality. He told Ottoline:

> You would have fallen in love with a certain huge Indian whom I saw the other day. He was standing unromantically upon the back end of a train. He towered over the rest of us, and looked beyond us, not in a stage manner, but in utter obliviousness of us, the train, the noise, and the city itself. One would have said, what a noble creature, what composure, what dignity, yet very possibly he was a clerk in a bank.[15]

Prewett's "dark depression and spiritual animation"

The combination of Prewett's physical attractiveness, his Indian ancestry, and his aspirations to become an important poet, all attracted Sassoon and others, but it was these attributes combined with Prewett's sporadic moodiness in itself interspersed with what Sassoon dubbed "spiritual animation," that they found truly spellbinding. Robert Graves always held Prewett in the utmost esteem, but was also exposed to a great deal of his bad feelings.[16] In between jokes about the "primitive deficiencies" of Prewett's work in correspondence, the two often discussed these periodic prolonged bouts of mental bad weather Prewett experienced. Even following his marriage early in 1925, Prewett told Graves morosely, "I feel, if one survives February, one is safe for another year. It is the month nature is most like to death." Again, after a visit between the two, on November 16, 1925, Prewett told Graves, "My mind has been negative almost a year, but ought to awaken again."[17]

Admittedly, some of Prewett's Garsington acquaintances found his depression less than alluring, but for the most part the inspirational charisma he also possessed struck a chord with those who encountered him. The painter Gertler was one of those who eventually found Prewett's moodiness wholly irritating, describing him as someone "who mooches about like a faded Hamlet," and who "doesn't know what he wants and is always trying to gain the ladies' sympathy by his grumblings—even to Julian [Morrell, daughter of Ottoline Morrell] he grumbles and whines, and looks at her with glossy eyes. Ugh! Every view he expresses is romantic, unreal and sickly. In fact, he has a sickly soul . . ." (Gertler 209). Sassoon for the most part, and especially in 1921 after a bracing trip the two shared to Rome, consistently stressed that "Toronto's "alterations of dark depression and spiritual animation suggested a streak of genius." He summed up the relationship they shared in his diaries, stating that after the two had banished the sexual attraction that Prewett could not reciprocate, "we established a very solid and sympathetic understanding which ranks very high among the amicabilities of my existence." He added however, "Toronto's character lacks that . . . sweetness which makes little [Edmund] B[lunden] so delightful. Toronto is always rather enigmatic. He is inclined to sulk and grumble and retire into resentfulness. One does not always feel that he trusts one. He does not give himself wholeheartedly to his friends" (quoted in Precosky 133; see also Sassoon 1981 162). Prewett's character remained something of an enigma. Sassoon suggested that "Toronto's" moodiness and aloofness could be explained "by his having served in the Ypres Salient, from the horrors of which he had been delivered by a huge shell bursting near him," while Graves merely stated that Prewett "felt it his duty to write at the orders of the daemon who rode him" and quoted Prewett's own words, that he heard "a hard but true music" (quoted in Precosky, 136).

In an important sense, Prewett's spasmodic depressions were fashionable. At the turn of the century, elites on both sides of the Atlantic increasingly expressed doubts about, and symptoms resulting from, modern life. This was a time of psychic crisis, as T. Jackson Lears has pointed out, an era of self-punishing depressions or "neurasthenia" concurrent with the emergence of what he terms "a therapeutic world view." George Miller Beard's *American Nervousness* had first described the term neurasthenia, a disease characterized by a lack of nerve force, in 1880. Neurasthenia's mental symptoms included "desire for stimulants and narcotics . . . fear of responsibility, of open places or closed places, fear of society, fear of being alone, fear of fears, fear of contamination, fear of everything, deficient mental control, lack of decision in trifling matters, hopelessness . . ." (Beard quoted in Lears 51). This paralysis of will was something Ottoline and Prewett shared. Indeed, one of the reasons why Ottoline fell out so decisively with another sometime Garsington habitué, D. H. Lawrence, following the publication of his novel *Women in Love* in 1920, was that the character he used within it to caricature her (Hermione Roddice), had "a lack of robust self, she had no natural sufficiency, there was a terrible void, a lack, a deficiency of being within her. And she wanted someone to close up this deficiency. To close it up forever." Her illness was something also discussed by Ottoline's friends. Lytton Strachey wrote to Dora Carrington on May 28, 1917, "Her ladyship is more fevered, jumpy and neurasthenic than ever, though as usual there have been moments (especially at first) when my heart melted towards her. She seems to me to be steadily progressing down to the depths of ruin" (quoted in Darroch 204).[18]

Prewett's mental health issues were at the core of a fundamental upset that occurred between him and Ottoline in mid-1919. The recriminations were such that she expressed the wish to cease to know him. They centered upon Prewett's "physical incapability" and her disillusionment at his "deficiency of normal manly instincts." In response, Prewett explained that while he may have appeared to have been simply a cad, the truth was much more complex and akin to textbook neurasthenia. He wrote:

> I have no passionate feeling. . . . One time, perhaps, I might have been passionate, but the war made me old, body and mind, and, unfortunately, while my mind has had sufficient elasticity to recover its youth, my body has not. When you condemn me, do not forget this thing. I move about the world in a maze, an uncomprehended vagueness. I see the eagerness of life, but I feel none of it. It is so hazardous, so short, so mysterious, so ironic, this life of humanity, that I cannot bring myself to plunge seriously and enthusiastically into it. The blue-and-gold existence knows neither event nor change.[19]

Of course, the neurasthenia Prewett as a veteran felt was in a different category to that felt by the jadedly rich Ottoline, the daughter, as Lytton Strachey put it, of a thousand earls. Prewett was suffering from war trauma, as close study of his correspondence reveals. On October 17, 1919 he told Ottoline:

> I suffer from moments of panic which no one suspects, I hope, & it is the dread which, in some measure, gives an admiration for all that is most English. Virtue is gone out of

me, I cannot write,—, because I experience no deep emotion.
I am still and the world spins around me.

Only his interest in music seemed to assuage "the obsession of war despair" that weighed upon him, a feeling he described elsewhere as "the sharpness of the injustice of war, the greed and incredible callousness of it."[20] At times, as he expressed it to Ottoline, Prewett's despair was exceedingly deep. He wrote, for example, on November 5, 1920:

> What is the reason of life? Why since life is so short, do we permit it to be so dull, and why, since it is so dull, do we cling to it. I feel that somewhere in these rather sordid speculations lies a valuable truth, but I cannot hit upon it.

The month before he contemplated suicide and told Ottoline, "I wish, not that I were dead, for then there is the question of the spirit, but that I had never become differentiated from the general life-substance into an individual."[21]

Interestingly, given Prewett's "Indian" identity and the links customarily made between things Indian and the natural world, in much of his poetry Prewett expressed the opposite, an almost total alienation and impassiveness in relation to nature. For example, in the poem "Burial Stones" the earth and nature are depicted as indifferent to the suffering caused by war:

> For they are gone, who fought;
> But still the skies
> Stretch blue, aloof, unchanged,
> From rise to rise. (2000, 36)

Again in "I Went Out Into the Fields," the poet described how in his "anguish of mind" (42) he sought fruitlessly for comfort from the trees. In "If Life Be Happiness" (51), Prewett as poet asked to live as he supposes river-birds do, devoid of consciousness, and in "Hated by Stars," the poet described how the very stars pressed down upon him for, he explained, they "hate me for the heat that is mine" (1964, 27). A number of poems by Prewett do exist in the archive, however, that could be said to express the unbounded sense of kindred with the natural world that is characteristic of a number of Indian lifeways. One such begins,

> Be kind to animals, for who knows
> What kin they be, if they might say;
> Be kind to every weed that grows
> And shares our own ancestral clay.

and ends:

> Be kind to friend, be kind to foe,
> To frail, what have we else to mind?
> Weep for the fallen beast and slow,
> For all is kindred, of be kind.[22]

There were also points, such as in the autumn of 1922, when Prewett's spirits lifted and he seemed to wed his purpose as a poet to the land and the landscape. On September 6, 1922, he wrote, "I begin to warm and come to life, and with this revival awakes once more the old and fixed belief that it is my business to translate the fields to man, and man to the fields."[23]

Yet there were many times when even Garsington could not shake Prewett's pervading sense of ennui, passive moroseness, and alienation from nature. He told Ottoline in September 1919:

> Garsington is at its loveliest today, everything shining mistily, the distances an elusive pale blue. A flock of migrating swallows has settled in the farm buildings, where they chirp in a plaintive and mystified way. I know what they feel, little wretches, all nicely coloured, full of food, and yet lacking self-determination.

Bizarrely, an aversion to things animal was what lay at the heart of his celibacy. As he explained to Ottoline Morrell when discussing one partner:

> We have never committed the sexual act, not because she would have refused, but simply because I am, in my heart, happier without it, and she, no less happy. I dread animalness. I hate to know that the organs of my body are those also of the pig. You perhaps know this.[24]

"Toronto's" anti-materialism was one attribute that did tally with popular notions of "Indianness." Prewett had expressed qualms about the sordid getting and spending he detected in Canada before he left to fight, but when he was forced to return to his native country in 1919, he was utterly disgusted by it. He wrote to Ottoline late in 1919, that he had found there "nothing but business, selling motor cars, land stock, anything." He feared becoming trapped into a Babbitt-like marriage and resolved that even though "Life is so isolated here that people must marry, and marriage is a bad thing for very young and ambitious men," he was not about to become a "bank clerk with slicked hair" or a "veneered barbarian" in order to find a mate.[25] The problem with Canada, he told Ottoline, was that "Man cannot live by bread alone, and Canada offers only the bread." Prewett felt he must escape if he was to become "anything other than a fat and nasal American."[26] Critics such as Meyer and Callaghan, echoing aspects of Paul Fussell's interpretation of the Great War, have tended to present Prewett as a figure who is part of the cultural shock caused by World War I, a shock that brought about a modernist upheaval in Canada. However, it may be more accurate to think of Prewett primarily as a figure who militates against Canada's myth of the Great War, to use Jonathan F. Vance's term. Prewett's poetry spoke directly to the mythic image of the innocent Canadian abroad, steeped in nature and the life of the farm but brought to a new consciousness and sense of nationhood by experience in the trenches. Yet for Prewett, the sense of Canadian identity that solidified after the war was of a nation bereft of "Indian" values, a nation losing cultural direction because of its blind attachment to capitalism. This rejection of what Prewett once described to Graves as "clinking profit and loss," can be felt in Prewett's own "Indian" poem entitled "The Red-Man" (1964, 5). The poem speaks to a seemingly immutable gulf between the non-Indian and Indian worlds, between "a breathless dusty town" and "a red-man in his robes." Quite where Prewett, as both Indian and modern poet, stands in this Manichean division is unclear. The impact of "The Red-Man" in Prewett's poem is to make the townsfolk "feel ashamed of toil and heat, And dream of springs and grass." The tone throughout is of nostalgia. The Indian figure relates to the town impassively but at the same time moves through it like a startled stag.

The poem begins:

From wilderness remote he breaks
With stealthy springing tread,
And in the town a vision makes
Of time and manners dead.
He scorns to see the things we own,
And steadfast stares beyond,
Alone, impassive, cold, unknown;
With us he feels no bond.

It concludes on a note of incomprehension and utter mystery:

And whence he came, and whither fled,
And why, is all unknown;
His ways are strange, his skin is red,
Our ways and skins our own.[27]

Rather than in his native Canada, Prewett seems to have found much more of the rural idyll he craved in Garsington with Ottoline and her set. As well as the beautiful house, the setting was sublime. As Sandra Darroch puts it, "It could almost have been a Constable landscape—tall elms, drowsy cows munching the spring grass, fields dotted with wild-flowers, and a hill around which a small village and a church clusters" (157). Ottoline saw it as a place where she could create "an oasis perhaps, isolated not only from war but from all material values, a place where artists, writers and other sensitive people might relax and express themselves in a congenial atmosphere" (Gertler 209). Its effect on Prewett was deep and abiding. He wrote to her, "I have been happier in your house than anywhere in my life."[28]

How then, should Prewett's popularity with the British literary elite be understood? Indisputably, a series of factors made him an attractive figure. In a period that lauded the strenuous life, Prewett was an outdoorsman and decidedly rural, a far cry from the sallow "industrial man" so often bemoaned in the British and American press. It would also seem that for many of the literary gatekeepers he met, he had an erotic vigor that was irresistible in short enough doses. His Indian identity made him especially attractive. This was an era focused upon the quest to heal the fragmented individual self through pursuing the quest for "authenticity," a quest which ironically, as Lears shows us, was easily assimilated to the concerns of the increasingly bureaucratic, corporate state. The modern elite was keen to find in Indians, and in Prewett, an antidote to the spiritual homelessness and "unrealness" of the times. To modernist sensibilities, Prewett was a representative of "Indians," a group of peoples thought of as being enviably psychologically whole and self-sufficient. Prewett was therefore able to speak to the Indian within; that is, to the anti-modern and primitivist impulse that has always been subsumed within the hegemonic project of cultural modernism (see Lears, Part 1, "Antimodernism").

Frank Prewett may or may not have been an impostor, but those he met in England did not seem to care. After all, this was an era fascinated with impostors and deceit, as evidenced by the popularity of books such as Herman Melville's *The Confidence-Man* (1857), by the character of Madame Merle in Henry James's *The Portrait of a Lady* (1881), and by the invented Indians who persisted into the twentieth century such as Long Lance and Grey Owl. Prewett may have had a significant degree of Indian heritage and, unless it is proven otherwise, he should probably be thought of as the Indian poet who prospered amid the post-World War I Bloomsbury set, treading the almost impossibly difficult path of assimilation and survival following the horrors of combat. However, if it were established that Prewett was definitively not Indian, then perhaps we might conclude that following the war, he chose to be "authentic" in the sense that another Canadian, Charles Taylor, uses the term, that is, that Frank James Prewett chose values that were true to his inner self. Prewett, it is strongly suspected, was treated (as was Sassoon, Wilfred Owen, Edmund Blunden) for shell shock by the anthropologist and psychologist William Halse Rivers of St John's College Cambridge. Previous to treating mentally wounded soldiers in convalescent homes during the First World War, Rivers wrote pioneering studies of tribal life based on his fieldwork in India and the Solomon Islands. One of his key contributions to the field of post-traumatic treatment was to encourage his patient-friends to write creatively out of their unconscious as therapy (see Slobodin 71). If Prewett was not in fact Indian, it is possible that his adopted Indian identity stemmed from this experience, and served as an important bulwark against inner recognition of the terrors he had suffered.

Notes

1. Virginia Woolf to Lytton Strachey, August 29, 1921. Quoted in "the introduction" to Prewett (2000, 1).

2. Frank Prewett appears in *Georgian Poetry, 1920–1922*, ed. Edward Marsh (1922); in *Harper's Anthology of Twentieth Century Native American Poetry*,

ed. Duane Niatum (1988); in *We Wasn't Pals: Canadian Poetry and Prose of the First World War*, ed. Callaghan and Meyer (2001); and in *Lads: Love Poetry of the Trenches*, ed. Taylor (2002). He is discussed critically in *The Cambridge Companion to Native American Literature*, ed. Porter and Roemer (2005). Here Norma C. Wilson describes him both as "an Iroquois" and as "the best known Native poet of his generation," connecting his work in tone and style to some of the poetry of Jim Barnes, N. Scott Momaday, and Elizabeth Cook–Lynn (148). Frank Prewett is also listed as an Iroquois author from Mount Forest Ontario in the Internet Public Library Native American Author's Project http://www.ipl.org/div/natam/bin/ browse.pl/A398

3. See for example Coppolino's suggestion: "Perhaps Prewett fancied himself as a 'red–man' and slyly offered such information to those around him" (n.p.).

4. Compare Prewett's "Three Broadcast Talks: Farm Life in Ontario Fifty Years Ago" (Meyer and Callaghan, 81–95) with biographical aspects within Ernest Hemingway's *The Nick Adams Stories* and *The Torrents of Spring*. Further discussion of Prewett's early life can be found in Coppolino.

5. Hemingway also rejected his early exposure to the Protestant religion; see Grimes.

6. It is perhaps worth noting that the painter Mark Gertler was jealous of Prewett's skills with women and that there was friction between Ottoline Morrell and her friend Dorothy Brett, daughter of Lord Esher, over Prewett in 1919 (Darroch 232).

7. Siegfried Sassoon to Ottoline Morrell, August 20, 1918; September 4, 1918 (quoted in the introduction to Prewett 1964, 6–7).

8. For more on Iroquois and Sioux history, see Snow, DeMallie, Meyer, and Cook-Lynn.

9. One of the most intriguing instances of this phenomenon was on July 9, 1998, when President Clinton told Sherman Alexie and others on the PBS show "A Dialogue on Race with President Clinton," hosted by Jim Lehrer, that his grandmother in Arkansas had one-quarter Cherokee blood. Further specifics on the Clinton family Indian connection were not provided thereafter.

10. Historically speaking, only recently have "Sioux" peoples started to use "Sioux" as a means of expressing their identity. The "alliance of friends," that is the Sioux group of nations, translates in Santee as "Dakhota," in Yankton dialect as "Nakhota," and in Teton dialect as "Lakhota."

11. Another "white Indian" of the period, who fought in Canadian forces during World War I, was Sylvester C. Long (1890–1932), also known Chief Buffalo Child Long Lance. For more on each figure see Dickson and Smith.

12. Wilson points out that Sassoon noted, in an annotated copy of *Picture-Show* held at the Harry Ransom Humanities Research Center, The University of Texas at Austin, that "Fancy-Dress" was written at Lennel in September 1918 (Wilson, 581).

13. Frank Prewett to Ottoline Morrell, November 6, 1919, Lady Ottoline Morrell Collection, 17.6, Harry Ransom Humanities Research Center, The University of Texas at Austin.

14. As Henry W. Wells pointed out as early as 1945, in literary terms Canada was thought of as lagging well behind the more populous countries before the First World War (6).

15. Frank James Prewett to Ottoline Morrell, December 9, 1919; January 3, 1920, Lady Ottoline Morrell Collection, 17.6, Harry Ransom Humanities Research Center, The University of Texas at Austin; Frank James Prewett to Lady Ottoline Morrell, March 13, 1920 (quoted in the introduction to Prewett 1964, 8).

16. Graves scrawled upon the edges of a postcard to Prewett, "I was thinking today is there any poet in England at the moment for whom I have any respect left? 'If so,' I said, 'I'll send him this postcard.' " Robert Graves, at Deya to Frank Prewett, n.d., F.1–8, Correspondence, Frank Prewett Fonds, National Library of Canada, Ottawa.

17. Frank Prewett to Robert Graves, September 11, 1921; February 22, 1925; November 16, 1925, F.1–8, Correspondence, Frank Prewett Fonds, National Library of Canada, Ottawa.

18. Lawrence is quoted to the same purpose in Darroch (193).

19. Frank Prewett to Ottoline Morrell, October 8, 1919, Lady Ottoline Morrell Collection, 17.6, Harry Ransom Humanities Research Center, The University of Texas at Austin.

20. Frank Prewett to Ottoline Morrell, October 17, 1919; February 18, 1920; April 14, 1920; Lady Ottoline Morrell Collection, 17.6, Harry Ransom Humanities Research Center, The University of Texas at Austin.

21. Frank Prewett to Ottoline Morrell, October 17, 1919; February 18, 1920; April 14, 1920; November 5, 1920, September 5, 1920; Lady Ottoline Morrell Collection, 17.6, Harry Ransom Humanities Research Center, The University of Texas at Austin.

22. Frank Prewett to Edmund Charles Blunden, n.d. Recipient series, Harry Ransom Humanities Research Center, The University of Texas at Austin.

23. Frank Prewett to Ottoline Morrell, September 6, 1922; Lady Ottoline Morrell Collection, Harry Ransom Humanities Research Center, The University of Texas at Austin.

24. Frank Prewett to Lady Ottoline Morrell, July 9, 1919, February 18, 1920, Lady Ottoline Morrell Collection, Harry Ransom Humanities Research Center, The University of Texas at Austin.

25. Frank Prewett to Lady Ottoline Morrell, November 17, 1919, Lady Ottoline Morrell Collection, Harry Ransom Humanities Research Center, The University of Texas at Austin. For more on Prewett's resistance to marriage at this time and his relationship with Muriel Slee, of Humber Bay, Lake Ontario, see Fullerton n.p.

26. Prewett to Ottoline Morrell, n.d. HRC, quoted in Darroch (238); Prewett to Ottoline Morrell, 17/10/1919, Lady Ottoline Morrell Collection, 17.6 Harry Ransom Humanities Center, The University of Texas at Austin.

27. Frank Prewett to Robert Graves, October 21, 1924, F.1–8, Correspondence, Frank Prewett Fonds, National Library of Canada, Ottawa.

28. Frank Prewett to Ottoline Morrell, n.d., Lady Ottoline Morrell Collection, Harry Ransom Humanities Research Center, The University of Texas at Austin.

Works Cited

Barsh, Russel Lawrence. "American Indians in the Great War." *Ethnohistory* 38.3 (Summer 1991): 276–303.

Callaghan, Barry, and Bruce Meyer, eds. *We Wasn't Pals: Canadian Poetry and Prose of the First World War*. Toronto: Exile Editions, 2001.

Cook-Lynn, Elizabeth. *Anti-Indianism in Modern America: A Voice From Tatekaya's Earth*. Urbana: U of Illinois P, 2001.

Coppolino, Andrew. "A Canadian in the Gasington [*sic*] Circle: Frank Prewett's Literary Friendships." *Studies in Canadian Literature* 12.2 (1987). http://www. lib.unb.ca/Texts/SCL/bin/get.cgi?directory=vol12_2/&filename=Coppolino.htm

Darroch, Sandra Jobson. *Ottoline: The Life of Lady Ottoline Morrell*. New York: Coward, McCann & Geoghegan, 1975.

DeMallie, Raymond J. "Sioux until 1850." *Handbook of North American Indians: Plains*. Vol. 13, Part 2. Washington, DC: Smithsonian Institution, 2001. 718–60.

Dickson, Lovat. *Wilderness Man: The Strange Story of "Grey Owl."* Ontario: Macmillan Company of Canada, 1973.

Fullerton, Carol W. "Frank Prewett: A Fragment of Biography." http://www. canadian poetry.ca/cpjrn/vol24/fullerton.htm

Fussell, Paul. *The Great War & Modern Memory*. New York: Oxford UP, 1975.

Gertler, Mark. *Selected Letters*. Ed. Noel Carrington. London: Rupert Hart-Davis, 1965.

Grimes, Larry. "Hemingway's Religious Odyssey: The Oak Park Years." *Ernest Hemingway: The Oak Park Legacy*. Ed. James Nagel. Tuscaloosa: U of Alabama P, 1996. 37–58.

Hemingway, Ernest. *The Torrents of Spring*. New York: Charles Scribner's Sons, 1926).

———. *The Nick Adams Stories*. New York: Charles Scribner's Sons, 1972.'

Lears, T. J. Jackson. *No Place of Grace: Antimodernism and the Transformation of American Culture, 1880–1920*. Chicago: U of Chicago P, 1981.

McPhail, Helen, and Philip Guest. *Robert Graves and Siegfried Sassoon: On the Trail of the Poets of the Great War*. Barnsley: Leo Cooper, 2001.

Marsh, Edward, ed. *Georgian Poetry, 1920–1922*. London: The Poetry Bookshop, 1922.

Meyer, Roy W. *History of the Santee Sioux: United States Policy on Trial*. Lincoln: U of Nebraska P, 1967.

Niatum, Duane, ed. *Harper's Anthology of Twentieth Century Native American Poetry*. San Francisco: Harper, 1988.

O'Prey, Paul, ed. *Selected Letters of Robert Graves, 1914–1946*. Vol. 1. London: Hutchinson, 1982.

Porter, Joy, and Kenneth Roemer, ed. *The Cambridge Companion to Native American Literature*. Cambridge: Cambridge UP, 2005.

Precosky, Donald. "Frank Prewett, a Canadian Georgian Poet." *Studies in Canadian Literature* 4.2 (1979): 132–36.

Prewett, Frank. *The Collected Poems of Frank Prewett*. Introduction by Robert Graves. London: Cassell, 1964.

———. *Selected Poems of Frank Prewett*. Ed. Bruce Meyer and Barry Callaghan. Toronto: Exile Editions, 2000.

Prewett, Frank James. *The Rural Scene*. London: Heineman, 1924.

Sassoon, Siegfried. *Picture-Show*. New York: E. P. Dutton & Company, 1919.

———. *Siegfried Sassoon Diaries 1920–1922*. London: Faber, 1981.

Slobodin, Richard. *Rivers*. Stroud: Sutton Publishing, 1997.

Smith, Donald B. *Long Lance: An Imposter*. Lincoln, NE: Bison Books, 1983.

Snow, Dean R. *The Iroquois*. Oxford: Blackwell, 1994.

Taylor, Charles. *The Ethics of Authenticity*. Cambridge: Harvard UP, 1992.

Taylor, Martin, ed. *Lads: Love Poetry of the Trenches*. New Edition. London: Duckbacks, 2002.

Vance, Jonathan F. *Death So Noble: Memory, Meaning, and the First World War*. Vancouver: U of British Columbia P, 1997.

Wells, Henry W. "The Awakening in Canadian Poetry." *The New England Quarterly* 18.1 (March 1945): 3–24.

Wilson, Jean Moorcroft. *Siegfried Sassoon: The Making of a War Poet, a Biography (1896–1918)*. London: Routledge, 1999.

6

Transdifference in the Work of Gerald Vizenor

Helmbrecht Breinig

There is no better way to start a discussion of authenticity than by rereading that greatest of all American satires of the nineteenth century, Herman Melville's *The Confidence-Man: His Masquerade*. This work without a coherent plot, without a self-identical protagonist, without any unambiguous message, this medley of fictional and metafictional sections, inset stories, intertextual allusions, repeated reflections on the nature of language and the meaning of words, this "novel" presents American society as a collectivity of fools and knaves, bent on their respective versions of the pursuit of happiness. No other literary genre requires the same level of authenticity in the sense of a confident and confirmed speaker position than satire because the communicational triangle of speaker, satiric target, and audience erected by this type of literature and the methods of indirection usually employed demand a high degree of thematic authority and communicational control, and these, in turn, imply an "authentic" position where the speaker's opinions can be located. It is an indication of Melville's genius that he pursues his satiric goals while demonstrating that there can be no such thing as a positive, firmly grounded authenticity even where there is so much to criticize satirically, because the epistemological weakness of any human perspective reduces concepts like identity, essence, and authenticity to constructions shaped by context and interest. The three-pole satiric communication collapses, and readers are forced to reconsider their own preconceptions in order to arrive at an independent reaction to whatever appears as negative, that is, to postulate norms in the middle of the void and thus to become satirists in their own right (see Breinig 149–89).

There is a long critical debate as to which of the characters the term "confidence-man" refers, but there is a consensus about the protean, shape-shifting nature of this figure, or agent, or should I say, this *idea* of an interactive catalyst, creative and destructive, and endowed with sardonic humor. Obviously this figure is a superb example of that textual function where tribal tradition and postmodernism meet: the trickster. It is this type of trickster as persona, satiric commentator and, indeed, punisher of the representatives of what he calls "terminal creeds" that is employed by the Ojibwa author Gerald Vizenor, the leading Native American satirist of today. And one of these terminal creeds might be the idea of authenticity itself. Undoubtedly, Vizenor is the most intellectual of Native North American writers, and although he does not share the tragic vision informing much of Melville's work, he resembles him in that he combines his superb faculties as a storyteller with a profound curiosity about the nature of reality, in his case particularly the social, intercultural reality, but also that underlying level of existence best approached by looking at nature or, rather, that which humans see as residing in stones, rivers, and birds. For a person so eminently endowed with the faculty of speech he shows a remarkable fascination with silence or, as I take it, the limits of language. The uncertainties he both creates and explores by his innovative use of words and metaphors, his plural plots and tentative characterizations, may remind us of some of Melville's texts.

What is more important for my further argument is that these and other aspects of his work contribute to conveying the idea and experience of transdifference. I will approach this term by drawing upon Melville for the last time. At midnight of April 1st, the last avatar of Melville's confidence man hands his last victim what he calls a life preserver: a chamber pot. As is well known, in *Moby-Dick* a coffin served this very function, and what is indicated by this shift is not only the tonal difference between the two books, between tragedy and satiric comedy, but also the continuity of human needs, a common range of experience aboard the ship of life. To realize that the tragic and the comic are radically different and may yet simultaneously define the situation of an individual or a society, a situation experienced as emotional or cognitive dissonance, as irritating tension, as a suspension of fixed categories, to realize that is to become aware of the phenomenon and the idea of what I have termed "transdifference." The concept of transdifference is one of several under discussion in the current search for models of non-linear thinking. It was developed in the context of a discussion of the hermeneutics of intercultural contact but it also describes phenomena outside the realm of cultural theory. "The term *transdifference* refers to phenomena of a co-presence of different or even oppositional properties, affiliations or elements of semantic and epistemological meaning construction, where this co-presence is regarded or experienced as cognitively or affectively dissonant, full of tension, and undissolvable" (Breinig and Lösch 105). For instance, it refers to persons and groups of plural ethnic or other affiliation. In contrast to models of *mestizaje*, creolization, or transculturation it does not point to cultural synthesis, an overcoming of difference. And in contrast to Homi Bhabha's postcolonial concept of hybridity it does not refer to an ongoing and radically Derridean deconstruction of difference. Notwithstanding Derrida's profound questioning of difference and his temporalizing of it into *différance*, difference as a simultaneous experience of the non-identical remains a basic part of our structuring of reality. Binary thinking, difference and sameness, are essential for living with contingency. Therefore, we see difference such as the distinction between self and other as indispensable and inevitable in the reduction of world complexity, which, in Niklas Luhmann's theory, is what the creation of meaning and thus of cultural systems is all about.

However, contingency will not go away although we may repress or disregard it by applying binary categories. And transdifference refers to that area of thought and experience that we try to exclude by binary differentiation. To take transdifference into consideration may be an act of liberation from the confines of a basically structuralist model of society and of reality at large. But it makes for an often disconcerting, uncomfortable experience. It requires what Keats, in one of his letters, has called "negative capability," that quality "when a man is capable of being in uncertainties, mysteries, doubts, without any irritable reaching after fact and reason" (50).

This is the negative capability that characterizes the writing and thinking of Gerald Vizenor. His whole *oeuvre*, therefore, is a treasure trove of transdifference. And this does not mean only the intercultural

existence of the mixed-blood or "crossblood," as he would have it. Everywhere in Vizenor's work there is an acceptance of limitation, a philosophical and humanistic relativism that begins in the smallest things.
Let us look at some of his haiku, from *Seventeen Chirps* (1964), poems
that are among his earliest literary publications.

> october sunflowers
> like rows of defeated soldiers
> leaning in the frost

This is a simple, comprehensible simile, and yet, if we ignore the "like,"
an exemplification of Pound's famous definition: "An 'Image' is that
which presents an intellectual and emotional complex in an instant of
time" (4). Haiku and imagist poetry and, indeed, Anishinaabe dream
songs, at least in the Densmore translations, share an exploratory quality:
language as discovery on the level of minimalist observations. At first,
the poem establishes a visual similarity between the leaning flowers bereft
of their bright petals and the dejected soldiers. But this analogy, this
de-differentiation, immediately raises questions regarding the nature and
implications of difference. There is the emotional aspect of "defeated"
and the uncertainty of the soldiers' fate, which tend to emphasize the difference between nature and the sphere of humans. And thus, the simile
that seems to improve understanding creates an oscillation of notions
of similarity and difference. Does frost refer to the flowers, the soldiers,
or both? How about the applicability of the seasonal life-death-rebirth
cycle to the soldiers? As we all know, much of the evocative potential of
this—and any—haiku lies in what is to be read, or heard, between the
lines, or between the words. Thus, a range of transdifference is opened
up by the semantic difference of the two central terms, which in turn
is made apparent only by an initial analogy. Another example:

> mounds of foam
> beneath the waterfall
> floating silently

Here is a text that does not even contain a metaphor or simile but
opens up a space of wonder about the nature of sound and silence.
The roaring of the waterfall and the inaudible movement of the foam's
bubbles form a contrast that makes us wonder whether the meaning of

"silence" is the same against a background of noise as it is in the context of encompassing stillness. And along with this, there arise innumerable questions about the nature of difference as an organizing principle of nature or of human constructions of nature. "Haiku hermeneutics," as Vizenor calls his technique, may be "a natural habitude in tribal litera- ture" (1994b, 32); for me it means a letting go of conventional modes of understanding. It is for this reason that one should consider going beyond the good, but often harmonizing, readings of the haiku in Kim- berly Blaeser's valuable monograph on Gerald Vizenor. He is a radical even at that early stage of his career.

Vizenor has often emphasized the centrality of metaphor for his writings. And innovative metaphors provide first-rate examples of the mental processes started by transdifference. According to recent inte- ractional theory, innovative—that is non-habitualized—metaphors are nutshell models of what is going on when we try to grasp reality, to understand it, and to communicate with one another. I translate a pas- sage from a recent study by Werner Kogge on *Die Grenzen des Verstehens* (*The Limits of Understanding*):

> the metaphoricity of language reveals two mutually encom- passing movements: an opening one that breaks with an ordinary mode of speaking and establishes a reference to a remote semantic sphere, and a closing one that deals with this reference and investigates what are initially alien concepts for common elements and then establishes a link between them. In these two movements the innovative nature of the metaphor connects the mental worlds of the people communicating. Mutual understanding is not simply assumed as given like it is in ordinary linguistic usage but such commonality results from mental movements that mutually induce and open one another up and that are interdependent. (246–47)

And yet, "creative metaphors often leave us with the feeling that we do not really understand in a rational way but 'somehow' get an idea, an intuition of what is being talked about and in this way see things in a new light. Rather than understanding this means a heightened awareness of the spaces of the ineffable that language can grasp only inadequately" (Breinig and Lösch 111). To quote from Vizenor's essay "Literary Ani- mals": "Metaphor and simile are the traces of creations, memories, and narrative conversions, the nature and presence of animals in the literature of survivance" (135). This metaphoricity of his writings covers a wide range. To stay with animal and nature metaphors: there is the mildly surprising imagery at the beginning of the "Bone Courts" chapter in *The Heirs of Columbus*: "The crows debased the dawn with their wicked celebrations in the tender birch. The sun bounced over the panic holes on the spring meadow, and a warm wind rushed the season in the loose willows, the wild cherries; the otter pawed the rim of tenuous ice near the headwaters of the great river, and the heirs were at the wild borders of the New World" (63). Even here the Vizenorian invention of the panic hole, familiar from other texts, may be startling enough. A much stronger challenge to our understanding is presented by animal characters whose metaphoric quality works in two directions, as in "Samana, the crossblood black bear and hand talker . . ." (12): is this a bear with human qualities or a bear of a woman? One should keep in mind that this isn't an animal character as we know it from traditional tribal narratives where "Bear" may be a figure at home in all of the spheres we distinguish so assiduously, the realm of nature, the human world, and the sphere of the superhuman, and thus indicates a basic coherence of reality. Since Vizenor writes within the context of Western culture, rationalism, the modern, as it were, his transgressions of categorial boundaries open quite different, much vaster areas of uncharted terrain. His neologism "holotrope" nicely hints at the resulting comprehensive nature of much of his imagery. In other words, Vizenor's language games tend not to make understanding easier; often he does not use his metaphors in the traditional way for the purpose of making the elusive become graspable. On the contrary: he extends the area of transdifference, for instance when he questions cause and effect, as when "Caliban, the great white reservation mongrel" (16) tells his listeners, " 'Once there was a crossblood who wrote about the mongrels we inspired. . . . We imagined the author, gave him the names, the mongrel healers and tricksters in his stories' " (18). Who is being invented here by the literary characters is the author Gerald Vizenor himself; the allusion concerns his novel *Bearheart*. Vizenor uses the disruptive techniques introduced by postmodernism not for the purpose of indicating the fictionality of so-called reality but with the aim of extending the scope of the real, the possible, the thinkable. Anti-Luhmannian, he creates meaning not by reducing, but by enlarging world complexity, by allowing for as much transdifference as possible.

This makes for hard reading, and anybody who has studied not only Vizenor's fiction but also his complex, erudite essays in, say, *Fugitive*

Poses, will agree. The introduction to this volume contains a number of definitions of terms Vizenor has (a) newly coined or (b) resurrected from some remote corner of the dictionary or (c) at least endowed with new connotations. An example of (a), neologisms: "The connotations of transmotion are creation stories, totemic visions, reincarnation, and sovenance; transmotion, that sense of native motion and an active presence, is *sui generis* sovereignty. Native transmotion is survivance, a reciprocal use of nature, not a monotheistic, territorial sovereignty." "Sovenance" is a case of category (b), resurrected terms: "Native *sovenance* is that sense of presence in remembrance, that trace of creation and natural reason in native stories; once an obscure noun, the connotation of sovenance is a native presence in these essays, not the romance of an aesthetic absence or victimry." And finally (c), "*indian*" (with lowercase *i*): "The *indian* is a simulation, the absence of natives; the *indian* transposes the real, and the simulation of the real has no referent, memories, or native stories. The *postindian* must waver over the aesthetic ruins of *indian* simulations" (15). Those who have read Heidegger and other advanced thinkers know that the limits of language have to be bent to accommodate new ideas and insights, but Vizenor's language games make one feel in utter awe, as if just barely hanging on. Language games? What Vizenor is doing here is what the Russian Formalists have called *ostranenye*, defamiliarization. What we seem to know is defamiliarized by being put in new contexts or by being used with fresh or freshly rediscovered semantic fillings.

Not surprisingly, the interaction of ethnic and cultural groups is thus turned into a subversive and liberating process. In an interview with Klaus Lösch and me some years ago, Vizenor describes the situation of the mixed-blood as "a tension of discovery and liberation. . . . What difference do we make out of the differences? That's my interest. In the past the differences have been violent and terribly damaging, and I'm arguing that the differences are liberation; they're the discovery of a whole person" (Vizenor 1995, 163). Small wonder then that Vizenor has received much opposition from essentialists, both among the dominant society whose images of "The American Indian" he has exploded and ridiculed ever so often and among the advocates of tribal autochthony, authenticity, and apartheid.

What distinguishes Vizenor from many postmodern writers is the ethical impetus behind his writing. Where Gayatri Spivak asks, "Can the subaltern speak?" Vizenor introduces the concept of the *postindian*—not postnative!—a self-invention that presupposes the "indian" as a simulation and invented category. The postindian is presented not as status or fixed position but as a transdifferent fluctuation between the reservation and the city, between tribal storytelling and the academy, between oral and written genres, certainly not subaltern, and decidedly capable of speech in any form, of taking sides with those who are marginalized not only by the dominant society but by so-called opinion leaders of many varieties. His favorite stance is that of having his readers find out for themselves, of teasing them into a maze of ironies, wordplay, nicknaming, and other tricks, into the world of transdifference. It is the fluctuating position of the trickster that makes his writing both elusive and effective. But contrary to Melville's confidence-man, the role he creates for himself as for many of his characters is that of a benevolent, compassionate trickster even where he may be sharply and wittily critical.

In this context, a look at Vizenor's 2003 novel *Hiroshima Bugi* may offer some concluding insights. This is a novel without a coherent plot, consisting of a series of scenes and dialogues as remembered and put down by the central trickster character, Ronin Browne, an Anishinaabe-Japanese crossblood. Ronin has much in common with his creator, for instance: "Ronin creates words, names, and turns combinations of words, some native words, to intimate desire and the critical thrust of new ideas. 'Survivance,' for instance, is not merely a variation of 'survival.' . . . By survivance he means a vision and vital condition to endure, to outwit evil and dominance, and to deny victimry" (36). But each of Ronin's remembrances is commented upon in the complementary "envoy" chapter written by a former member of the U.S. Army who has also collected and arranged Ronin's texts and who shares even more qualities with the author. I will only mention the wordplaying possibilities offered by the name Ronin, a nickname that reminds us of his father Orion, bearing echoes of "irony" but also sharing some linguistic elements with "Nori, the wise *nanazu* poet" (34), and hence the Japanese tradition of tricksterism, and unmistakeably also with "Vizenor." The commentary chapters provide almost as much information as we find in Nabokov's *Pale Fire*, but what might possibly kill the aesthetic and moral effect of the Ronin chapters actually leaves us in some kind of reader-response limbo, wondering about the power of poetic language to do so much more than just provide information and opinion. The double narrative of scene and commentary thus turns into a fruitfully irritating play with the reader who finds much else to be irritated about. The book explores the most basic differences: life and death, peace and war; but Ronin makes us equally unhappy with the sentimental and apolitical peace celebrations of the Hiroshima memorials as with the warmongers. He makes us furious about those who developed and used the atomic bomb but at least as furious about the Japanese war cabinet. He will not even allow us to retire to a cheap sympathy-with-the-victims position but asks us to reconsider any given position, without providing ready-made answers, and without withdrawing into total despair about mankind, as we find in his satiric cousin Mark Twain during the last phase of his career. The differences are there: Japan and America, the tribal and the urban worlds, nature and commerce, the past and the present, war and peace, life and death. But they are always simply not enough to structure reality, to create an order of values. The simultaneity of presence and absence, of identity and non-identity, take us to that trembling ground of transdifference.

Therefore it is not sufficient to call Gerald Vizenor a leading exponent of contemporary Native American literature and hence a "mediator between two worlds," as the saying goes. I would much rather describe his role in the words and, once again, the animal metaphors he uses for Ronin, his character and persona:

> Ronin strongly resists any association with cults or the mythic concoctions of animal tenancy. Animals do not haunt him, or by guile penetrate his body. Clearly, his creative, perceptive powers are innate, similar to the poses of an ascetic or shaman, and his tricky visions are not imitations or derived from others. He is the animal of his mind, a spirit by stories not by the possession of sorcerers. He is a unique and ironic healer, a trickster by stories, not by character simulations. . . . His native stories evade closure and victimry. (64)

His is the authenticity of one who has the courage to endure and represent transdifference as a subject position and as a source of satiric authority resting not on the power of argumentative coercion but on that of creative liberation.

Works Cited

Bhabha, Homi K. *The Location of Culture*. London and New York: Routledge, 1994.

Blaeser, Kimberly M. *Gerald Vizenor: Writing in the Oral Tradition*. Norman and London: U of Oklahoma P, 1996.

Breinig, Helmbrecht. *Satire und Roman: Studien zur Theorie des Genrekonflikts und zur satirischen Erzählliteratur der USA von Brackenridge bis Vonnegut*. Tübingen: Gunter Narr Verlag, 1984.

Breinig, Helmbrecht, and Klaus Lösch. "Transdifference." *Journal for the Study of British Cultures* 13.2 (2006): 105–22.

Keats, John. "Letter to George and Thomas Keats," 28 December 1817, *The Complete Works of John Keats*. Vol. 4. Ed. H. Buxton Forman. New York: Thomas Y. Crowell & Co., n.d.

Kogge, Werner. *Die Grenzen des Verstehens: Kultur—Differenz—Diskretion*. Weilerswist: Velbrück Wissenschaft, 2002.

Luhmann, Niklas. *Soziologische Aufklärung: Aufsätze zur Theorie sozialer Systeme*. Vol. 1. Opladen: Westdeutscher Verlag, 1970.

Melville, Herman. *The Confidence-Man: His Masquerade* (1857). The Writings of Herman Melville: The Northwestern-Newberry Edition, Vol. 10. Ed. Harrison Hayford et al. Evanston and Chicago: Northwestern UP and The Newberry Library, 1984.

Pound, Ezra. *Literary Essays*. Ed. T. S. Eliot. London: Faber, 1954.

Spivak, Gayatri Chakravorty. "Can the Subaltern Speak?" *Marxism and the Interpretation of Culture*. Ed. Cary Nelson and Lawrence Grossberg. Urbana and Chicago: U of Illinois P, 1988. 271–313.

Vizenor, Gerald. *Seventeen Chirps: Haiku in English*. Minneapolis: Nodin Press, 1964.

———. *Darkness in Saint Louis Bearheart*. St. Paul, MN: Truck Press, 1978. Reprinted as *Bearheart: The Heirship Chronicles*. Minneapolis: U of Minnesota P, 1990.

———. *The Heirs of Columbus*. Hanover and London: Wesleyan UP/UP of New England, 1991.

———. *Manifest Manners: Postindian Warriors of Survivance*. Hanover and London: Wesleyan UP/UP of New England, 1994a.

———. "Envoy to Haiku." *Shadow Distance: A Gerald Vizenor Reader*. Ed. A. Robert Lee. Hanover and London: Wesleyan UP/UP of New England, 1994b. 25–32.

———. "Gerald Vizenor." Interviewed by Helmbrecht Breinig and Klaus Lösch. *American Contradictions: Interviews with Nine American Writers*. Ed. Wolfgang Binder and Helmbrecht Breinig. Hanover and London: Wesleyan UP/UP of New England, 1995. 143–65.

———. "Literary Animals." *Fugitive Poses: Native American Indian Scenes of Absence and Presence*. Lincoln and London: U of Nebraska P, 1998. 119–43.

———. *Hiroshima Bugi: Atomu 57*. Lincoln and London: U of Nebraska P, 2003.

7

Traces of Others in Our Own Other

Monocultural Ideals, Multicultural Resistance

Juan Bruce-Novoa

While it is undeniable that to some extent the quality of "authenticity" within human groups is linked to physical characteristics, it is far more commonly a matter of a set of customs made up of performance codes and rules that determine membership in and status within the particular group. Performance is a matter of cultural discourses designed to render actions meaningful within the group's system of attributing value and assigning relative position to its participants. This is certainly nothing new. In *The Structure of Evil*, Ernest Becker observed that humans use language, play, work, ritual, and art to create systems of self-signification intended to provide the means to achieve, in Kant's words, maximum individuality within maximum community. Patterns of behavior are institutionalized through repetition and rewards—or ritualized through the same process if one prefers to focus on the religious and sacred aspects of the same phenomenon, as Mircea Eliade demonstrated thoroughly in his vast opus. Participation in these institutionalized rituals, whether in the strictly controlled forms of the central events of a culture's calendar or the daily routines of pragmatic interaction, garners recognition from one's peers while simultaneously earning one a sense of significance within the established system of values. This is possible as long as all participants agree on or at least acquiesce to the pattern of rules and goals. Even those who do not consent to the pattern at least accept that their non-compliance is exactly that, eccentric behavior in relationship to the centric rule. In this way, discordance ironically reaffirms the communal concordance even as measures—defined by the system for handling anyone who strays off course—are taken to control miscreants.

In *The Denial of Death*, Becker argued that performance of the cultural ideal of community could be interpreted as a pattern of codes for achieving the status of hero in the eyes of one's society. A symbolic action system lays out for participants a wide range of performance possibilities, from those simple acts that reaffirm compliance with basic expectations up through those that would merit extraordinary recognition and rewards.

> A structure of statuses and roles, customs and rules for behavior, designed to serve as a vehicle for earthly heroism. . . . each cultural system is a dramatization of earthly heroics; each system cuts out roles for performances of various degrees of heroism: from the "high" . . . to the "low" . . . [even] the plain, everyday, earthly heroism wrought by gnarled working hands guiding a family through hunger and disease. (4–5)

Cultural authenticity would be judged, then, on how well one performs one's role as defined by this code of communal heroics.

However, Becker recognized several problems with the description of society as a homogeneous system, somewhat utopian in the present situation of high rates of mobility of all sorts and proven patterns of heterogeneity in most areas of the world. A fundamental, significant problem is the extreme difficulty in maintaining the communal exclusivity necessary to assure total adherence to the rule of behavior. The outside, or Other, is a menace that represents to the homogeneous cultural ideal, according to Becker, the menace of an impoverishment of meaning.

> The exclusive group stages its own ideal dream, which all members live in unison. It draws on the combined personalities of all its members, including ancestors with whom the group

feels intimate ties . . . the outsider represents an immediate impoverishment in a joint drama. (229)

When outside influences begin to permeate through the communal defenses, or insiders begin to desire alternative forms of behavior, the question of authenticity—that is, the adherence to cultural norms of performance—becomes central to the preservation of the culture's ideal dream of itself . . . or the culture's dream of its ideal self.

When a group migrates from its traditional space to another, it takes with it those codes of performance. A comparison can be drawn with what Mircea Eliade refers to in his discussions of the function of the talisman or touchstone in times of migration or diaspora. Something—a rock, a plant, a relic of a hero or saint, or customs themselves, like dances, rituals, etiquette—of the original place must be brought along to serve, more than as mere reminders, rather as the actual presence of that which has remained behind. In this way, distance is erased and the new settlement, even while in transit, still centers round the "same place."

However, the new setting for the transported "sameness," no matter how elaborate and thorough the efforts to reproduce the original, introduces de facto adaptation. In the mere fact of the effort to be faithful to the model introduces a new ritual that in the original site was not necessary since "back there" the context was a given with no need to be evoked in words or gesture. And when the new setting forming the context is shared with other groups, contact and competition ensue. Differing codes of performance compete for the generations of new initiates, even when those who administer them on either side of the migration act express no interest in recruiting one from the other. It should surprise no one that the young would be attracted to whichever code promises the most fulfilling rewards, that in turn provokes regulatory reactions from the elders less flexible in their adaptation potential. And mastering the techniques of performance that will garner rewards from the inner or outer group becomes paramount; "authentic performances" with "authentic objects" are at a premium. One learns to imitate, improvise, perfect, even surpass the original, until the rewards are achieved from the new host; or one learns to duplicate the gestures and attitudes of the traditional inner culture to reap the rewards offered to those who remain faithful to the old ways. And despite the negativity of such imitative performances of acculturation found in the works of, for instance, Homi Bhabha—negativity bordering on fanatical rejection among post-colonialist critics and radical cultural nationalistic ethnics—the author's example of successful mastery at performing the crossover rituals into the hierarchies of colonial power is much stronger than his textual warnings of its perils. Authenticity changes meaning in the process, but it is still a value.

Survival also becomes a premium, although I must confess that, while I understand the emotions and the motivation, I do not feel the need—and never have felt it personally—to preserve anything. (For me culture is what one makes in working toward the future, not what one manages to impose on the present in the name of fidelity to the past.) In the 1960s the desire or need to create a group identity as "Other" within what was perceived to be the "National One" became a central concern of youth. We called it counterculture: a discourse of self-identity within the greater "national" or "mainstream" that most often assumed the position of opposition. From the start structural/functional assumptions of binary opposition based on contrast established mutual dependencies. Not simply the gathering around a once-cohesive national identity as imagined within the national boundaries of a country that would have been home territory of the group, but the assumption of all of that plus the experience of it being now reduced to and reproduced in a minority group within the larger unit, one that claims its own symbiotic relationship between territory and communal characteristics.

In the case of the people of Mexican descent, what was the basis of that formulation? The following, admittedly simplified enumeration offers some items that were and still often are cited as the assumed characteristics of what some call Chicanos and other, Mexican Americans.

1. Origin
   a) National/cultural: Mexican
   b) Racial: *mestizaje* or Caucasian/Native American miscegenation, with emphasis on the contribution of the latter.
2. Language: Mexican Spanish as the supposed native language, with a decidedly working-class register.
3. Common Experience: U.S. experience with Mexican immigrant origins in the past.
4. Ideology: cultural nationalism based on Mexican origins and on claims to previous territorial possession of the U.S. Southwest.

It has been further assumed that these characteristics could be found in early works of Chicano cultural production, such as *I Am Joaquin* (1967), *El Plan Espiritual de Aztlán* (1969), *Flor y canto en Aztlán* (1975), the Teatro Campesino's *Actos* (1965–1970), or the novels that won the Quinto Sol prizes: *. . . y no se lo tragó la tierra* (1971), *Bless me, Ultima* (1972), *Klail City y sus alrededores* (1976). Implicit in this assumption is yet another that appears in much current Chicano criticism: Chicanismo or the Chicano Movement's failure to maintain a cohesive, unitary proposition can be viewed as almost a natural consequence of the passing of the 1960s and the onset of the more individualistic and less idealistic subsequent periods. In short, the Chicano Movement is placed in the same general framework with other counterculture phenomena and given the status of another victim of the relentless swing of the ideological pendulum from liberal to conservative. While I have no objection to placing Chicano activism within the context of counterculture with which it in effect shares many characteristics, we must be careful to avoid one of the pitfalls of sixties nostalgia, that of confusing the ideals with reality. To surrender to such nostalgia would, by default, maintain the illusion that there once existed a Chicano Camelot: a period when there actually was a unified cultural and political *Movement* based on homogeneous cultural foundations. If that were true, then we could simply examine the cultural production of that period to find what was the authentic Chicano code of cultural heroics and offer it as the standard for future generations—a practice not unfamiliar to old guard Chicano studies programs. I, however, prefer to remain focused on that period in a more analytical fashion to show that the illusion of unity was always already a delusion—that there was never a clear homogeneous Chicanismo to oppose to the national Other. The reality was more heterogeneous, with Chicanismo harboring within itself its own oppositional, or at least differential, others, all competing for the role of *axis mundi* of authenticity.

Into the Chicano Hall of Mirrors: Others of Our Others

To begin at the center of the ideal construction, and the first point on our list of assumed characteristics, there has never existed a homogeneous national state on either side of the border to which one could fix a model to be followed or rejected in order to create a clear ethnic nationalist program of otherness, whatever its relation to the other two might be. Neither the United States nor Mexico are homogeneous cultures, not even in the realm of the imagined communities postulated by Anderson. When Anderson first defines his concept of the imagined nation, he explains that the nation "is *imagined* because the members of even the smallest nation will never know most of their fellow-members, meet them, or even hear of them, yet in the minds of each lives the image of their communion" (5). At no time in either country is there proof of this uniformly held image of communion with a common fellowship as members of the same unit. Instead, we find the history of a consistent pattern of only partial participation, with notable groups of residents who have felt themselves excluded. One could even say that perhaps the definition of Anderson's imagined nation must be corrected to include the presence within the "limits" of the nation of excluded, "othered" minorities. Perhaps this lack in Anderson stems from his having placed the origin of the nation in the Enlightenment, ignoring that the first modern national state was Spain, a phenomenon that quite self-consciously recognized that not everyone within its boundaries shared in the unifying principles. Be that as it may, there is no unified United States for people of Mexican descent to resist, nor—and perhaps more significantly—is there is a unified Mexico for them to preserve, except that which the state apparatus attempts to create through public education and media. And it is in the ideals of that ideal nation, for good or not, that much of the Chicanos' imagined Mexico has its origin. But since there is no homogeneous Mexican nation, it can hardly serve as a clearly defined set of characteristics. More realistic is to see Mexican culture as regional, even local, with marked differences that will logically filter through to produce distinct and different ethnic formations in Mexican American communities in the United States.

As for being a *mestizo* race, the concept, while appealing as an ideal principle, presents difficulties from the start. *Mestizaje* is a process, not a racial classification. One can rightfully say that Mexico is characterized by the presence of a large majority of people of biological mixture of Native American and non-native bloodlines. Within this mixture, however, the percentages vary tremendously, and at either end of the spectrum one finds a number of non-*mestizos*, who have as much right, legal and moral, to be considered Mexicans. Moreover, the identification with Native Americanness will differ from region to region, family to family, period to period—on both sides of the border. And often, tribal specificity is lost in the process of *mestizaje*, not to speak of immigration to the United States. Then within the United States, there is the question of *mestizaje* with "non-Mexican" Native Americans, a difference that despite some efforts to erase it as a colonial imposition, seems to have a historical rationale predating the arrival of the European. The acceptance of the various admixtures and the value attributed to each, or the process as an abstract concept, differs from period to period. Admittedly, during the 1960s and 1970s, the desire to reconnect with Mexican native roots was promoted by cultural nationalist activists. Equally, in some areas, like New Mexico and to some extent Arizona and California, the local connection to U.S. tribes has been acknowledged and cultivated, although not often carried over into political or cultural production.

Just as the native base differs from region to region and period to period, its reception is a matter of the shifting discursive field in which the interpretive act is performed. For example, United States versus Mexico, Northern versus Central New Spain, New Mexico versus California or Texas, Pueblos versus Apache or Navajo, Nahua-based versus Non-Nahua, Mexica versus Non-Mexica, permanent residence versus nomadic tribes, mission tribes versus non-mission ones, "high culture" tribes versus . . . the vocabulary of politically correct attributions fails us, although the implications are often clear in a given text. As a result, what is left of native specificity, when differences are erased for the sake of cultural cohesion, is often a vague pan-Indianism that names the most familiar of the possible choices as the base of the present *mestizaje*. The acknowledged master foundational poem of Chicano cultural nationalism, *I Am Joaquin*, achieved this effect by offering enumerations of tribes in the development of its program of encapsulation of five years of historical development of the Mexican American community: Mexicas (referenced through "Cuauhtémoc"), Mayas and Chichimecas (3, 5); "Yaqui/Tarahumara/Chamula/Zapotec/Mestizo/Español" (9). The second enumeration flows into the category of *mestizo* that acts as a bridge to the Spaniard. The total effect of the enumerations is to produce a multi-tribal native base for the "racial" category formed by fusion with that last term that enters from the outside, the non-native side.

Observers of Chicano literature might assume that the multiplicity of indigenous Mexican tribes is subsumed "naturally" under the term "Aztlán." Certainly its power to function as a central myth of Chicano discourse cannot be denied. Entire books have been written to analyze its significance. Yet, the same problem arises yet again. The myth of

Aztlán pertains to the Mexica tribe—commonly, though inaccurately, known as Aztecs—of central Mexico. The tribe emerged from servitude to dominate the area of the present Mexico City in the fifteenth century and exercised hegemony over a coalition of tribes that controlled a vast emporium of economic and military relationship far beyond the central valley when the Spaniards arrived in the early sixteenth century to end their rule. Aztlán is the myth of the Mexicas' origins supposedly lying somewhere to the north of central Mexico, a homeland from which they migrated south to that central valley.

Aztlán, however, does not now, nor did it ever, pertain to the majority of tribes in what is now called Mexico. In the attempt to turn it into a symbol of all Mexico, Chicano cultural nationalism actually mirrors the ideological program of countless Mexican regimes dating back into the nineteenth century if not earlier. The tactic places all the other tribes in an evolutionary pyramid supporting the Mexicas at the summit.

This was already the tactic of the first conscious program of Mexican historiography from the 1880s: *México a través de los siglos* (Tenorio-Trillo 66–73). Alberto Urista's *Flor y canto en Aztlán* (1971), one of the most influential publications of those years, seems to accept and promote this investiture of national representation in the Mexicas and their myth.

At least one Chicano writer of equal if not higher status than Urista among that generation of cultural producers, Luis Valdez of Teatro Campesino fame, disagreed with the Mexica investiture. In his "Pensamiento Serpentino" (1971), that can be read as a response to both *I Am Joaquin* and *Flor y canto en Aztlán*, Valdez chooses to seek the roots of Chicanismo, not in the Mexica, but the Maya. Valdez did not argue with the need for Chicanos to Mexicanize themselves (172), but when he sets out the process for returning to their "PROPIO PUEBLO" (their own people), his enumeration of elements traces a different genealogy than Gonzales's: the Chicano must be liberated "BY HIS POPOL VUH / HIS CHILAM BALAM / HIS CHICHEN ITZA / KUKULCAN, GUCUMATZ, QUETZALCOATL" (173). The references are to Maya texts, places, and gods, culminating not in a Mexica reference, but a Toltec one, the god Quetzalcoatl.[1] Despite the efforts by the Mexica to link themselves to the Toltec tradition, Quetzalcoatl is not a Mexica and can be read in opposition to the Mexica cult of warrior gods. Hence, Valdez constructs a non-Mexica Chicano family tree, and leaves no room for ambiguity when he states: "We must all become NEO-MAYAS" (173). Later, in his masterpiece of Teatro Campesino theater, *La Gran Carpa de los Rascuachi* (1973), the play culminates in a quotation in Maya also found in the "Pensamiento Serpentino": In Lak'ech [You are my other I] (173).

Which is the authentic Chicano genealogy, Mexica or Maya? Unbiased observers might respond, neither exclusively and both, of course, but the two sources are not the same and each engenders different heirs. To collapse them into pan-Mexicanism is like lumping Catholic and Calvinist missionaries under the title of Christians: correct, generally, but certainly not without violence to both. To elide the differences that obviously existed in the 1960s is to ignore realities that continue in opposition in contemporary ideological conflicts within Chicano culture. That the image and concept of Aztlán can be seen to have triumphed, especially among intellectuals, is a case for reception theorists to ponder and explain, but it cannot erase the intracultural dissonance present in the dialoguing texts that remain as a record of the early struggle to define Chicano models of identity.

One can ponder what happens to the peoples of tribes left out of these and other efforts to represent the multiplicity of indigenous peoples through a selection of a few exemplary names. In the case of *I Am Joaquin*, what does it mean in ideological and biological terms that no U.S. tribe is mentioned as a feeder source of Chicano miscegenation? Could one read this as prejudice—even implicit racism—that excludes U.S. Native Americans from the process of Chicanismo? While it can be read as a symptom of the ideological mind-set of the mid-sixties among Chicano cultural nationalists, someone less generously inclined could say that it veils a U.S.—and reflects a Mexican, why not?—tradition of exclusion of the Native American from participation in the national identity, other than as a silenced "another other," present, but not counted. Could this not be a trace of the U.S. national "other" within the constructing core of the Chicano self-imagined otherness? Perhaps.

The assumption that Chicanos share a common language, Spanish, was and is still yet another ideal. However, anyone who has taught Spanish-language courses in areas where Chicanos reside need not be told how far reality and ideal fall mutually off target. Regional differences are manifold even within that common base. There is the question of whose Spanish is the most "authentic," whose the closest to the center of the imagined national identity? Most would prefer Mexican to, say,

Caribbean or even New Mexican Spanish. This choice seems logical and natural. Focusing south of the border, then, one is struck by the tremendous variety of "Mexican" forms of speech. Which of the Mexican regional types of Spanish is to be chosen as the preferred source, Mexico City, northern states, southern, urban or rural? The difference can be as subtle as a variance of accent or a shift within phrasing rhythms, or even of vocabularies that do not travel from one region to another. A *bolillo*, the compact, French-style bread in Mexico City, becomes an American man along the northern border. The Yucatecan accent and regional vocabulary are almost totally absent from Chicano expression. "Chilanga Banda," a song Juan Jaime López performed by the Mexican punk rock group from the national capitol, Café Tacuba, illustrates the same point and more. The text must be translated for Mexicans themselves, revealing levels of class and regional estrangement.[2] Moreover, its use of slang reveals the intervention of time in fracturing the ideal of homogenous ethnicity among immigrant Mexicans. The song features slang words that no longer mean what Chicanos who immigrated in the fifties or sixties understood them to mean. As Mexican slang changes, it shifts the sense of what is "authentic" in national and regional Mexican colloquial usage, producing a then and now of authenticity among immigrants who tended to bring with them the speech patterns of their moment. And while since the 1960s Spanish-language mass media has become ubiquitous in the United States, the local, subaltern sectors of Mexican culture, to which a resident of Mexico may have access, hardly ever form part of the mass media exports.

To return to *I Am Joaquin*, in its initial bilingual publication, the first edition features a Spanish translation composed in colloquial speech. It served to locate the poem's Spanish voice within the register of popular speech, with a tendency toward usages familiar to immigrant readers of the working class. In the bilingual publication, with the English and Spanish texts appearing in facing columns on the page, the Spanish appeared as an equal, occupying fifty percent of the space, a provocative visual metaphor bespeaking the ideology of cultural miscegenation and a bold statement in areas where English was considered—and sometimes legislated as—the primary language. However, the colloquial tone of the Spanish also set a social and cultural level for the performance of that ideology. It achieved what the English could only do in terms of content: by speaking from the register of the working and poor classes, more than proclaim, the translation embodied an ideology of justice for the social "other." However, in the last authorized version of the translation made before the author's death for the publication of his collected works, *Message to Aztlán*, the language, according the editor's note, has been corrected.

> We have translated the original English version . . . adding accent marks, Spanish punctuation and articles, as appropriate. We used verb tenses that agree with the English version. In places where the original Spanish version used the preterite tense, we changed them to the present perfect tense to agree with the original English version. In some cases we substitute Spanish words that best convey the sense of the English Text. (2)

In other words, the new translation seeks a more standard Spanish. In addition, the explanation clearly privileges the English version as the original text, destroying the impression that the two languages were equal: this impression is driven home by the separation of the texts, leaving each solitary and singular. And printing the Spanish version first in *Message to Aztlán* is an all too transparent effort to give it priority, an effort countermanded by the editor's statement that clearly declares its secondary status to the "original English." The possibility of close, interlingual reading of which I wrote years ago, praising it as one of the poem's highest achievements, is voided (Bruce-Novoa 1982, 48–68). It is, however, in the substitution of words, the changing of verb tenses, and the inclusion of accents where striking difference becomes most noticeable. A comparison of the English with the first and second translation is enlightening.

	1967	2001
I am Joaquin	Yo soy Joaquín	Yo soy Joaquín
Lost in a world of confusion,	Perdido en un mundo de confusión	Perdido en un mundo de confusión
Caught up in a whirl of an [sic] gringo society	Encanchado en el remolino de una Sociedad gringa	Atrapado en el remolino de una Sociedad gringa

Only one word is altered: *encanchado* becomes *atrapado*. The first thing one asks is how is this more faithful to the original? *Atrapado* means to be trapped, not necessarily a synonym for *caught up in*. But the first translation rendered it as *encanchado*, literally caught on a hook, which is not a synonym either. However, *encanchado* captures the sense of the original better in its evocation of something lifted off the ground and exposed to the whirlwind; while *atrapado* conveys a more closed off connotation and none of the lifting sensation of *encanchado*. Also, while *atrapado* communicates the idea of being caught and held, *encanchado*, through its colloquial connotations, communicates that and much more: to be caught up in a migrant worker contract is to be *encanchado*, and to make a down payment on something—that is, to enter into a contract to make payments and go into debt—is called an *encanche*. Thus, the colloquial Spanish usage was more poetic if one of the characteristics of poetic language is to open the word to multiple meanings that enhance its impact on the reader's imagination. Moreover, in this case the colloquial was more ideologically powerful, evoking images of capitalist repression that the text seeks to denounce.

A comparison of the verb tense corrections renders a similar impression.

1967	2001
Fui dueño de la tierra hasta donde veían	Yo era el dueño de toda la tierra que se podía
los ojos debajo la corona Española,	ver bajo la corona española,
Y yo trabajé en mi tierra	Y trabajaba mi tierra
Y di mi sudor y sangre india	y daba mi sudor y sangre india

Without entering into the subtleties of the difference between the preterite (1967) and the imperfect (2001) in Spanish, one can say in general terms that both convey past, historical action in the two versions. However, as poetry, the 1967 text takes advantage of the accentuated last or single syllable in the preterite—*Fui, trabaje, di*—to accelerate the rhythm, while the imperfects of the 2001—*era, trabajaba, daba*—slow the text down, underscoring Spanish's tendency to favor accentuation on the penultimate syllable to create a more tedious overall effect. One could also question the need to add *Yo* and *el* in the first line when they are not necessary—Spanish does not need the personal pronoun since it is contained in the verb; the article is not necessary either—and the prosaic rendering of the end of the first line and start of the second are a regrettable undermining of the poem's lyric potential. The question of adding accents where they were omitted may seem the least important point among all the rest, but actually it is a key signifier of the general effect caused by the changes. Evoking again the image of teachers of Spanish in Chicano classrooms, one of the commonest points of discussion among us is the surprising lack of ability among Chicano students to write the diacritical accent marks in Spanish. One could say that it is close to a Chicano characteristic that transcends regional and generational lines. To correct all the accents is to practice an elitist, universalizing intervention in popular ethnic culture. To add all the unnecessary articles and pronouns is pedantry.

The general effect of the corrections is to alter not only the poem's persona, but the image of the author as well as that of his intended audience. When the poem loses the popular touches and the lyric quality of the first version, the new text shifts all those products of its performance to a more elite class of Spanish speaker and implies an author with a less creative poetic imagination: although actually we must remember that it is not the author, rather the translator, who has changed. The text seems to level out at a register devoid of local color, colloquial flavor, and not a little poetic interest. The question for us here is less which of the two is the more authentically Chicano version—though certainly an interesting and valid concern for those who assume that it speaks from, for, and to the poor—but what kind of Chicano imaginary does each version create? And unvoiced questions linger: does this not at least echo old prejudices against the Mexican immigrant worker, that prejudice many of us experienced in the Spanish classroom when we were told that our Spanish was "too Mexican" and that we should try to lose the colloquial tone in favor of standard usages. But then that was the ethnic "other" who misunderstood us, and in the 1960s we could go to texts like *I Am Joaquin* to find our way of speaking verified right there on the page alongside the English. And now?

When we speak of language as an indicator of culture, we cannot avoid issues of social class. Here, too, it is a matter of choice, and the possibilities cover the range from urban or rural working class to middle class, to highly sophisticated, in either language. Granted, since the sixties there has been a tendency to invest the working-class register with a charge of authenticity. Yet the majority of Chicano literary texts do not reflect that level. Writers tend to come from an educated sector of the community where colloquial language is often a recuperation of a language no longer actively spoken by the writer. That is why a text like *I Am Joaquin* carried such a high charge of sentimental value as well as ideological impact. It spoke the language of the class that the political movement claimed to represent. The learning of that language was clearly stated as a problem to be addressed by political activists in Oscar Zeta Acosta's *The Revolt of the Cockroach People* where the narrator/protagonist sets out to learn the language of the young Chicanos he finds himself involved with in Los Angeles. Not only is it Spanish he must learn, but he chooses to associate ideologically with the sector known as the "Vatos locos" (Crazy guys) of gang culture. Acosta's book is most useful because it is one of the few texts from those critical years of communal self-definition that consciously described the great variety of social and ideological sectors present in the Mexican American community. Even more telling, Acosta shows us that among those who presumed to be Chicanos there also existed ideological and class differences. He takes this knack for revealing the fissures in the community and ironically presents an image of union. Toward the end of his novel, when he is defending Chicano militants in a Los Angeles court, Acosta calls as witnesses César Chávez and Rodolfo Corky Gonzales. Both were admired Chicano leaders at the start of the 1970s, but while Chávez had already won recognition as a Gandhi-style pacifist, Gonzales advocated the right to use violence to achieve the movement's goals. Ideologically they had little in common, yet they appear together in Acosta's book, standing beside him, one on each side. That was exactly the function of literature: to create the semblance of unity. Yet, as Acosta states, if the political situation reached a crisis point, he—and we—would have to choose between the two, and in that case he knew the difference between them. Acosta conveyed a message it would be wise to remember: not all Chicanos or their ideology are the same, and the differences are significant.

Conclusion

There is no common U.S. Chicano experience; rather there are only highly regional ones with degrees of difference. In the period of the sixties it was not the same to have grown up in Texas, New Mexico, Illinois, Pennsylvania, California, or Colorado. Each had its own regional context and local variations within that. In 1975 a then-young Chicano folklorist presented his work on "Chicano dance" to students at Yale University. Slowly, in reaction to interruptions and questions by the students who came from different communities scattered across the southwestern states, the scholar had to admit that his research had been done in only a small area of the Rio Grande border in south Texas. Faced with the indisputable denials of his thesis by representatives of the areas he was attempting to force under the umbrella of Texas Valley culture, he had to abandon, if only for the moment, the bid for hegemonic power in the ethnic performance. Years later, one of his students appeared on a California campus and proceeded to tell the students that one version of a recording was the "real" Chicano one while the other was the "agringado" or assimilated version. The problem was that the California students felt the second version to be more to their liking and did not appreciate being implicitly cast out from the inner circle of authenticity. I, on the other hand, having grown up in urban Denver, considered both recordings to be much too rural, completely divorced from the rock and roll every Chicano band worth its salt played. There is a saying in Spanish, *Para los gustos, los colores*—for tastes, there are colors.

For maximum individuality within maximum community, perhaps the best possibility is within, not a unitary, homogeneous culture, but in a variegated, heterogeneous one with many, and even contradictory, ways to be authentic. To those who fear the Other's invasive potential, perhaps it will be reassuring to realize that even before Mexicans migrate, and even from the start of Chicano literature, the role of the Other—and Others—was already well considered and inscribed from within. One could say that without the Other within, there would be no Mexican culture. Nor Usonian or Chicano either.

Notes

1. *Popol Vuh*, transcribed by a Quiché Mayan shortly after the Spanish conquest, preserves Maya origin myths and is considered their bible. The books of *Chilam Balam* "form the most important part of this native Maya literature. Written in the Maya language, they reflect more closely the thought of these Indians than any other records that have come down to us . . . they contain a wealth of historical and ethnological information . . . [and] also furnish a record of the reactions of the native mind to the European culture and of the manner in which the latter was adapted to suit its new environment" (Roys xi). Chichén Itzá was one of the main Mayan ceremonial centers; the

archeological site lies about midway between Cancún and Mérida. Kukulcán, Gucumatz, and Quezalcoatl are variants of the feathered serpent, snake god in Maya mythology in charge of the four elements—air, water, fire, earth; one of the gods responsible for the creation of the earth and humankind, he brought agriculture and, hence, civilization to humans. Among the Toltecs (his original followers) he was revered for having taught them also the use of laws; having come from the ocean, he returned to it, and, some thought, returned in the form of Cortés to reclaim his land from the Mexicas. Hence, Valdez's choice of origins includes an ancient element of resistance to Aztlán hegemony.

2. The text of the López song is as follows:

> Ya chale chango chilango,
> ¡qué chafa chamba te chutas!
> No checa anda de tacuche
> ¡y chale con la charola!
> Tan choncho como una chinche,
> más chueco que la fayuca,
> con fusca y con cachiporra
> te pasa andar de guarura.
> Mejor yo me echo una chela
> y chance enchulo una chava
> chambeando de chafirete
> me sobra chupe y pachanga.
> Si choco saco chipote
> la chota no es muy molacha
> chiveando a los machucan
> se va a morder su talacha.
> De noche caigo al congal
> 'No manches,' dice la "Changa,"
> 'hay chorros de toporochos
> y chifla y pasa la pacha.'
> (Chorus)
> Pachuchos, cholos y chundos
> Chichifos y malafachas
> Acá los chómpiras rifan
> Y bailan tibiritábara
> Mejor yo me echo una chela
> y chance enchufo una chava
> chambeando de chafirete
> me sobra chupe y pachanga.
> Mi ñero mata la bacha
> y canta *La Cucaracha*

su cholla vive de chochos
de chemo, churro y garnachas
(Chorus)
Transando de arriba abajo
¡ahí va la chilanga banda!
Chinchin si me la recuerdan,
Carcacha y se les retacha.

For a translation of the slang terms into standard Spanish, see http://www.
jergasdehablahispana.org/mexico.htm

Works Cited

Acosta, Oscar Zeta. *The Revolt of the Cockroach People*. San Francisco: Straight
    Arrow Books, 1972.
Anaya, Rudolfo. *Bless Me, Ultima*. Berkeley: Quinto Sol Publications, 1972.
Anderson, Benedict. *Imagined Communities: Reflections on the Origin and Spread
    of Nationalism*. London and New York: Verso, 1991.
Becker, Ernest. *The Denial of Death*. New York: Free Press, 1973.
———. *The Structure of Evil: An Essay on the Unification of the Science of Man*.
    New York: Free Press, 1976.
Bruce-Novoa, Juan. *Chicano Poetry: A Response to Chaos*. Austin: U of Texas
    P, 1982.
Gonzales, Rodolfo Corky. *I Am Joaquin: An Epic Poem*. Denver: El Gallo
    Newspaper, 1967.
———. *Message to Aztlán: Collected Writings*. Houston: Arte Público Press,
    2003.
Hinojosa, Rolando. *Estampas del Valle y otras obras*. Berkeley: Quinto Sol,
    1973.
López, Juan Jaime. "Chilanga Banda." On *Café Tacuba, Un viaje*. DVD/CD.
    México City: Universal Music México S.A., 2005.
Rivera, Tomás. . . . *y no se lo tragó la tierra*. Berkeley: Quinto Sol Publications,
    1971.
Roys, Ralph L. *The Book of Chilam Balam of Chumayel*. Washington, DC:
    Carnegie Institution, 1933.
Tenorio-Trillo, Mauricio. *Mexico at the World's Fairs: Crafting a Modern Nation*.
    Berkeley: U of California P, 1996.
Urista, Alberto "Alurista." *Flor y canto en Aztlán*. Los Angeles: Chicano Studies
    Center, UCLA, 1971.
Valdez, Luis. "El Pensamiento Serpentino." *Early Works: Acots, Bernabé and
    Pensamiento Serpentino*. Houston: Arte Publico Press, 1990. 168–99.

8

Sacred Community, Sacred Culture

Authenticity and Modernity in Contemporary Canadian Native Writings

Richard J. Lane

The claim that Canada's First Nations have existed in the land since "time immemorial" is one of immense importance. While Westerners can understand the claim as an assertion of mythic identity and precontact history, fewer understand the claim as an assertion of modernity. That is to say, the location of an "immemorial" authentic identity does not mean that identity is located in a distant or unremembered past, which subsequently needs to be developed in a progressive manner (an evolutionary model of culture); rather, the phrase is indicative of cultural maturity and a self-present, complete, or modern culture (nonetheless, one which is open to productive change and growth). Much recent literary criticism has focused on the performativity of native culture, especially with the explosion of contemporary native drama as an expressive form, one which is deeply critical of the colonial era. However, it is important to maintain another "aspect" (although this is too feeble a word) of native modernity: that it is a sacred culture, one which is foremost community based. Often, contemporary western critics will bring postcolonial, postmodern, and/or poststructuralist paradigms to bear on native texts, and subsequently there is a "pick-and-mix" approach to which elements of indigenous culture are allowed to remain visible, or, are foregrounded; the focus on a critique of colonialism, while definitely a core strand of contemporary native texts, still maintains the "evolutionary" model.

Native writers, such as Thomas King, reject the term "postcolonial" precisely because of the way in which indigenous culture, instead of being "too early" (located in a mythic, lost past), is now in the postcolonial sense "too late" (located almost entirely *after the fact* of the impact of colonialism). Authentic native identity, following the standard postcolonial paradigm and King's critique of it, is thus *eccentric*, elsewhere, in some other time, instead of existing in "now time" (to steal Walter Benjamin's phrase). In this essay I will explore the coincidence of literary-critical models of authenticity and modernity in contemporary Canadian Native writing, exploring some theoretical aspects of Linda Griffiths' and Maria Campbell's *The Book of Jessica: A Theatrical Transformation* (1989), and the indigenous images that Kwantlen First Nations writer Joseph A. Dandurand reappropriates in *Looking into the Eyes of My Forgotten Dreams* (1998) and *Please Do Not Touch the Indians* (2004). I shall utilize a number of interpretive strategies to reexamine the temporality and spatiality of indigenous writing, to reveal a contradictory clash within the *Western* desired signs of native authenticity.

The Red Cloth

The Book of Jessica is a complex, hybrid book, written through collaboration, drawing upon Campbell's Métis and Griffiths' Canadian backgrounds. The complexity is furthered by the position of Métis heritage in Canada. Government Orders-in-Council dealing with Métis land title in the late 1800s, for example, produced a negative outcome whereby the land/money scrip on offer "meant loss of entitlement to be registered as an Indian and exclusion from the Indian Act" (Dickason 294). Land scrip could be legally sold, and due to the exigencies of Métis life at that time, the need for such sales in turn led to further disinheritance and dispossession. Maria Campbell's autobiography, *Halfbreed*, narrates personal, community, and historical journeys of repossession and recovery of Métis identity, but such a transformational process does not end with her use of one genre; rather, she extends and transforms it again with the trilogy of "trans-genre" texts called *The Book of Jessica: A Theatrical Transformation*, incorporating among other modes of writing, native theater. As Egan notes: "Theatre was a natural choice for the author of *Halfbreed* precisely because it works as live performance and blurs the boundaries between contingent reality and its narrative interpretation. . . . It provided one more way in which Campbell could extend the story she needed to tell beyond the limitations of the printed word and ensure its return to the community" (22). The theatricality of *The Book of Jessica* also creates a trans-genre contact zone where a discursive field or "third space" of transcultural communication is generated. The phrase "transcultural communication" indicates a move beyond binary thinking, where one cultural system is simply contrasted, often negatively, with its opposite; in other words, with transcultural communication there is a desire to go beyond centered, hierarchical systems of power, being, and knowledge, thinking through subjects who are instead "multiply located and presented with a set of relations to a variety of other cultural identities and therefore not fixed in any given center" (Davies 105). There is also a certain fluidity and flexibility in transcultural communication that pertain to native orality and writing. As Crispin Thurlow argues: "I . . . prefer the sense *trans*-cultural creates of moving *through* and *across* cultural systems, in whatever way they may be constituted or conceived. It allows better, I think, for the fluidity of these systems, their porous boundaries and constantly reorienting expressions, as well as the conceptual spaces that open up between traditionally defined cultural systems—the putative " 'Third Space' " of Bhabha (1994) and the borderlands of Anzaldúa (1987)—that emerge between shifting patterns of sociocultural organisation and practice."

In a theoretically related essay on "The Gendered Space of Auto/ Biographical Performance" (Lane 2006a), I note how Homi Bhabha regards an "enunciative split" as being central to expression within the transcultural third space, in other words, the subject's *enunciation* is constituted, disrupted, and made other through writing, literally the necessary shift via *différance* to the state that (for example, with postcolonial notions of ethics) is expressed with the phrase "not I." As Bhabha notes: "The implication of this enunciative split for cultural analysis that I especially want to emphasize is its temporal dimension. The splitting of the subject of enunciation destroys the logics of synchronicity and evolution which traditionally authorize the subject of cultural knowledge" (36). In "The Gendered Space of Auto/Biographical Performance" I argue that it is important to think of the third space not just as a complex interlacing of identities and a spatial mapping-out of these new formations, and not simply as something that occurs in writing (since the speech/writing opposition is here deconstructed), but also, if not primarily, as a complex temporality:

> It is often taken for granted in materialist and idealist prob-
> lematics that the value of culture as an object of study, and
> the value of any analytic activity that is considered cultural,
> lie in a capacity to produce a cross-referential, generalizable
> unity that signifies a progression or evolution of ideas-in-
> time, as well as a critical self-reflection on their premises or
> determinants. . . .
>
> The intervention of the Third Space of enunciation,
> which makes the structure of meaning and reference an ambiva-
> lent process, destroys this mirror of representation in which
> cultural knowledge is customarily revealed as an integrated,
> open, expanding code. Such an intervention quite properly
> challenges our sense of the historical identity of culture as a
> homogenizing, unifying force, authenticated by the originary
> Past, kept alive in the national tradition of the People. In other
> words, the disruptive temporality of enunciation displaces the
> narrative of the Western nation which Benedict Anderson so
> perceptively describes as being written in homogenous, serial
> time. (Bhabha 36–37)

At one level, "serial" time clashes in *The Book of Jessica*, with sacred/symbolic time, that is to say, the narrative strictures of putting together or editing the book clash with the ritual theater that is transformational and "ambivalent" in its results. Laura J. Murray focuses on the way that a three-part trade took place in the autobiographical process: Maria Campbell wanted to learn the tools of the theatrical trade, and went to Paul Thompson, a workshop theater director, "to learn his improvisatory method of creating political theatre" (91). The contract is described by Campbell as follows: "We'd do a play together—no, he couldn't teach me what he knew, but that was okay, I was never a good student. Instead, we'd exchange. I'd learn from him in 'the process,' and in return I'd give my bag of goodness knows what" (16). Griffiths, an experienced actress and improviser was then brought into the process to work closely with Campbell. Murray summarizes the remaining process:

> After a draining and conflictual collaboration, which did eventually result in two productions of the play *Jessica* (1982 and 1986), Campbell suggested that Griffiths and she write an account of their work together. In so doing, they would put Griffiths forward as herself, not in brownface, but "exposed, small and white" . . . Working from memory, notes, and tape transcripts, Griffiths prepared the final version of both the introduction and the play; the final editing took place while Campbell was running for President of the Métis Society of Saskatchewan and had no time to participate. (92)

Murray argues convincingly that the "triangular" relationship between Campbell, Thompson, and Griffiths is downplayed by the book and by the majority of its critics. Yet there may be a good reason for this downplaying, since the actual collaboration between Campbell and Griffiths is reflected in the dialogic nature of the text, and such a dialogism is in itself massively disruptive of "the mirror of representation," to use Bhabha's phrase. I am focusing on form—the shape of the contract, the dialogic trans-genre text, and collaborative writing—because it reveals a transcultural disruption of time, with the shift into sacred time. Focus on *The Book of Jessica* as postcolonial critique, for all of its good intentions, may in fact continue to locate the entire experience, to quote Bhabha again, as once more being part of "the narrative of the Western nation . . . written in homogenous, serial time" (37). As Lorraine York asks: "Why is it that the criticism of *The Book of Jessica* seems to replicate the property dispute that lies at the heart of that text: the theft of stories by white artists?" (174). York in no way downplays or disregards the importance of the postcolonial reception of *The Book of Jessica*, but her question is important in focusing on the open-ended dialogism at work in the text. Two statements by York are germane: "It may be more accurate to say that the text engages the oppositional and thus works toward a mutual recognition that is, I think, posited as a horizon but never achieved" (177), and, "Campbell . . . locates 'property' as an unstable site of ethical meaning for her, a site that is arguably associated with her sometimes uneasy negotiation of 'white' and 'Indian' in her Métis subjectivity" (179).

Rather than locate "authentic" identity as eccentric, what *The Book of Jessica* reveals is the encounter of authentic identity as always taking place in the face-to-face; it is writing that is deliberately mimetic of that encounter, which is why York's insights are so valuable. The (again deliberately) vague and conflicting descriptions given by Campbell and Griffiths, concerning what the play *Jessica* is even supposed to be about, engage in this "instability" of "property," while replacing the critical drive for certainty and closure with the face-to-face encounter. Griffiths' statement that "Paul and Maria wanted the project to deal directly with the spiritual world" (16) is countered with Maria's question, "What is she talking about anyway?" and her statement that "This was not supposed to be a play about spiritual worlds, it was supposed to be a play about a woman struggling with two cultures, and how she got them balanced; because when she leaned into one, a part of her got lost, so she had to lean into the other one and try to understand and find a balance" (17). In the dialogism of the text—the shuffling back and forth of contradictory desires, dreams, rebuttals, and disavowals, among many other emotions and intellectual strategies—not only is the historical background revealed, but also the engagement with history via the symbolic space of text and performance. That is to say, a critical understanding that merely perceives Griffith's misreadings or appropriations as being countered by Campbell's revelation of native truth ignores the two-way trading that takes place, and what Campbell wants to achieve through her engagement with Griffiths. The position consistently offered by Campbell is that of her hybrid identity: it is one that means that the production of the play *Jessica* and the engagement with Thompson and Griffiths has to be transformed once again with the production of *The Book of Jessica*, and that further, the latter does not become a final, but rather a provisional, meta-text.

Levinas writes that "in order that I be able to see things in themselves, that is, represent them to myself, refuse both enjoyment and possession, I must know how *to give* what I possess" (171). One of the most critically explored sections of *The Book of Jessica* is that of "The Red Cloth," where Campbell discusses her pain, when she was a child, at giving away her most precious possession (the red cloth) at a Sun Dance: "My grandmother waited until I finished crying and said, 'The give-away should hurt, that's your sacrifice' " (110). Griffiths responds by saying that *Jessica* is her give-away. Murray argues that there are two conceptions of gift-giving culture at work here; the first is the native conception, where gift-giving involves sacred "flow" and the second is that of a Western feminine, non-native, non-Métis economy (102–03).

From a postcolonial perspective, *Jessica* is not owned by anyone; from a capitalist perspective, it is "value-added" by Griffiths' investment in it, and thus it can be "offered back" to Campbell as a potential campaign fundraising contribution. Murray notes the discrepancy between such a capitalist notion, and that of an entirely different indigenous gift-giving, which is "the way Native societies originally bound themselves to each other and to the land. Within such societies, gift-giving was economic exchange, but also exchange or flow of the sacred" (103). Bizarrely, the examples given by Murray are Maori, drawn from the anthropological works of Marcel Mauss, but Murray does raise a key point: that there is an "obligation" attached to a gift in indigenous societies that transcends that of the capitalist notion of return, and the trading bond of Western reciprocal friendship, an obligation that is one of being held within spiritual power.

Campbell's injunction to "not tell," but "tell," that occurs in the text suggests that her desire for a mediating role within Métis culture functions as one that needs to find a new language, one which can repudiate the appropriative colonial narratives. Paradoxically, Campbell and Griffiths replay or perform the trust/betrayal chiasmus (don't tell, but you must tell . . . don't tell, but you must tell . . . etc.) as a way of creating this new language, one that is open-ended, open to the power of indigenous gift-giving, that is also a transformational experience. If such an experience has taken place, then, again paradoxically, Griffiths does have power over Campbell, but this time, it is not the "colonialist" power of appropriation or stealing. What I am suggesting is that *The Book of Jessica* is always a *doubled* text: it simultaneously plays or performs *two* overarching narratives: one narrative is that of Griffiths' colonial appropriation of Campbell's identity and stories; the other narrative is Campbell and Griffith's transformational journey, away from appropriation and into a gift-based economy of knowledge, spiritual power, and friendship (with all the tensions still in place). Because these two narratives are simultaneously overlaid, the text is extremely elusive and slippery: at any one point in the text the signs of appropriation, for example, are also the signs of having learned the lessons that Campbell is teaching Griffiths. The "give-away" concept is appropriated (as Hoy and Andrews argue), but it is also a lesson that has been learned: that gifts have spiritual power. Which is it to be?

In *The Book of Jessica*, both readings are available, the latter suggesting that Griffiths has entered, to whatever degree, the sacred space of Campbell's understanding and experience of authentic—hybrid, modern Métis existence, and the former screaming at the reader that this is impossible, dangerous, and simply a repetition of the acts of colonialism. In this doubled performance, Griffiths' revealing of ceremonial secrets, for example, is thus both a violation of trust and a cultural performance "directed to multi-ethnic audiences," to use Susan Roy's phrase (62). As Roy argues: "While much scholarship emphasizes how intercultural events serve the interests of dominant society, commentators should not lose sight of the fact that Aboriginal peoples autonomously 'confer meaning on the circumstances that confront them' " (62). In other words, Griffiths' mimetic reenactment of her spiritual experience performs both an unauthorized colonialist revealing and a "framed," authorized encounter with indigenous spiritual forces; the *staging* of *The Book of Jessica* is precisely the two-way conferring of meaning. But this is still to ignore the ways in which the coincidence of claims concerning native authenticity and modernity in the text leads to a reworking of form: Griffiths and Campbell do not just create a doubled text, they also *ritualize* the Western genres of autobiography, meta-textual commentary or interpretation, and drama; in other words, they take the linear, progressive time and the appropriative space of Western master narratives, and they transform them into symbolic time/space. "I thought it was over," says Griffiths (13), but of course it is never "over," since the symbolic charge of *The Book of Jessica* always overrides the conceptual attempts at closure and commodification.

Indigenous Images

Indigenous images have long been created and then commodified by Western settler-invader cultures. One of the most bizarre images to be given three-dimensional form is the "cigar store" wooden Indian. Daniel Francis notes that this image "refers to the association between Native North Americans and tobacco, a product which originated in the New World" (85). He also argues that the image is coded with negative and positive stereotypes: "On the negative side, the wooden-Indian . . . suggests a lack of emotional range, a failure of feeling. . . . On the positive side, this stereotype says that Indians do not wear their hearts on their sleeves; they do not reveal their emotions capriciously" (85–86). Of course, the so-called "positive" stereotype is also massively reductive and part of a romantic view of so-called "primitive peoples": ". . . inside we are convinced that they contain all the world's wisdom. Once again, the imaginary Indian is almost anything Whites want it to be" (Francis 86). Why attempt to make sense of a ridiculous, outmoded stereotypical image? Because in the world of commodity culture, certain image tropes continue to have vitality, and function as signs of Western desire: for example, in the search for the "exotic" in Western tourism to Canada. Canadians may not have noticed these images for quite some time now, but they are in fact still present, as Diana Brydon points out:

> This figure stands at the entrance to the large grocery store where I sometimes do my shopping. Rushing in and out, I never saw him until he was pointed out to me. A brief survey of my students revealed the same thing. All had shopped at this store; none had noticed this stereotypical "wooden Indian." Indeed, when they encountered the parody of the "cigar store Indian" in Monique Mojica's *Princess Pocahontas and the Blue Spots*, these students had to ask me what a "Cigar Store Squaw" was. (50)

Once again, the double nature of the image is noticed and analyzed, in this case in relation to Graham Huggan's work on the "post-colonial exotic": "the wooden Indian can carry a double message," notes Huggan, since it can both cater "to white colonialist sensibilities" (Huggan 263), but "it may also carry the potential, when remobilized in other contexts, as it is in Mojica's play and on the cover of Drew Hayden Taylor's book, *Further Adventures of a Blue-Eyed Ojibway: Funny, You Don't Look Like One Two*, to turn such stereotypes back against the system that has produced them" (Brydon 51). I call these images "image tropes" because of the way in which they are countercultural and counter-discursive, not just functioning as synecdoches (where the stereotypical image is a part that stands in for the stereotyped whole), but also as recoding devices. And what is recoded?

The answer, in Joseph Dandurand's case, is the power of the invader-settler/tourist *visioning* in the first place. Dandurand questions the invader-settler or tourist's ability to create authentic images of native culture. Doubling with a difference occurs in his play *Please Do Not*

Touch the Indians: there are two "cigar store" or "wooden Indians" who are the protagonists: "Centre stage there is a wooden bench and sitting on the bench are two wooden Indians. Their clothing is simple and not quite traditional but more of a Hollywood taste" (7). "Wooden Indian Woman," as she is called in the play, is holding flowers that have been placed in her hand; "Wooden Indian Man" has his eyes closed, and he wears a sign that hangs from his neck that says *Please Do Not Touch the Indians*" (7). Throughout the play, both "wooden Indians" cheekily and playfully subvert a series of tourists who are attempting to photograph them. Slowly both protagonists come alive, sharing their stories and visions, at first in monologue, but eventually in a powerful and touching dialogue.

The individual memories and visions of an entire ensemble of characters—the protagonists, Sister Coyote, Brother Raven, and Mister Wolf—at first appear to be at cross-purposes, the audience not entirely aware, beyond intimate glimpses, of the significance of these revealed stories. After a sequence of French, English, and German tourists attempting to photograph the protagonists, a shift occurs in the play as a "Mountie" sets up a camera; the ensemble of indigenous characters are all now frozen and they subvert the photograph *en masse*. There is a qualitative shift in the reading of the play at this point, since the intervention of an RCMP officer undertaking photography signifies not just the gaze of the tourist, but also the juridical intervention in, and policing of, native lives, where the "image of the Indian" becomes one that represents criminality and deviance from the colonial norm. Later in the play, the tourist is dressed in a military outfit: "Tourist enters now dressed in a blue U.S. Cavalry uniform. He is holding freshly taken scalps, his old camera and tripod. He places the scalps in the hands of Wooden Man and Wooden Woman, goes and takes their picture" (42). The transformation of the tourist into one of the participants in the Amerindian colonial wars creates a historical backdrop, through which the indigenous ensemble now live their lives; the tourist further becomes a movie director, a sexually abusive priest, and a present-day tourist who now carries the overdetermined coding of all of these identities. The complexities of the transhistorical yet still highly personal memories and visions that the indigenous ensemble recount, as well as their transformations throughout the play, are too complex to go into detail here. What is of immediate concern is the way in which the play as a whole performs the subversion of, and resistance to, externally imposed vision, symbolized through the reactions to the act of photography (and in the case of the priest, his painting at an easel). The more the action of freezing aboriginal peoples into a static image is *resisted*, the more Wooden Woman and Man come alive. This simple correlation, however, leads not to catharsis, but rather, the shocking journey in the play to suicide.

What Dandurand has achieved in *Please Do Not Touch the Indians*, among many other things, is to reveal the multiple layers of the "image of the Indian" as represented by the image trope of the "wooden Indian": he shows how the constructed image/object, the wooden or plastic sculpture itself, is a simulacrum, which then stands in for the real (however we interpret or understand the latter); in the process of being photographed, the image trope becomes a simulacrum of a simulacrum. In other words, the photographed image is hyperreal, functioning at the level of pure semiosis. As Jean Baudrillard says, such "a sign attempts to mislead: it permits itself to appear as totality, to efface the traces of its abstract transcendence, and parades about as the reality principle of meaning" (162). *Please Do Not Touch the Indians*, at one level, resists the shift to the third level of simulation, recoding the simulacrum with a new reality, a new set of native stories, which are also the old stories. Once more, authenticity is the coincidence of native characters who have existed since time immemorial, with that of contemporary native reworkings and understandings of native history. While the play is far more powerful, disturbing, and moving than this brief account intimates, the underlying resistance to the hyperreal is an important factor in controlling image tropes from a native perspective.

In a previous work by Dandurand, *Looking into the Eyes of My Forgotten Dreams*, anthropological photographic images are physically incorporated via juxtaposition with Dandurand's poems. Focusing briefly on one poem, called "Fort Langley," the photograph that Dandurand places into the text to create a montage is by Frederick Dally, and it is titled "Indians, Fraser River circa 1868." The poem reads:

Fort Langley

you can see the fort from where I live.
wooden walls,
trees,
desperate voices.
they call to me,

come on over,
come on over,
come on.
shut up,
I say.
shut up and stay over there.
used to drink at their bar,
used to sip whiskey,
used to fight,
used to be blind from it all.
now
I stare at their walls.
wooden walls.
thick with history.
many men and women never made it home.
they found them trying to climb over the walls.
whiskey bottles broken and empty roll down to the
river,
laceless shoes sit silent as if waiting for someone else,
a picture of someone's mother blows away and over the
walls,
the gate is closed.
the fort.
over that way.
over past the mass grave.
smallpox.
you ever seen smallpox?
pretty ugly.
not as pretty
as wooden walls. (6–7)

The image, one of the many that Dandurand found while browsing
in his local library at Fort Langley, British Columbia, is also one of
a group that he recodes and reclaims. The image is cropped, which is
understandable, given Frederick Dally's caption, handwritten by Dally
directly onto the photograph: "Indians shamming to be at prayer for the
sake of photography. At the priests request all the Indians kneel down
and assume an attitude of devotion. Amen." The word "shamming" is

intriguing, as it suggests a negative performativity, but also creates a spurious homonymic etymology that produces a link with "shaman."

Through image cropping and juxtaposition, Dandurand becomes the "shaman" and recodes the "sham": instead of indigenous peoples performing a mode of belief that was imposed upon them by colonialism, *the image is now seen as a "sham" imposed by Dally*. Instead of indigenous peoples looking foolish in this piece of colonial theater, Dandurand creates a pathos in his juxtaposition of photograph and poetic text. The recoding creates a dialectical image, a "now of recognizability" (see Lane 2005) whereby images are subtracted from "sham" narratives of progression or evolution, and exposed instead to a different configuration that has an explosive potential. Why explosive? Because dialectical images simultaneously function as memorial aesthetics and a rupture in time: after a great deal of excellent work has been done by Western researchers cataloguing, critiquing, and rejecting inauthentic images of indigenous peoples (such as the staged work of Curtis), indigenous peoples in the United States and Canada are reappropriating those very same images and giving them a new value, inserting them into a new context, with *recoded memorial significance*. This is a radical gesture of re-recognition and a temporal intervention: "Look, there is my grandfather" or "Look, there is my grandmother"; or "Look, there is my ancestor wearing ceremonial dress that I would otherwise have not seen."

Such statements go against everything that the Western academy has recently taught itself and generate what Jean François Lyotard has called "a *différend*"; non-indigenous academics want to condemn "sham" colonialist images while respecting at the same time the right of indigenous peoples to assert critical and creative autonomy. Holding both of these contradictory positions together is a *différend*, or, the recognition in law that both sides here have a legitimate claim. From either side of the issue, the *différend* does not exist; but juxtaposed, as in a montage, the *différend* does exist, with powerful repercussions. In *Looking into the Eyes of My Forgotten Dreams*, the haunting poems about the residential school experience for Kwantlen First Peoples also reveal the intersection of the homely and the unhomely (or uncanny): the residential school, a place of care, was of course also a place of abuse; those in charge, who had the legal status of guardians or parents, also engaged in a project of cultural genocide. Dandurand's dialectical images reject mainstream Canadian narratives of humanistic progress, and instead return to specific architectonic sites and imagistic sights for reasons of critical, historical, and political intervention.

Conclusion and Transformation

In this essay I have concentrated on postcolonial and semiotic readings of the texts, suggesting that Campbell and Griffiths *ritualize* the Western genres of autobiography, meta-textual commentary or interpretation, and drama, and Dandurand fundamentally *questions* the invader-settler or tourist's ability to create authentic images of native culture. All three authors create not just aesthetically and intellectually complex texts, but texts that generate a level of discomfort, either in terms of content or interpretation (for example, mimetically reenacting the "arguments" embedded in *The Book of Jessica*). Jacqueline Rose, in another context, suggests that such a discomfort may be an effect of "the way universality as a concept starts to break up under scrutiny" (412; Lane 2006b). Colonial and postcolonial notions of authenticity both begin to "break up" with the texts in question, that is to say, with the transformation of modernity into sacred, and symbolic, time and space.

Works Cited

Andrews, Jennifer. "Framing *The Book of Jessica*: Transformation and the Collaborative Process in Canadian Theatre." *English Studies in Canada* 22.3 (September 1996): 297–313.

Baudrillard, Jean. *For a Critique of the Political Economy of the Sign*. Trans. Charles Levin. St. Louis: Telos, 1981.

Bhabha, Homi K. *The Location of Culture*. London and New York: Routledge, 1994.

Brydon, Diana. "Canada and Postcolonialism: Questions, Inventories, and Futures." *Is Canada Postcolonial? Unsettling Canadian Literature*. Ed. Laura Moss. Waterloo, Ontario: Wilfrid Laurier Press, 2003. 49–77.

Dandurand, Joseph. *Looking into the Eyes of My Forgotten Dreams*. Wiarton, Ontario: Kegedonce Press, 1998.

———. *Please Do Not Touch the Indians*. Candler, NC: Renegade Planets Publishing, 2004.

Davies, Carole Boyce. "Beyond Unicentricity: Transcultural Black Presences." *Research in African Literatures* 30.2 (Summer 1999): 96–109.

Dickason, Olive Patricia. *Canada's First Nations: A History of Founding Peoples from Earliest Times*. Don Mills, Ontario: Oxford UP, 2002.

Egan, Susanna. "*The Book of Jessica*: The Healing Circle of a Woman's Autobiography." *Canadian Literature* 144 (Spring 1995): 10–26.

Francis, Daniel. *The Imaginary Indian: The Image of the Indian in Canadian Culture*. Vancouver, BC: Arsenal Pulp Press, 1993.

Griffith, Linda, and Maria Campbell. *The Book of Jessica: A Theatrical Transformation*. Toronto: Coach House, 1989.

Hoy, Helen. " 'When You Admit You're A Thief, Then You Can Be Honorable': Native/Non-Native Collaboration in 'The Book of Jessica.' " *Canadian Literature* 136 (Spring 1993): 24–39.

Huggan, Graham. *The Post-Colonial Exotic: Marketing the Margins*. London and New York: Routledge, 2001.

King, Thomas. "Godzilla vs. Post-Colonial." *New Contexts of Canadian Criticism*. Ed. Ajay Heble, Donna Palmateer Pennee, and J. R. (Tim) Struthers. Peterborough, Ontario: Broadview, 1997. 241–48.

Lane, Richard J. *Reading Walter Benjamin: Writing Through the Catastrophe*. Manchester and New York: Manchester UP, 2005.

———. "The Gendered Space of Auto/Biographical Performance: Samuel Beckett and Hans Bellmer." *Theatre and Autobiography: Essays on the Theory and Practice of Writing and Performing Lives*. Ed. Sherrill Grace and Jerry Wasserman. Vancouver: Talon Books, 2006a. 72–88.

———. *The Postcolonial Novel*. Cambridge: Polity, 2006b.

Levinas, Emmanuel. *Totality and Infinity: An Essay on Exteriority*. Trans. Alphonso Lingis. Pittsburgh: Duquesne UP, 1998.

Lyotard, Jean-François. *The Differend: Phrases in Dispute*. Trans. Georges Van Den Abbeele. Manchester and New York: Manchester UP, 1988.

Murray, Laura J. "Economies of Experience in *The Book of Jessica*." *Tulsa Studies in Women's Literature* 18.1 (Spring 1999): 91–111.

Rose, Jacqueline. "On the 'Universality' of Madness: Bessie Head's *A Question of Power*." *Critical Inquiry* 20 (Spring 1994): 401–18.

Roy, Susan. "Performing Musqueam Culture and History at British Columbia's 1966 Centennial Celebrations." *BC Studies* 135 (Autumn 2002): 55–90.

Thurlow, Crispin. "Transcultural communication: a treatise on *trans*." http://faculty.washington.edu/thurlow/research/transculturalcommunication.html

York, Lorraine. *Rethinking Women's Collaborative Writing*. Toronto: U of Toronto P, 2002.

Postindian Reflections

Chickens and Piranha, Casinos, and Sovereignty

Gerald Vizenor and A. Robert Lee

A. ROBERT LEE: Let me lead into this latest Vizenor-Lee exchange, an epilogue of sorts to our *Postindian Conversations* (1999), with an old, dare one say possibly even less than true, anecdote (told to me first by a New Englander about his home state). A local country preacher, heir to hellfire Puritanism, found himself moved to speak to his male parishioners, farm people for the most part, about certain "practices" that had come to his attention to do with farm animals. Appealing to them as dutiful churchgoers, and aware that, well, things do happen "on the farm," he nonetheless invoked the Bible as to unnatural man-beast conjunctions. Rumor had reached him of activity with cows (there was a terrible silence). Furthermore the word was that there had been congress with pigs and sheep (more silence). "Why," he continued, "some of you have even been having congress with chickens." At which there was a near collective response, at once offended and deeply envious, "Chickens?"

Few, save the odd trickster Minnesotan, have hitherto fully recognized the connection between chickens and piranha. Fowl to fin, as it were. But Gerald wants to open with a few words about piranha.

Gerald Vizenor does a few sign language signals, in response to this introduction.

167

GERALD VIZENOR: I've been trying, since the first day I met Robert, to find some way to anticipate his irony—and dominate him. And I thought I had just the person, a year ago, in Santa Fe: the Chief Justice of the New Mexico State Supreme Court was one of the finest storiers I'd ever met—a different kind of teller than Robert. He had stories committed to memory with all kinds of variations to suit any occasion, like chickens. And he also had a powerful, and dominant, and interesting delivery. And I thought, this is going to be a great contest . . . to see who survives. We carefully placed the justice at one end of the table, with gin in hand; and at the other end of the table, Robert Lee, with two gins in hand. The judge started with his story, and Robert tried to butt in with his masterly ironic play. The words never touched the judge. Robert was so desperate, after two or three ironic intrusions, that he pretty much gave up, and therefore started a conversation on the side with an FBI agent—he was so desperate—a retired FBI agent! He turned to the agent for counsel. He then looks up and finds just the right moment, and makes a comment about vegetarian piranha. It was just a long shot—he lobbed that out there, and the words circled around the judge. The image of vegetarian piranha did not land at first. But then the judge stopped and frowned and turned around to Lee and asked: "What the fuck did you say?" And I knew Robert had ended the contest, defeated the judge and his stories with vegetarian piranha. He went on a long lecture about vegetarian piranha and chickens, and the judge almost died by laughter that night, he was so into it.

ARL: Fowl to fin. Chicken to piranha. That story, too, might, er, almost be true. Iguanas were going to come next but, given the actual focus of this book, we thought it more appropriate to highlight a few of the issues we visited on the world in *Postindian Conversations*. So, at the cost of no small amount of iguana scholarship, we *are* going to talk about some of the Native cultural landscape. And to open—Casinos. Casino facts and figures. Casino semantics. What, Gerald, do you see as the impact of this gaming, slots and tables, reservation economies, sovereignty?

GV: This is the serious part. Let me make a declaration, provocatively. Casinos are likely the end of Indian, but not Native, sovereignty. The end of Indian sovereignty, that is the obscure sentiments of Western sovereignty, borders, boundaries, and rights, but not the end of Native sovereignty, or the sense of transmotion and a visionary presence. The Native sense of sovereignty is the sense of motion, mobility, not a boundary condition. Casinos have raised a lot of money, of course, more than twenty million dollars last year, at more than a hundred casinos. And probably much less than a third of this money finds its way directly to Natives and Native communities. Most of the money goes to management, paying off investors, and also mortgages for construction. The problems that arise from this are the obvious ones—luring people into gambling when the odds are about 95 percent against them and luring them into losing money. But I should say also that the majority of gamblers are not Native American Indians. Robert and I share a good lunch story in the monstrous casino on the White Earth Reservation. We went there for lunch, Robert, his wife Pepa, my wife Laura. And because it is the best food in a hundred miles in any direction, we had to stand in line. While we were in line, a group of people behind us were speaking a language we couldn't quite recognize. So Robert disappears, approaches the speakers, tries introductions in a half dozen different languages (Robert is the last British monarch of irony, and is quite desperate to play at double meaning in any language), and discovers the language is Tagalog of the Philippines. This came as a great surprise on the White Earth Reservation in remote northwestern Minnesota. There, in the woodlands, in a lunch line at an obscure casino, a group of Tagalog speakers from the Philippines. Am I in a postmodern world, or what? Robert chats and teases the group who are laborers brought from the Philippines to nearby Winnipeg, Canada. The Canadians want to accommodate their visiting workers, so they arrange bus tours to casinos because, apparently, they believe certain people are born to gambling. Bussed in for a weekend, across the international border, they gamble away their Canadian money. They return to work, and then come back again the next weekend to lose money at a reservation casino.

ARL: Not quite what Marxists mean when they speak of "an exchange economy"?

GV: A sick business, and yet there is some comedy in the rush to casinos. The money is enormous, but not much of the money gets to ordinary people in terms of direct payments. There are nonetheless great examples of generosity—for instance, in Connecticut, the Pequot Casino, one of the largest in the country, does give enormous payments, paid off every debt, and built a cultural museum. Many communities near casinos are not happy about the traffic, crime, and narcotics. As the reservation has no responsibility toward any surrounding municipality or community, the roads, bridges, municipal, and police services have to be paid for by nearby residents. Also, because Natives have been buying a lot of land, real estate prices have risen. This has changed completely the pleasant, rural values of the community.

ARL: There has also been a slew of lawsuits has there not?

GV: Indeed. Many of them turn on questions of sovereignty. Let me briefly describe the law that made all this possible, for all these casinos to flourish, and consequently, the lawsuits. The Indian Gaming Regulatory Act was passed in 1988, the first federal law to regulate casinos on treaty land. The reason there is such a law is that Indians had just started opening casinos, and many states complained that trust land is exempt from state taxation. Indeed, many states passed laws to regulate or forbid casino-style gambling. What's the difference in gambling styles? Bingo and lotto are not casino games, because the money invested in bingo games, for instance, goes into the pot to pay off the expenses of the operation, and the rest of the money is given away to winners. Casino-style gambling (slot machines and other games) set the odds of winning against the players. Most states had laws against this, so when Indian casinos opened, a lot of friction and legal challenges arose. Hence, Congress passed a law named the Indian Gaming Regulatory Act, which had three provisions:

> Indians can practice any traditional games of chance.
> Any tribe can organize bingo or lotto games. No permission is needed, but the state government must be notified of the games.
> The third style, the casino style, where you bet against the house, or manipulated games of chance, requires a compact or negotiated agreement with the respective state government.

ARL: What, in this light, about relationships between Native communities and each state where casinos operate?

GV: Many states have very strict gambling laws. Arizona proscribed casino gambling, and California had a constitutional amendment against gambling with the hope of fighting off corruption. California, however, changed the amendment by referendum. Native groups opened casinos and challenged the law, and citizens voted to allow casino gambling. Arizona did not change the law, but allowed Indian casinos to operate for a few years. Natives started with bingo, moved to slot machines and black jack. Indeed, the politics were such that Arizona officials did not want to arrest Natives. Here is the sympathetic image of Natives trying to make a living, after living in such poverty, after being victims for five hundred years; a powerful sentiment. No state government wanted to arrest anyone. Arizona did obligate Federal marshals to close down casinos, and they tried but were not successful. So, law enforcement backed away and the state tried once again to negotiate. Arizona probably has the strongest laws against gambling, any gambling. The state permits municipal gambling but did not want Indians going into the casino business. Minnesota, Wisconsin, Michigan, and many other states have actively negotiated compacts or agreements, according to federal law, that provides for a percentage of gaming profits to the state. Ten percent, and in some states twenty percent, of casino profits becomes a significant source of income, a substitute for increased state taxes. Arizona, on the other hand, negotiated a short-term agreement to avoid a political crisis. California Indians had already made so much money in non-compact casino gambling that they invested almost a hundred million dollars in a campaign to persuade the voters to change the Constitution of California. The state referendum passed, now the state is in a difficult position to increase the percentage of the contracts to avoid the political risk of raising taxes. Florida refused to negotiate a casino compact with the Seminoles. Federal law provides that states must reach an agreement for Indians to open casinos. Florida refused to negotiate. So the Seminoles sued Florida and the case was appealed to the United States Supreme Court. The Court decided in favor of Florida based on the principle of the right of states in the Constitution. The federal government does not have the authority, based on the Constitution, to order the state to negotiate with anyone. This is an example of how complicated the issue of Indian casinos has become, and thus each challenge raises new questions about Indian sovereignty.

ARL: What, in this context, does sovereignty mean?

GV: The concept of sovereignty is not absolute, and is not easily understood because the word is used in at least two general contexts. The first is the concept and history of Western sovereignty, and the second is a sense of Native visionary sovereignty. Indian sovereignty is ironic, forgive me for this disabuse, because boundary sovereignty was negotiated by treaties and endorsed by the United States Congress. Congress has plenary power, absolute power, to protect or terminate treaty sovereignty. Congress created a sense of sovereignty by treaties, but it should be referred to as limited sovereignty. And, as the negative criticism grows over Indian casinos Congress could vote to end the concept of treaty sovereignty. Federal policies have never been stable, and there is no reason to believe that Indians have absolute sovereignty in a constitutional democracy. Many times in the past century federal policies have been reversed to suit the ideology of the time.

ARL: So how do you see the "public" image of Natives evolving?

GV: The romantic sympathy is changing and not many natives are writing about the change brought about by casinos. Most news stories about Natives today are about casino politics, and related issues of sovereignty. The negative sentiments seem to increase because of casinos. In the past, there was a romantic manifest that inspired foundations, public funding sources, to support Native programs by sympathy, if for no other reason. Natives were favored because they had been excluded for so long, were encouraged to apply for philanthropic grants; there was a sympathy factor and a romantic response that was constructive, and productive, at the time. A good motivating force that many Natives benefitted from, learned to manipulate the metaphors of, and for good causes, such as medical services, education, and other essential support and assistance—not just funding to produce literary concepts.

ARL: Politics enters with a certain vengeance and as you and others have pointed out, the president in modern times who has perhaps been the most sympathetic to the Native cause, of all people, was Richard Nixon. Hard to think that Nixon had that disposition, but in the last forty, fifty years, from the sixties forward, we've seen a succession of "Indian politics" (the quotes around the phrase essential)—at federal, state, and local level. But one kind of politics that still persists is that of Russell Means and the movers and shakers of AIM. Can we take another estimation of what AIM is, isn't, what it has or hasn't achieved, and on whose behalf it's acting—not to mention in this latter respect the issue of electedness and un-electedness. Gerald, you've been writing about the American Indian Movement from your early Minnesota journalism through to *Manifest Manners, Fugitive Poses,* and well beyond. Anyone who knows the book [*Manifest Manners*] will recall its cover portrait of Russell Means by Andy Warhol of that gay blond wig. Who better, in a sense, to have recognized the artifice, the sheer constructedness, of "the Indian"? Certainly Means himself looks up for the part, a Native playing Indian—sober demeanor, braided, choker, eyes seemingly full of pensiveness, stately. How do you interpret this profile?

GV: I must respond to this with a story, of course. About ten or fifteen years ago, there was an encampment protesting the government's insistence that tribes give up their claims to the Black Hills. Russell Means was sort of the de facto significant figure there (wherever there is a large group of Natives, he would be there, claiming the stage and leadership). First, you need to know that back in Germany, a group of dedicated simulators, pretentious members of the Oglala Lakota Indian Club in Germany. The German Oglala Lakota club decided to attend the encampment in South Dakota. They had a lot of experts to teach them about the fixed context of Oglala culture, and how to perform in this absolute concept of culture. They had absolutely magnificent, beautifully polished tepee poles, hides that were seamless, flawless, everything made with real bones, not plastic. They had decided after many years of vacations to play Indian, well, to spend their summer among the real Oglala Lakota in South Dakota. So they did just that. They traveled with their tepee poles across the ocean. Old World Indian fantasies return to a new Indian World. The German Oglala pitched their perfect tepees right in the middle of the political encampment in the Black Hills. The encampment was a demand for treaty rights and the return of stolen land, most notably the Black Hills. Along with the actual Lakota were gay, spirited nudists, and ecstatic supporters from around the world. The Indians were outnumbered by the lively partisans who supported the great cause of treaty rights. The Germans, in the center of this marvelous circus, in their perfect tepees, were apparently offended by the spectacle. They packed up in less than three days and returned to Germany. They decided it was better be "real" Indians back home in Germany. Several German Lakota were interviewed by a National Public Radio reporter about the event. When asked why they were leaving, the German Indians replied: We're leaving because these are not real Indians. And it was true. Most of them weren't, even if there were many Lakota people at the encampment. The Germans were asked: What do you mean? And they said: Well, the Indians here live in canvas tents, and they use briquettes, gas fired stoves, and Coleman lanterns. These are not traditional Indians, said the Germans. A reporter asked Russell Means about the critical comments of the Germans. Means acknowledged that it was too bad they left, according to the radio reporter, and he challenged the Germans to come back in a few years. Means apparently responded with unintended irony. We are making progress! Yes, progress, progress into the past?

ARL: And the American Indian Movement leadership now?

GV: Many of the early American Indian Movement leaders were felons, and not just literary criminals. They served sentences in prison for crimes against people, which has nothing to do with the romantic crimes against property. They were convicted as felons and served time in federal and state prisons. And the irony is that most of them came to their sense of Indian identity through special state programs in prisons. The programs delivered instruction to the inmates about the culture and religion of Native American Indians. They had a lot of free time to practice religious ceremonies, and by the time they got out of prison they were inspired and transformed by the experience. And, the militants seemed to walk out of photographs by Edward Curtis. Dennis Banks was different. He came out of prison and decided to wear a summer suit and tie before he converted to outfits in photographs. I think he had a book of Curtis photographs. Some Natives teased him about that: Where is this outfit from? The mixedblood trapper? These early militant leaders were convicted felons. I am offended by the liberal sentiments and stupidity of some people who celebrate criminals as leaders. The cynicism is radically offensive to common sensibilities, cultural values, and manners. Many Natives were troubled by the huge amount of federal and foundation money that was given to these felons, as if they were elected tribal leaders. They assume authority and were never elected to represent anyone on reservations, or anywhere else. The money probably came from shame and guilt for the romance and adventure of the radical cause, and because of a Jesse James kind of mentality. They were outlaws and without even asking for it, they were given money. Some people actually delivered money to them. They raised hundreds of thousands of dollars without even a job application.

ARL: What do you make of Russell Means's recent declaration of independence from the United States and his proposed Republic of Lakota?

GR: Natives are forever distracted by inventions, and by cultural and national simulations. Russell Means is a tricky militant poser, his tease of traditional manners is forceful and persuasive. The Indian spectacles are dubious, even comical and ironic, and he is a habitual source of news reports. The invention of a nation, however, is a melodramatic farce. Means has been a master of simulations, and he would no doubt be the absolute master of his own new nation, the Republic of Lakotah. How would he determine citizenship, provide medical care, education, negotiate trade and treaties, create an economic system, and control the borders of his burlesque nation?

ARL: Notice of a burlesque nation is a natural point to shift to a larger subject. How does this relate to reservation money issues, land, and sovereignty?

GV: The White Earth, Leech Lake, and other reservations in Minnesota, for instance, were created by treaty as removal reservations. That is, the federal government removed Natives from vast areas and located them on a new treaty reservation. Later the communal land according to the treaty boundaries was divided into allotments. Most of these individual allotments have been privately sold or foreclosed by the state, leaving only a fraction of the original reservation treaty boundaries. Over the years, what's actually left of treaty land, collective and individual, because of the failed allotment program, is only about ten percent. The percentage varies from reservation to reservation. The purpose of the allotment program was assimilation, the primary policy of the federal government. Nevertheless, federal law defined the treaty boundaries and even though non-Indians may own treaty land, they are obligated to comply with tribal rights within the treaty boundary. The federal government was the first to violate the treaties by the grant of huge sections of land for missionary and educational purposes. Government agents gave the land to mission groups, and in particular to the Episcopal Church. They gave away a square mile section of the land—the most beautiful part of the reservation, including an island on Cass Lake, which is located on the Leech Lake Reservation. The Episcopal Church had not used the land as an active mission for many years. Instead, the church built a resort. Later, they probably felt guilty about owning treaty land on the reservation. The Episcopal Church, by an act of supreme irony, granted the American Indian Movement the use of the resort camp for an armed resistance on the Leech Lake Reservation. AIM declared they were on the reservation to restore Indian rights. What they had in mind countered a federal lawsuit that the Leech Lake Reservation had already filed against the federal government, claiming that the state had no jurisdiction to enforce game and fish laws. They won the lawsuit, and, while specific issues were negotiated by the state and reservation government, and elected government, AIM leaders decided to muscle in with firearms and such things, to turn the decision around, as if militant intervention would restore reservation treaty rights. I was living in the area at the time, and all these urban Indians arrived on the reservation with a single message: Kill the white fishermen! Reclaim our rights. The militant recreation of the reservation was indirectly supported by the Episcopal Church. The church provided cabins, lakeshore property,

islands, canoes, and the huge kitchen at the resort. And it was on treaty land. The scene was treaty land by betrayal, reservation treaty land
manipulated by a monotheistic institution and the federal government.
So these young people arrived in the early 1970s with new firearms and
a marginal view of reservation politics. The urban road Indians came
from Chicago, Denver, Los Angeles, and many other cities. They never
had any experience in the woodlands, and they showed up with new
guns. The dangerous comedy started when the militants unpacked their
new rifles. They actually stopped in small towns, just outside the reservation, to unpack their weapons, and their behavior naturally worried the
merchants. What they didn't know was that at least a hundred federal
agents were camped in every motel and hotel around the reservation.
Federal disguises were feather thin, they drove the same model and color
of federal cars, but the agents did not wear white socks. And probably
several hundred National Guard troops were located near the reservation. This was all rather scary. I was, as a former journalist, an advisor
to the reservation chief at the time. The strategy was to mitigate any
surprise problems, so we scheduled two meetings a day, and after each
meeting, a press conference. We held two large press conferences every
day to mitigate the enormous ego demands of the putative leaders of
the American Indian Movement.

ARL: Who is Simon Howard in this story?

GV: Simon Howard was the elected chief, at the time, of the
Leech Lake Reservation in Minnesota. Forgive me, but he was a "real"
Native who had lived on the reservation his entire life. In the context
of this story, he was one of the real people, and he was elected to
serve the residents of the reservation, unlike the leaders of the American
Indian Movement. Dennis Banks arrived in his leathers and feathers,
a simulation of a photograph by Edward Curtis. Howard wore Hush
Puppies boots, side zippers undone, cheap synthetic trousers, a bowl-
ing jacket, his standard reservation attire. I was working with him to
mediate the potential of violence, a war with white fisherman. Everyone
carried firearms, the tension was high on the opening day of the fishing
season. Howard was a very perceptive leader. He decided to hold two
daily meetings of the militant leaders in an elementary school classroom.
Everyone had to sit on tiny chairs. Here come the tough guys, all dressed
up in furs, leathers, feathers, and armaments. The thing that broke me
up was that some of the militants had bandoliers of ammunition that
did not match the bore of their rifles. Practically everyone carried a big

knife, rifles, and other weapons. Dennis Banks was the only warrior who carried a revolver. The warriors were obviously nervous, dressed for a war and they circled around tiny chairs in a classroom. Howard walked into the classroom, nodded to the warriors, slowly sat in a tiny chair, and folded his hands. OK boys, take your seats, let's have a talk. The warriors were reduced to the position of a schoolchild in a tiny chair. Banks was the only one who refused to sit in a tiny chair. He roamed around and stood by the window, a perfect stoical pose for a photograph. Perhaps he was waiting for the magical return of Edward Curtis. OK boys, said Howard, you didn't check with me when you arrived on the reservation. I know a lot of you, but now, to get started, why don't you stand up and introduce yourself and say what you think, tell me why you are here. Howard looked around the classroom. The warriors were silent, the fear of elementary school in a tiny chair. I was shy too. I did not want to stand in front of a classroom and announce my name. One warrior from Milwaukee stood up and said in a trembling voice: My name is Robert Lee and I came here to die. By the end of the first week it got a little easier. But still, when you get into that little chair, you regress. So to overcompensate for this, they all acted real tough. A consequence I had not anticipated. If they had not been humiliated in tiny chairs, the warriors might have been more moody and angry, and that would not have been good news. A federal agent decided he was going to try a new strategy of law enforcement and surveillance. The agent approaches Banks and said: Dennis, I'd like to make a deal with you. I'm going to be following you everywhere, so why don't I just be your chauffeur? So Dennis had a federal agent as a chauffeur, and that was perfect law enforcement. The whole thing was a marvelous, dangerous comedy. The others just couldn't stand this of course. The whole tense situation almost ended in a reservation war over fishing rights that had already been recognized by a federal court.

ARL: In fact, am I not correct, there was shooting?

GV: Right, one warm spring day sudden, rapid gunfire, rifles and shotguns, broke the silence about midnight. I can still hear the sound of rifle fire in my memories. Then the urgent sound of voices on shortwave radios. Federal agents cautiously moved closer to the sound of gunfire and strategically circled the war zone. Dennis Banks' chauffeur, the federal agent, had not yet reported to his superior. Luckily Howard was respected as the responsible leader to order assistance in an emergency, this way the National Guard would not move without word from the elected tribal chief. Otherwise it would have been total bloodshed. These new urban warriors went out hunting, and shining. Do you know what I mean by that, to catch the eyes of the animal with a bright light? Of course you do, surely you have been caught in the bright lights of the academic world. Now, you need to know that most of this land had been allotted and was owned by whites. And some of the land was foreclosed by the state and sold to farmers. So there were many white farmers in the area and they had cattle. These urban simulated warriors were out hunting and shined an ordinary milk cow. The warriors aimed and fired at the bright shiny eyes of the cow. The farmer came out, and, of course, he shot back in the dark. Unbelievably, no one was dead or wounded. Not even the milk cow. Hundreds of rounds were fired by fear. Then, the highway patrol decided that they had to do something about these guys going around hunting and shining, so they decided to collect any roadside animal hit by a car, and deliver it immediately to the camp, to provide some wild food for the warriors in cabins at the Episcopal Church camp and resort. A day later a deer was killed on a nearby highway and promptly delivered by highway patrolmen in uniform. Picture this scene, a highway patrolman delivers a warm dead deer to the camp. The urban hunters pull the carcass out of the trunk of the patrol car. Others rush forward with their knives and start cutting at the hide against the ribs. One warrior said: Can't get in, can't get in. The unbelievable scene was record by a local television news crew and broadcast that night. Anyone who lived in the northern part of the state, any scout or hunter, and even many people in the cities, know generally how to dress an animal. The young ersatz warriors hacked away at the dead deer. That was quite a scene. So they never did cook anything. They sent people out for fast food in nearby towns.

ARL: Doesn't Mrs. Howard get in on the act?

GV: Yes, she certainly does save the day. She quieted one last incident in the reservation war. The federal court ruled in favor of treaty rights, as you know, so a war was not necessary on the Leech Lake Reservation. And, most of the warriors were weary and bored after more than a week so they started to leave the reservation. Two press conferences on tiny chairs in the elementary school twice a day were not what the warriors had in mind, especially those who came to the reservation to die in a war for reservation rights to hunt and fish. Simon Howard and his wife were relieved that the American Indian Movement decided to return to the city. Then there was an emergency shortwave radio message. Several warriors had blocked one of the main roads on the reservation and intended to abuse white fisherman. Mrs. Howard who had been silent and calm during the entire occupation of the reservation by militants, jumped out of her chair on the porch of her house, ran to her car, and drove at high speed to the area of the reported roadblock. By the time she got there, dozens of warriors had taken off their shirts, sported breechclouts, painted their faces, and they were apparently ready die at the last minute. The scene was perilous, but, at the same time, it was a woebegone comedy. I got there just behind Mrs. Howard. She walked directly toward the warriors, pointed her finger at them, and said: What the hell are you boys doing here? The young armed warriors were shied by the voice of an older woman. Now, she said, you pick up your stuff and you go on home. And they did. That was the end of the war. Who could resist the firm voice of a Native grandmother?

ARL: How, next, about a move into literary matters?

GV: Yes, the tricky sight, site, cite of literary matters and manners. But, first, let me ask you, in turn, about some of the figurations of Natives in commercial literature, or at least other writing that you tackle in a number of places in your own critical work.

ARL: Well, if nothing else, it virtually makes for a tradition in its own right, starting with Cotton Mather's "black people of the forest" and onward. As early as 1786, Philip Freneau—one of the literary names of the then New Republic—writes his poem "The Indian Burial Ground." It's nothing other than an early version of the Native as Vanishing American. In the novel there's a pioneer like Charles Brockden Brown writing about ten years later in *Edgar Huntly* (1799)—"brown and terrific Indians," all Gothic harlequins and threat. Washington Irving is also early on to the page in his *Tour of the Prairies* (1835), *Astoria* (1835), and *The Adventures of Captain Bonneville* (1837). His "Indians" are all a kind of savagist heroism, redemptive biological figures as against a supposed weak and white masculinity. There's also a fair bit of that in James Fenimore Cooper who invents the Chingachgook (pronounced Chicago according to Twain) of *The Last of the Mohicans* (1826). Natty Bumppo as cultural whiteness, Chingachgook as heroic indigeneity—it's been a longtime equation. Not surprising that Russell Means would be irresistibly drawn to playing the role, when the time came (1992), with Daniel Day-Lewis, the most beautiful Irishman since Yeats, in the white role. The line, of course, continues; Poe's Dirk Peters in *The Narrative of A. Gordon Pym* (1838) as gargoyle Saroka mixedblood to Twain's Injun Joe in *Tom Sawyer* (1876), Longfellow's Hiawatha to Faulkner's Chief Doom, Ken Kesey's Chief Bromden to Tony Hillerman's Jim Chee and Joe Leaphorn—the line explored in Leslie Fiedler's *The Return of The Vanishing American* (1968) and latterly Fergus M. Bordewich's *Killing the White Man's Indian: Reinventing Native Americans at the End of the Twentieth Century* (1996).

GV: May we now consider Herman Melville? Does the mighty *Moby-Dick* stir your global literary gonads?

ARL: Who better understood the play of reality and mask in figurations of the Native than Melville in the person of Queequeg in *Moby-Dick.* Scottish-kilted, cosmically tattooed, "George Washington cannibalistically developed," bearer of a war and peace tomahawk-pipe, and from "Kokovoko . . . a place not down any map"—is not that the perfect *trompe l'oeil* of "The Indian"? Few, too, have ever bettered the chapter in *The Confidence-Man* (1857) on savagism that he called "The Metaphysics of Indian-Hating." Melville knew, as if by instinct, that what becomes in due course Johnny Weissmuller Tarzan-Indians was always fake. His genius was to make imaginative treasure out of that simulation.

GV: Your tricky sources are impeachable, almost memorable.

ARL: With which, back to you Gerald. In your many disquisitions and creative writing on Native culture, casinos to sovereignty, you've created almost a Vizenor lexicon—postindian, survivance, storier, varionative, even panic holes. Why the need for this language? How does it attach to, and enact, your visions of Native culture?

GV: Native stories and narratives have been closed translation and simulations, an inconvenient nationalism. Natives became a commercial literary cause, for a time, and that detracted from a sense of presence. I created characters of survivance not victimry to overturn the simulations and narratives of the vanishing, tragic Indian. My postindians are liberated from these simulations and the marvels of commercial literature. I must create selected words to undermine simulations and narratives of dominance, and to provide a more original sense of Native experience.

ARL: A closing thought. It has always, actually, been the imaginers, Native storytellers, oral and scriptural, and Native visual artists who have come closest to articulating the human resonance of the tradition. Centuries, not just a few modern years, of art, signature, poetry, memory, talk, and print. Even if his chicken and piranha scholarship has sometimes been less than solid, Gerald (he won't mind my saying) has played a simply major role in its continuance.

Contributors

Helmbrecht Breinig is Professor Emeritus at the University of Erlangen-Nürnberg. He has published widely on nineteenth- and twentieth-century American fiction and poetry, intercultural and inter-American topics as well as Native American literature. His recent book publications include *Multiculturalism in Contemporary Societies: Perspectives on Difference and Transdifference* (coeditor, 2002) and *Imaginary (Re-)Locations: Tradition, Modernity, and the Market in Contemporary Native American Literature and Culture* (2003).

Juan Bruce-Novoa is Professor of Spanish and Portuguese at the University of California, Irvine. His many publications include: *Only the Good Times*, a novel (1995); *RetroSpace: Collected Essays on Chicano Literature* (1990); *Chicano Poetry: A Response to Chaos* (1982); and *Chicano Authors: Inquiry by Interview* (1980).

Richard J. Lane is Professor of First Nations Literatures at Malaspina University College, British Columbia. His major publications include: *Jean Baudrillard* (2000); *Beckett and Philosophy* (editor, 2002); *Contemporary British Fiction* (coeditor, 2003); and *The Postcolonial Novel* (2006) He has published widely on postcolonial literatures and theory, and currently writes the "Canadian Literature" section for *The Year's Work in English Studies*.

A. Robert Lee is Professor of American Literature at Nihon University, Tokyo. Recent publications include: *Gothic to Multicultural: Idioms of Imagining in American Literary Fiction* (2008); *Multicultural American Literature: Comparative Black, Native, Latino/a, and Asian American Fictions* (2003), which won the 2004 Before Columbus Foundation's

American Book Award; *Postindian Conversations* (with Gerald Vizenor 2000); *Designs of Blackness: Mappings in the Literature and Culture of Afro-America* (1998); and the essay collections *Other Britain, Other British: Contemporary Multicultural Fiction* (1995) and *Making America / Making American Literature: Franklin to Cooper* (with W. M. Verhoeven 1996).

Paul Lyons is Associate Professor of English at the University of Hawai'i-Manoa. His current research centers on American Pacific Orientalism, about which he has published in *boundary 2*; *ESQ: A Journal of the American Renaissance*; *Arizona Quarterly*, and *Inside Out: Literature, Cultural Politics, and Identity in the New Pacific*. His book *American Pacificism: Oceania in the U.S. Imagination* (2006) deals with the U.S. production of knowledges about the Pacific from early shipboard narratives of encounter through contemporary tourist narratives.

Deborah L. Madsen is Professor of American Literature and Culture at the University of Geneva, Switzerland. She works in the field of Postcolonial American studies, with a focus on issues of nation and transnation. Her publications include *Allegory in America: From Puritanism to Postmodernism* (1996); *American Exceptionalism* (1998); *Post-Colonial Literatures: Expanding the Canon* (editor, 1999); *Beyond the Borders: American Literature and Post-Colonial Theory* (editor, 2003); and *Understanding Gerald Vizenor* (2009). She is coeditor with Gerald Vizenor of the State University of New York Press series Native Traces.

David L. Moore is Professor of English at the University of Montana, Missoula. He has published widely on Native American literary history and critical legal theory in relation to tribal sovereignty, American and Native American identity issues, and cultural property. His current book project is entitled *Native Knowing: American Identity and Native American Sovereignty*.

Joy Porter is a lecturer in American studies at the University of Wales, Swansea. She is best known for her work on Native American themes and is the author of *To Be Indian: The Life of Seneca-Iroquois Arthur Caswell Parker, 1881–1955* (2002) and *The Cambridge Companion to Native American Literature* (coeditor, 2005). Her work can also be found in a variety of journals such as *New York History* and *Presidential Studies Quarterly* and in books such as *The State of U.S. History* (2002). Previously she was Senior Lecturer in American History at Anglia Ruskin University,

Cambridge. Her next book is *Native American Freemasonry*, the research for which is supported by a Leverhulme Research Fellowship.

Malea Powell is Associate Professor and Director of Rhetoric and Writing at Michigan State University. Her research focuses on examining the rhetorics of survivance used by nineteenth-century American Indian intellectuals, and on the material cultural rhetorics of American Indian artists. She has published essays in *College Composition and Communication, Paradoxa*, and several critical essay collections. Powell is the editor of *SAIL: Studies in American Indian Literatures*. Malea Powell is a founding member of the National Center for the Study of Great Lakes Native American Culture—an organization dedicated to the preservation of Great Lakes indigenous history, art, and culture—and a participant in the Myaamia Project for the preservation of Miami Language and Culture (located at Miami University).

Lee Schweninger is Professor of English at the University of North Carolina, Wilmington, where he teaches early American, ethnic American, and American Indian literatures. Author of *The Writings of Celia Parker Woolley* (1998); *John Winthrop* (1990); and *N. Scott Momaday* (2000), he has also published recently in *Studies in American Indian Literatures* and *MELUS*. His latest book is *Listening to the Land: Native American Literary Responses to the Landscape* (2008).

Gerald Vizenor is Professor of American Studies at the University of New Mexico and Emeritus Professor of the University of California, Berkeley. He was born in Minneapolis, but spent much of his childhood on the White Earth Reservation in northern Minnesota. Vizenor attended New York University for two years, transferring to the University of Minnesota where he earned his BA in 1960. His graduate studies include University of Minnesota and Harvard University. His career includes work for the Minnesota Department of Corrections and the *Minneapolis Tribune*. Vizenor's teaching career includes professorships at Lake Forest University, Bemidji State College, University of Minnesota, University of California at Berkeley, and the University of California at Santa Cruz. He is the single most prolific and most published Native American Indian writer, honored as a critic, theorist, novelist, poet, playwright, and screenwriter. His work has been recognized with the award of the Fiction Collective/ Illinois State University Prize, 1986; the American Book Award, 1988; and the Josephine Miles Award, PEN Oakland, 1990.

Index